Composing Humor

TWAIN, THURBER, AND YOU

domains
in language and composition

 Harcourt Brace Jovanovich, Inc.
New York   Chicago   San Francisco   Atlanta   Dallas

Composing
Humor
TWAIN,
THURBER,
AND
YOU

Jean Sisk
Jean Saunders

ACKNOWLEDGMENTS: For permission to reprint copyrighted material, grateful acknowledgment is made to the following:

Associated Press Newsfeatures: "Girl, 20, Jailed For Chasing Beau" from *The Baltimore Sun*, July 26, 1970. "Brazilian Town Has Night Clubs Shut by Police" from *The Baltimore Sun*, January 24, 1971. "Oh, God, the niggers are in the school!" by Relman Morin, The Associated Press, September 23, 1957.

The Baltimore Sun: Page 108, untitled article by Pran Sabharwal from *The Baltimore Sun*, July 26, 1970.

Harper & Row, Publishers, Incorporated: "Instructions in Art" from *Europe and Elsewhere* (pp. 315-325) by Mark Twain. "Running for Governor" from *Sketches New and Old* (pp. 377-383) by Mark Twain. FROM pp. 22-26 of *Tom Sawyer Abroad & Other Stories* by Mark Twain. FROM pp. 276-278 of *The Gilded Age* by Mark Twain. FROM pp. 7-8, 11-12 of "How To Tell A Story" by Mark Twain. FROM *The Adventures of Huckleberry Finn* by Mark Twain. FROM *Life on the Mississippi* by Mark Twain. "My Late Senatorial Secretary-ship" from *Sketches New and Old* by Mark Twain. FROM "To the Person Sitting in Darkness" from *Europe and Elsewhere* by Mark Twain. FROM *Roughing It* by Mark Twain. FROM pp. 70-76, "Answers to Correspondents" from *Sketches New and Old* by Mark Twain. FROM *Puddn'head Wilson's New Calendar* by Mark Twain. FROM "The Story of the Old Ram" (pp. 99-101) from *Roughing It* by Mark Twain. "Curing a Cold" and "The Petrified Man" from *Sketches New and Old* by Mark Twain. FROM pp. 87-92 under the title "A Genuine Turkish Bath" from *The Innocents Abroad*, Vol. II, by Mark Twain. From pp. 56-57 "A Couple of Poems by Twain and Moore" (retitled "Those Evening Bells" and "Those Annual Bills") from *Sketches New and Old* by Mark Twain. "The Invalid's Story" from *In Defense of Harriet Shelley & Other Essays* by Mark Twain. All from Mississippi Editions of Mark Twain. Abridged from pp. 176, 181-182, "Mark Twain & the Public Reading" from *The Autobiography of Mark Twain*, edited by Charles Neider, copyright © 1959 by The Mark Twain Company; copyright © 1924, 1945, 1952 by Clara Clemens Samoussoud; copyright © 1959 by Charles Neider. FROM pp. 223-227, 228, 229-232 of "The Lowest Animal" from *Letters from the Earth* by Mark Twain, edited by Bernard De Voto, copyright © 1938, 1944, 1946, 1959, 1962 by The Mark Twain Co.

The McNaught Syndicate: Page 160, syndicated column by Dr. Peter Stein-crohn, © 1970 McNaught Synd. Inc., from *The Baltimore Sun,* April 27, 1970.

Media Features, Inc. and *The Baltimore Sun:* Pages 95-96, from the syndicated column "Ask Jennifer" by Jennifer Anderson, from *The Baltimore Sun,* July 26, 1970.

New York Post: "Prisoners with Midnight in their Hearts," by Harold A. Little-dale from the *New York Post,* January 12, 1917.

Simon & Schuster, Inc.: Page 118, from *The Enjoyment of Laughter* by Max Eastman, copyright 1936 by Max Eastman.

Mrs. James Thurber: "Where Did You Get Those Big Brown Eyes and That Tiny Mind?" from *Alarms and Diversions* by James Thurber, copr. © 1957 James Thurber. Published by Harper and Row. Originally published in *The New Yorker.* "Prehistoric Animals of the Middle West" from *The Beast in Me—and Other Animals* by James Thurber, copr. © 1948 James Thurber. Published by Harcourt Brace Jovanovich, Inc. Originally printed in *Mademoiselle.* "The Bear Who Let It Alone," "The Very Proper Gander," "The Rabbits Who Caused All the Trouble," "The Birds and the Foxes," "The Tiger Who Understood People," "The Fairly Intelligent Fly," "The Courtship of Arthur and Al," "The Crow and the Oriole," "The Moth and the Star," and two drawings for A.E. Housman's "Oh When I Was in Love with You" (from *A Shropshire Lad*), originally printed in *The New Yorker, from Fables for Our Time and Famous Poems Illustrated* by James Thurber, copr. © 1940 James Thurber; copr. © 1968 Helen Thurber. Published by Harper and Row. All fables originally printed in *The New Yorker.* "The Peacelike Mongoose" from *Further Fables of Our Time* by James Thurber, copr. © 1956 James Thurber. Published by Simon and Schuster, Inc. Originally printed in *The New Yorker.* FROM "The Case for Comedy," originally printed in *The Atlantic Monthly,* "Here Come the Dolphins," originally printed in *Punch,* and "The Trouble With Man Is Man," originally printed in *The New Yorker,* from *Lanterns and Lances* by James Thurber, copr. © 1961 James Thurber. Published by Harper and Row. "A Couple of Hamburgers," and from "Nine Needles" from *Let Your Mind Alone* by James Thurber, copr. © 1937 James Thurber; copr. © 1965 Helen W. Thurber and Rosemary Thurber Sauers. Published by Harper and Row. Both originally printed in *The New Yorker.* "A Box to Hide In," "Casuals of the Keys," "Guessing Game," "The Private Life of Mr. Bidwell," and "Mr. Preble Gets Rid of His Wife" from *The Middle-Aged Man on the Flying Trapeze* by James Thurber, copr. © 1937 James Thurber; copr. © 1963 Helen W. Thurber and Rosemary Thurber Sauers. Published by Harper and Row. All stories, but none of the drawings, originally printed in *The New Yorker.* FROM "Preface to a Life" and "The Dog That Bit People" from *My Life and Hard Times* by James Thurber, copr. © 1933, 1961 James Thurber. Published by Harper and Row. "Here Lies Miss Groby" from *My World—and Welcome to It* by James Thurber, copr. © 1942 James Thurber; copr. © 1970 Helen W. Thurber and Rosemary

Thurber Sauers. Originally printed in *The New Yorker*. "The Pet Department" (including selection on text page 86) from *The Owl in the Attic—and Other Perplexities* by James Thurber, copr. © 1931, 1959 James Thurber. Published by Harper and Row. Originally printed in *The New Yorker*. "And Keep Me a Normal Healthy American Girl"; "I Don't Want Him to Be Comfortable if He's Going to Look Too Funny"; "That's My First Wife Up There, and This Is the *Present* Mrs. Harris"; "All Right, Have It Your Way—You Heard a Seal Bark"; "You and Your Premonitions!"; "Touché!"; "Home"; "You Said a Moment Ago That Everybody You Look at Seems to Be a Rabbit. Now Just What Do You Mean by That, Mrs. Sprague?"; and "Have You Seen My Pistol, Honey-Bun?" from *The Thurber Carnival* by James Thurber, copr. © 1945 James Thurber. Published by Harper and Row. All drawings originally printed in *The New Yorker*. "Shake Hands with Birdey Doggett," story, not drawing, originally printed in *The New Yorker*, and "What's so Funny?", originally printed in *The Bermudian*, both from *Thurber Country* by James Thurber, copr. © 1953 James Thurber. Published by Simon and Schuster, Inc.

The Viking Press, Inc.: FROM Bernard De Voto's Introduction to "Letters from the Earth" by Mark Twain from *The Portable Mark Twain*.

CONTENTS

The Release of Laughter

Light Humor: The Quiet Smile

Satire

Contents

"Black" Comedy: The Scornful, Mournful Laugh

The Parroting Humorist

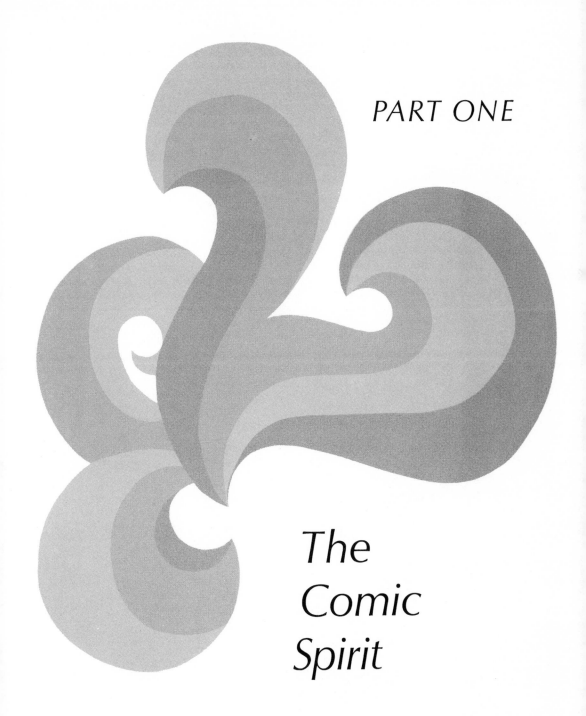

PART ONE

The
Comic
Spirit

1

The Comic
Point of View —
Not Always "Funny!"

If someone were to ask you, "Do you have a sense of humor?", your immediate response would almost inevitably be, "Of course. Doesn't everyone have a sense of humor?" Well, at least everyone thinks he has. And yet you must have had the experience of watching others laugh hilariously at some joke *you* didn't think was funny—or, worse still, of telling a joke that fell flat because no one laughed. Or maybe you've heard a particular film or television show described as being uproarious, and you don't find it humorous at all.

Not all comedy, however, is intended to evoke laughter. You may not remember that comics used to be called "funny papers," that most of the cartoon strips were devoted to laugh-provoking situations, to "fun" in the most basic, childlike meaning of that word. Think of the comics you read now. How many of them make you laugh, or even smile? How many are simply pictorial narratives? How many have a serious social intent? Yet the comics are indeed special forms of the comic mode in all its varied manifestations—from the "funny" quick laughs in "Andy Capp" and "Dennis the Menace" to the more subtle smiles in "Peanuts," the broad satirical comment of "The Wizard of Id" and "B.C.," and the often unfunny, at times bitter social criticism and ironic paradox, of "Li'l Abner" and "Pogo."

The sight of a clown skidding on a banana peel, the sniping digs of a witty critic, or the spectacle of a henpecked husband submitting meekly to a shrewish wife, may or may not evoke a smiling response. Yet most of us would consider the death of a young person in an avoidable accident to be tragic—or the deliberate harming of an animal to be pathetic and cruel. Apparently, a sense of humor is more personal, more capricious or dependent on cultural and social styles than a sense of the tragic or pathetic. Or perhaps comedy and humor are more difficult to classify or define than tragedy, realism, romanticism, and other modes frequently applied both to life and literature.

DEFINITIONS OF COMEDY, WIT, AND HUMOR

Ask yourself how you would define "comedy" or "humor." Then compare your answer with those of well-known students of comedy —writers and critics of various nations and times. For example, George Meredith, a nineteenth-century English novelist and critic, stresses the detachment of comedy, the fact that it views life from a rational, objective viewpoint rather than from the subjective, empathic one of tragedy or pathos. He points out that it is comedy that gives a sense of balance and proportion to life, that makes it possible for man to rise above his fate and to accept some of his disappointments in a philosophical and often good-natured manner. He considers the comic spirit a typically human affirmation of the value of life, even life at its worst. And he tells us that much comedy—especially the "comedy of manners"—deals with the problems of men in groups, in society, rather than with the unique problems of individuals.

Henri Bergson, the French philosopher and critic, agrees with Meredith that the essence of the comic spirit is its detached way of looking at both individuals and societies from the "outside." He especially emphasizes, however, the idea that comedy is a game that imitates life, that all humor has a childlike origin in its element of surprise or pleasure in repetition. Comedy, in this sense, helps us to preserve our childlike sense of wonder and play. It helps us to enjoy living and to make a game of it. Bergson says that laughter is caused whenever a man ceases to behave like a human being and begins to act like a mechanical toy or clock, wound up to respond to every situation in the same way. And he points out that the logic of comedy is often an upside-down, dreamlike logic that an individual tries to impose on the world in order to make it conform to his wishes. Such an individual seems funny to us because we detect the unreality of his reasoning, and perhaps because we feel superior to him in that *we* are more practical or reasonable.

William Hazlitt, a nineteenth-century English essayist, was interested in the distinctions between "wit" and "humor." He believed that humor arises from the imitation of the natural or acquired absurdities of men of certain personalities, in particular situations and times. Wit, according to Hazlitt, is more artificial than humor, more a playing with and on words that establish unexpected or surprising contrasts between words themselves or between words and things. His contemporary, the poet Samuel Taylor Coleridge, was equally concerned with the differences between wit and humor, but he considered wit a verbal artifice rather than a natural kind of comedy. His main contribution to a theory of comedy, however, is his insistence that all humor arises in the uniqueness of men, in some "peculiarity of individual temperament and character." This humor of idiosyncrasy is counterpointed, in his opinion, by a more universal, cosmic humor that acknowledges the "hollowness and farce of the world, and its disproportion to the godlike within us." It is this recognition of the idea that life itself can be a joke that carries us from the laugh that asserts our sense of childlike fun or our sense of delighted superiority over others to the comic awareness of detached and objective acknowledgment that human impotence is the rule rather than the exception. This kind of philosophic humor approaches the edge of tragedy in many cases.

And indeed, all attempts to classify comedy, to contain it in a single, concrete definition, fail. We can try to explain what is comic from the viewpoint of the reader or listener who smiles quietly, laughs, shares a critical view of man's social pretensions and hypocrisies, or comes to terms with life's bitterest ironies. Or, we can try to explain how the humorist, the comic artist, makes us laugh at his jokes and smile at his portrayals of humorous personalities; we can also try to explain how he pokes fun at sham or masks his tears with a bitter gibe. But any endeavor to constrict the meaning of the comic spirit breaks down simply because trying to apply rigid classifications or definitions to literature is as futile as trying to classify life itself into neat, mutually exclusive elements. To be helpful, discussions of the characteristics of

The Comic Point of View—Not Always "Funny!"

literary categories must be sufficiently general and flexible to permit some "exceptions" or debatable areas. It is often easier to think of what a particular type of experience or literary genre is *not* rather than what it *is*. Comedy is a number of things, but it is *not* "tragic."

REALISM, COMEDY, AND ROMANCE

The realism of the nineteenth and twentieth centuries, neither "tragic" nor "comic" in mode, attempted to reproduce, uncritically and without comment, a photographic likeness of man as he is—weak or strong, rich or poor, degraded or uplifted. But realism as a mode, rather than as a philosophy, often became "naturalism," or a tendency to depict only the sordid side of life; frequently it sentimentalized its protagonists, so that their fate became pathetic, or "bathetic," rather than tragic. The realists' initial interest, however, was in observable, verifiable data, and it is in its desire to unmask and expose rather than to aggrandize or mythologize that realism resembles comedy.

Comedy is like realism in its aim to unmask; it is unlike realism in its ability to value the good-natured acceptance of life and the use of reason to surmount one's fate, which is one of the benefits of being "human." Comedy is more likely than realism to view life's indignities with tolerance. And comedy always keeps its distance, its cool detachment—unlike realism, which often descends to sentimentality and bathos.

Romance, another literary mode or stance in life, idealizes life itself—the excitement of adventure, the quest for the unusual, the ecstasy of love. The "romantic hero" is the knight in armor who devotes his life to a liege lord, to an ideal, or to a beloved. A romantic hero is an idealist of sorts, like the tragic hero; but the ideal of the romantic hero is to find and slay the dragon, to attain his quest, to win his secret love rather than to challenge his destiny by seeking forbidden freedoms or superhuman rewards. He is, in this sense, less "realistic" than the tragic hero, who is aware of the risks he takes and of his own tragic fate. The romantic values happiness as the greatest good in life. Much of the pleasanter, good-natured comedy of low humor and of the idiosyncratic dreamer of obsessive character is essentially romantic in its pleasure-seeking objectives. Yet comedy aims for truth and the triumph of reason over desire; it rejects the romantic's wishful thinking and accent on youthful pleasures.

COMEDY AND TRAGEDY

Comedy and tragedy present different views of human nature, of man's possibilities, and of his stature in the universe. Tragedy views man as capable of great nobility, sacrifice, and courage in the face of the ultimate fact of his existence—his mortality. All things in the world of nature must die, but only man is aware of this fact. Most tragic endings come to men who dare defy fate, or who risk everything for freedom or for some other ideal. Often the tragic hero acts in behalf of a group, is a leader, the "best" of his kind, the epitome of the qualities most valued by the culture he represents and defends. The tragic view of man is at once idealistic—assuming man's ability to rise above his animal nature, and realistic—recognizing the odds against successful defiance of the limitations of fate and mortality. The tragic hero aims for whatever immortality is possible, whatever degree of perfection is attainable.

Because tragedy deals with the universal themes of human mortality and the hope that man's divine spark can lead him to ultimate perfectibility, it is considered by some people to be "superior" to comedy. Not so. Both tragedy and comedy reflect equally valid and complementary views of life. In an essay concerned primarily with the comic art of the theater, James Thurber —one of the two humorists with whose work this book is concerned—makes a case for comedy in our time.

FROM *The Case for Comedy*

JAMES THURBER

The decline of humor and comedy in our time has had a multiplicity of causes, a principal one being the ideological beating they have taken from both the intellectual left and the political right. The latter came about through the intimidation of writers and playwrights under McCarthyism. The former is more complex. Humor has long been a target of leftist intellectuals, and the reason is simple enough in it-

The Comic Point of View—Not Always "Funny!"

self. Humor, as Lord Boothby has said, is the only solvent of terror and tension, and terror and tension are among the chief ideological weapons of Communism. The leftists have made a concerted attack on humor as an antisocial, antiracial, antilabor, antiproletarian stereotype, and they have left no stereotype unused in their attack, from "no time for comedy" to the grim warnings that humor is a sickness, a sign of inferiority complex, a shield and not a weapon.

The modern morbid playwrights seem to have fallen for the fake argument that only tragedy is serious and has importance, whereas the truth is that comedy is just as important, and often more serious in its approach to truth, and, what few writers seem to realize or to admit, usually more difficult to write.

It is not a curious but a natural thing that arrogant intellectual critics condemn humor and comedy, for while they can write about Greek Old Comedy, Middle Comedy, and New Comedy with all the flourishes of pretension, they avoid a simple truth, succinctly expressed by the *Oxford Classical Dictionary* in its discussion of Middle Comedy. "Before long the realistic depiction of daily life became the chief aim in Comedy. Ordinary, commonplace life is no easy subject to treat interestingly on the stage; and Antiphanes contrasts the comic poet's more difficult lot with the tragedian's, whose plot is already familiar, and the *deus ex machina* at hand— the comic writer has no such resources."

The history of stage comedy, in both Greece and Rome, begins with cheap and ludicrous effects. In Greek Old Comedy there were the padded costumes of the grotesque comedian, the paunch and the leather phallus. The Roman Plautus, in freely translating Greek New Comedy, stuck in gags to make his rough and restless audiences guffaw, so that in the beginning comedy was, to use a medical term, exogenous—that is, not arising from within the human being, but dragged in from the outside. The true balance of life and art, the saving of the human mind as well as of the theater, lies in what has long been known as tragicomedy, for humor and pathos, tears and laughter are, in the highest expression of human character and achievement, inseparable. Many dictionaries, including the OED, wrongly hyphenate tragicomedy, as if the two integral parts were warring elements that must be separated.

I think the first play that ever sent me out of the American theater in a mood of elation and of high hope for our stage was *What Price Glory?* Amidst all the blood and slaughter there ran the recurring sound of congruous laughter. I still vividly remember the scene in which the outraged French father of an outraged daughter babbles his grievance for a full minute to the bewildered Captain Flagg, who then asks a French-speaking American lieutenant, "What did he say?"

"Rape," says the lieutenant.

And I can still recall the gleams of humor in R. C. Sheriff's *Journey's End*, as bitter a war play as any.

"What kind of soup *is* this, Sergeant?" asks Captain Stanhope.

"Yellow soup, sir," says the mess sergeant, apologetically.

Screen writers, as well as playwrights, seem reluctant, or unable, to use the devices of comedy out of fear of diluting suspense. A few years ago, in a movie about a bank clerk who stole a million dollars, crammed it into a suitcase, got into a taxi with his unaware and bewildered wife, and headed for an airport to flee the country, there came a scene in which he handed the driver a fifty-dollar bill and told him to "Step on it." Now I submit that the wife of an American male of modest income would have gone into a comedy scene at this point, but the writer or writers of the script must have been afraid that such an interlude would ruin the terror and tension, and terror and tension must be preserved nowadays, even at the expense of truth.

Katharine Hepburn recently said that our playwrights should "rise above their time," but, if they tried that, they would simply sink below themselves, or sit there staring at the blank paper in their typewriters. Separate molds turn out unvarying shapes. You can't make a Tennessee Ernie out of a Tennessee Williams, any more than you can turn a callin' back into a trough cleanin'. A callin' back, if you don't know, is a gatherin' of folks at the bedside of a dyin' man, to call him back. I hope this doesn't inspire one of the morbid playmakers to make a play in which the dyin' man drags all other folks down with him.

It will be said, I suppose, that I couldn't write such a tragedy because of the limitation of my tools and the nature of my outlook. (Writers of comedy have outlook, whereas writers of tragedy have, according to them, insight.) It is true, I confess, that if a male character of my invention started across the stage to disrobe a virgin criminally (ah, euphemism to end euphemisms!), he would probably catch his foot in the piano stool and end up playing "Button Up Your Overcoat" on the black keys. There are more ways than one, including, if you will, a Freudian stumble, to get from tragedy

The Comic Point of View—Not Always "Funny!"

into tragicomedy. Several years ago a book reviewer in the New York Sunday *Times* wrote: "The tragedy of age is not that a man grows old, but that he stays young," and, indeed, there is the basis of a good tragedy in that half-truth. The other half might be stated, in a reverse Shavian paraphrase, "The trouble with youth is that it is wasted on the old." There is where the comedy would come in to form a genuine tragicomedy. At sixty-six, going on sixty-seven, I think I can speak with a touch of authority.

Miss Hepburn (to get back to her) is devoted to the great plays of Shakespeare, who didn't rise above his time, but merely above the ability of his contemporaries. He often wrote about a time worse than his own, such as the period of Macbeth. In that drama he could proclaim that life is a tale told by an idiot, full of sound and fury, signifying nothing, but say it in a play told by a genius, full of soundness and fury, signifying many things. The distinguished Mr. Williams and his contemporaries are not so much expressers of their time as expressions of it, and, for that matter, aren't we all? The playwright of today likes to believe that he is throwing light upon his time, or upon some part of it, when his time is actually throwing light upon him. This, it seems to me, has always been the case, but it happens more intensely now, perhaps, than ever before. Moreover, there are two kinds of light, the glow that illumines and the glare that obscures, and the former seems to be dimming.

The American family, in spite of all of its jitters and its loss of cohesion, still remains in most of its manifestations as familiar as ever, and it is our jumpy fancy to believe that all fathers are drunkards, all mothers kookies, and all children knife wielders planning to knock off their parents. Our loss of form in literature is, in large part, the result of an Oral Culture into which we began descending quite a while back. This is the age of the dragged-out interview, the endless discussion panels on television; an age in which photographers, calling on writers in their homes, stay around the house as long as the paper hanger or the roofer. Everything is tending to get longer and longer, and more and more shapeless. Telephone calls last as long as half an hour, or even forty minutes by my own count; women, saying good-by at front doors, linger longer than ever, saying, "Now I *must* go," and, eventually "Now, I *really* must go." But nothing is accomplished simply any more. Writers of letters finish what they have to say on page two and then keep going. Khrushchev talks for five hours at press conferences, and may even have

got it up to ten by the time this survey appears. (Moral: Great oafs from little icons grow.)

As brevity is the soul of wit, form, it seems to me, is the heart of humor and the salvation of comedy. "You are a putter in, and I am a taker out," Scott Fitzgerald once wrote to Thomas Wolfe. Fitzgerald was not a master of comedy, but in his dedication to taking out, he stated the case for form as against flow. It is up to our writers, in this era of Oral Culture, to bring back respect for form and for the innate stature and dignity of comedy. We cannot, to be sure, evoke humorists, or writers of comedy, by prayer or pleading or argument, but we can, and must, hope for a renascence of recognizable American comedy. The trend of the modern temper is toward gloom, resignation, and even surrender, and there is a great wailing of the word "Decadence!" on all sides. But for twenty-five hundred years decadence has come and decadence has gone. Reading Webster on the subject might make a newly arrived visitor from Mars believe that everything in art and literature came to a morose end as the nineteenth century closed out. It was a period of Decadence and of the Decadents, led by Baudelaire, Verlaine, and Mallarmé in France. Writes old Noah: "They cultivated the abnormal, artificial, and neurotic in subject and treatment, tending to the morbid or eccentric, and to the mystically sensuous and symbolic."

> Well, we are still going on, and we have four decades left in this battered and bloody century. . . . It is high time that we came of age and realized that, like Emily Dickinson's hope, humor is a feathered thing that perches in the soul.

We must face the tragic events of life, and our own mortality, with dignity if possible, and occasionally with heroism. But we must also have a way of handling our disappointments, enjoying our moments of leisure, applying our reason to the problems of society and our wit to their exposure and remedy. Sometimes we have a choice of "laughing things off" or of going under. If our efforts are in vain and if our view of the world leads us to pessimistic conclusions about man's future, we can either sacrifice ourselves in a grand gesture and end our lives in defeat, or we can adopt a comic, ironic, or even sardonic view of the world that is, though serious and pessimistic, humorous rather than tragic.

To allow ourselves to be defeated is to deny the value of life itself. The grand gesture must be noticed to be effective; perhaps that is why classic tragedies usually dealt with the king-hero, the national leader. His gestures and sacrifices were occasions for national or group rejoicing or mourning. In today's world, where individuals are massed and herded, a grand gesture by the ordinary person—you and the rest of us—is scarcely commented on. We act our roles on a Chekhovian stage, where comedy and tragedy mingle, where the climax of the play is anticlimax, and where the "happening" is that nothing happens. Boredom and frustration are our enemies, as is the possibility of impersonality developing unnoticed into cruelty and destructiveness.

Because comedy stresses man's reason over his will, his ability to unmask the false, his striving for proportion and balance in a world gone mad, and his need to release his tension, his fears, his anger—comedy, equally with tragedy, recognizes the divine spark in man. Comedy recognizes man's ability to rise above his situation, not with the grand gesture but with the childlike laugh, the cheerful quip, the good-natured joke, the quietly retrospective smile, the satiric disclosure of falsity and weakness and, yes— even the bitterly sardonic gibe and the mournful, ironic laugh that betrays the feeling, temporary or permanent, that life itself is absurd and that tragic gestures are meaningless. When life itself is the joke, raillery and angry resignation are the "comic" human recourses of sane men in an insane world.

2

Meet Two Professional Humorists: Mr. Twain and Mr. Thurber

Among the world's great prose writers are relatively few humorists. Perhaps their absence from the classics of literature can be attributed to the difficulties of creating the kind of comedy that satisfies a broad variety of senses of humor, or perhaps it can be attributed to the nature of humor itself—its spontaneity and its dependence upon the language and customs of the moment. Or, more probably, it is the seriousness of life, its ultimate ending in death that explains why most prose writers respond to the natural human tendency to take ourselves seriously. Humorists face life's seriousness in a different way, one that is equally human but a little less hopeful of man's godlike possibilities—unless, of course, laughter is godlike, as well it may be.

This country has produced its share of comic writers. One of them, Mark Twain, is world famous. *The Adventures of Huckleberry Finn* is as familiar to many British, French, and Russian readers as it to us, which says something about the timelessness of its humorous statement about people and life. James Thurber is not as internationally famous as Mark Twain, but he is certainly one of America's great satiric writers of short prose pieces. In addition, he was a first-rate cartoonist.

Of the four degrees of comedy, from exaggerated low comedy to bitter ironic humor, Twain represents the two extremes, and Thurber the gentler humor and wit, the more measured, temperate satire. The selections in this chapter will introduce the great variety of comedy and varieties of techniques and devices that are discussed in the first part of this book.

My Late Senatorial Secretaryship

MARK TWAIN

"My Late Senatorial Secretaryship" employs all the major devices of humor and is typical of Mark Twain and the extravagant humor of his time. The situation in this story is ripe for exploiting in the comic manner. The wild inventiveness of Twain as private secretary contrasts sharply with the deadpan delivery of the narrator, who could be the prototype of Twain's "inspired idiot." The characters are stock comedy characters, the trickster or practical joker preying on the official who is caught with his hypocrisies down. As is typical of low comedy, the source of greatest humor lies in the author's use of language.

My Late Senatorial Secretaryship   I am not a private secretary to a senator any more now. I held the berth two months in security and in great cheerfulness of spirit, but my bread began to return from over the waters then—that is to say, my works came back and revealed themselves. I judged it best to resign. The way of it was this. My employer sent for me one morning tolerably early, and, as soon as I had finished inserting some conundrums clandestinely into his last great speech upon finance, I entered the presence. There was something portentous in his appearance. His cravat was untied, his hair was in a state of disorder, and his countenance bore about it the signs of a suppressed storm. He held a package of letters in his tense grasp, and I knew that the dreaded Pacific mail was in. He said:

"I thought you were worthy of confidence."

I said, "Yes, sir."

He said, "I gave you a letter from certain of my constituents in the State of Nevada, asking the establishment of a post office at Baldwin's Ranch and told you to answer it, as ingeniously as you could, with arguments which should persuade them that there was no real necessity for an office at that place."

I felt easier. "Oh, if that is all, sir, I *did* do that."

"Yes, you *did*. I will read your answer for your own humiliation:

" '*Washington, Nov. 24*

" '*Messrs. Smith, Jones, and others.*

" '*Gentlemen:* What the mischief do you suppose you want with a post office at Baldwin's Ranch? It would not do you any good. If any letters came there, you couldn't read them, you know; and, besides, such letters as ought to pass through, with money in them, for other localities, would not be likely to *get* through, you must perceive at once; and that would make trouble for us all. No, don't bother about a post office in your camp. I have your best interests at heart, and feel that it would only be an ornamental folly. What you want is a nice jail, you know—a nice, substantial jail and a free school. These will be a lasting benefit to you. These will make you really contented and happy. I will move in the matter at once.

" '*Very truly, etc.,*

" '*Mark Twain,*

"For James W. N——, U. S. Senator.'

"That is the way you answered that letter. Those people say they will hang me, if I ever enter that district again; and I am perfectly satisfied they *will,* too."

"Well, sir, I did not know I was doing any harm. I only wanted to convince them."

"Ah. Well, you *did* convince them, I make no manner of doubt. Now, here is another specimen. I gave you a petition from certain gentlemen of Nevada, praying that I would get a bill through Congress incorporating the Methodist Episcopal Church of the State of Nevada. I told you to say, in reply, that the creation of such a law came more properly within the province of the state legislature; and to endeavor to show them that, in the present feebleness of the religious element in that new commonwealth, the expediency of incorporating the church was questionable. What did you write?

*Meet Two
Professional
Humorists:
Mr. Twain
and Mr. Thurber*

15

" 'Washington, Nov. 24

" 'Rev. John Halifax and others.

" 'Gentlemen: You will have to go to the state legislature about the speculation of yours—Congress don't know anything about religion. But don't you hurry to go there, either; because this thing you propose to do out in that new country isn't expedient—in fact, it is ridiculous. Your religious people there are too feeble, in intellect, in morality, in piety —in everything, pretty much. You had better drop this—you can't make it work. You can't issue stock on an incorporation like that—or if you could, it would only keep you in trouble all the time. The other denominations would abuse it, and "bear" it, and "sell it short," and break it down. They would do with it just as they would with one of your silver-mines out there—they would try to make all the world believe it was "wildcat." You ought not to do anything that is calculated to bring a sacred thing into disrepute. You ought to be ashamed of yourselves —that is what *I* think about it. You close your petition with the words: "And we will ever pray." I think you had better—you need to do it.

" 'Very truly, etc.,

" 'Mark Twain,

"For James W. N———, U. S. Senator.'

"That luminous epistle finishes me with the religious element among my constituents. But that my political murder might be made sure, some evil instinct prompted me to hand you this memorial from the grave company of elders composing the board of aldermen of the city of San Francisco, to try your hand upon—a memorial praying that the city's right to the water-lots upon the city front might be established by law of Congress. I told you this was a dangerous matter to move in. I told you to write a non-committal letter to the aldermen—an ambiguous letter—a letter that should avoid, as far as possible, all real consideration and discussion of the water-lot question. If there is any feeling left in you— any shame—surely this letter you wrote, in obedience to that order, ought to evoke it, when its words fall upon your ears:

" 'Washington, Nov. 27

" 'The Honorable Board of Aldermen, etc.

" 'Gentlemen: George Washington, the revered Father of his Country, is dead. His long and brilliant career is closed, alas! forever. He was greatly respected in this section of the country, and his untimely decease cast a gloom over the whole community. He died on the 14th day of December,

1799. He passed peacefully away from the scene of his honors and his great achievements, the most lamented hero and the best beloved that ever earth hath yielded unto Death. As such a time as this, *you* speak of water-lots!—what a lot was his!

" 'What is fame! Fame is an accident. Sir Isaac Newton discovered an apple falling to the ground—a trivial discovery, truly, and one which a million men had made before him— but his parents were influential, and so they tortured that small circumstance into something wonderful, and, lo! the simple world took up the shout and, in almost the twinkling of an eye, that man was famous. Treasure these thoughts.

" 'Poesy, sweet poesy, who shall estimate what the world owes to thee!

"Mary had a little lamb, its fleece was white as snow—
And everywhere that Mary went, the lamb was sure to
    go."

> "Jack and Gill went up the hill
>   To draw a pail of water;
> Jack fell down and broke his crown,
>   And Gill came tumbling after."

" 'For simplicity, elegance of diction, and freedom from immoral tendencies, I regard those two poems in the light of gems. They are suited to all grades of intelligence, to every sphere of life—to the field, to the nursery, to the guild. Especially should no Board of Aldermen be without them.

" 'Venerable fossils! write again. Nothing improves one so much as friendly correspondence. Write again—and if there is anything in this memorial of yours that refers to anything in particular, do not be backward about explaining it. We shall always be happy to hear you chirp.

" 'Very truly, etc.,
" 'Mark Twain,
" 'For James W. N——, U. S. Senator.'

"That is an atrocious, a ruinous epistle! Distraction!"

"Well, sir, I am really sorry if there is anything wrong about it—but—but it appears to me to dodge the water-lot question."

"Dodge the mischief! Oh!—but never mind. As long as destruction must come now, let it be complete. Let it be complete—let this last of your performances, which I am about to read, make a finality of it. I am a ruined man. I had my misgivings when I gave you the letter from Humboldt, asking that the post route from Indian Gulch to Shakespeare

*Meet Two
Professional
Humorists:
Mr. Twain
and Mr. Thurber*

17

Gap and intermediate points be changed partly to the old Mormon trail. But I told you it was a delicate question, and warned you to deal with it deftly—to answer it dubiously, and leave them a little in the dark. And your fatal imbecility impelled you to make *this* disastrous reply. I should think you would stop your ears, if you are not dead to all shame:

" 'Washington, Nov. 30

" 'Messrs. Perkins, Wagner, et al.

" 'Gentlemen: It is a delicate question about this Indian trail, but, handled with proper deftness and dubiousness, I doubt not we shall succeed in some measure or otherwise, because the place where the route leaves the Lassen Meadows, over beyond where those two Shawnee chiefs, Dilapidated-Vengeance and Biter-of-the-Clouds, were scalped last winter, this being the favorite direction to some, but others preferring something else in consequence of things, the Mormon trail leaving Mosby's at three in the morning, and passing through Jawbone Flat to Blucher, and then down by Jug-Handle, the road passing to the right of it, and naturally leaving it on the right, too, and Dawson's on the left of the trail where it passes to the left of said Dawson's and onward thence to Tomahawk, thus making the route cheaper, easier of access to all who can get at it, and compassing all the desirable objects so considered by others, and, therefore, conferring the most good upon the greatest number, and, consequently, I am encouraged to hope we shall. However, I shall be ready, and happy, to afford you still further information upon the subject, from time to time, as you may desire it and the Post-Office Department be enabled to furnish it to me.

" 'Very truly, etc.,
" 'Mark Twain,
" 'For James W. N——, U. S. Senator.'

"There—now *what* do you think of that?"

"Well, I don't know, sir. It—well, it appears to me—to be dubious enough."

"Du—leave the house! I am a ruined man. Those Humboldt savages never will forgive me for tangling their brains up with this inhuman letter. I have lost the respect of the Methodist Church, the board of aldermen—"

"Well, I haven't anything to say about that, because I may have missed it a little in their cases, but I *was* too many for the Baldwin's Ranch people, General!"

"Leave the house! Leave it forever and forever, too."

I regarded that as a sort of covert intimation that my service could be dispensed with, and so I resigned. I never will be a private secretary to a senator again. You can't please that kind of people. They don't know anything. They can't appreciate a party's efforts.

For Writing and Discussion

1. One of the main devices of low comedy is the contrast between a seemingly literal or naive narrator and an outwardly more sophisticated, self-confident antagonist. The classic example is that of the country rube and the city slicker. How does this story use and vary this device? Why is it central to the comic confusion of the reader?

2. Each execution of the senator's orders is a variation on a routine. In each instance, what use does the secretary make of the senator's directions? What words does he seize upon to aid him in distorting the directions? What techniques or devices does he employ to achieve the opposite of what the senator wishes?

3. Contrast the first paragraph with the last. What is the effect of the understated first sentence of the last paragraph? What is the effect of the injured air of the narrator after the admissions of the first paragraph? Has the narrator fooled himself? Has he forgotten his role in the proceedings or is he not at all serious?

4. Cite examples from this story of the following humorous devices: exaggeration of incidents and characterization, understatement, contrast between levels of language in the dialogue and in the letters, contrast between the purpose and the tone of the letters, repetition. Is any one device primarily responsible for the humor of this story? Explain.

5. Reread the fifth sentence of the story. Notice that it begins quite seriously. What device makes the sentence funny? Compare this sentence with the first sentence of the second letter. Is the device the same? Explain.

6. Frequently the aim of humor is to serve as a corrective to the social scene. What might Twain be attempting to correct with this series of letters?

Meet Two
Professional
Humorists:
Mr. Twain
and Mr. Thurber

Casuals of the Keys

JAMES THURBER

Thurber's "Casuals of the Keys" contains obvious similarities to Twain's "My Late Senatorial Secretaryship." In this story too, the narrator relates, in a very cool, offhand manner, a series of idiotic happenings. "Casuals of the Keys," however, exemplifies a more sophisticated humor than Twain's. This greater sophistication is typical of much twentieth-century comic writing, but the difference in approach is due also to the basic personality differences between Twain and Thurber. In this story the romantic is exposed through parody. By means of irony, the reader is forced to accept the absurdity of it all. Introduced by the mechanical means of a narrator, an appealing set of strange and funny characters wander through the story. Not the least winning among them is the obsessive goldfish holder. Thurber's language makes great use of repetition both in incident and in a beautiful set of linking words. In addition and in contrast to finding the expected in repetition, the reader also finds the unexpected lurking in the commonplace.

Casuals
of the Keys

If you know the more remote little islands off the Florida coast, you may have met—although I greatly doubt it—Captain Darke. Darrell Darke. His haunted key is, for this reason and that, the most inaccessible of them all. I came upon it quite by chance and doubt that I could find it again. I saw him first that moment when my shining little launch, so impudently summer-resortish, pushed its nose against the lonely pier on which he stood. Tall, dark, melancholy, his white shirt open at the throat, he reminded me instantly of that other solitary wanderer among forgotten islands, the doomed Lord Jim.

I stepped off the boat and he came toward me with a lean brown hand out-thrust. "I'm Darke," he said, simply, "Darrell Darke." I shook hands with him. He seemed pleased to encounter someone from the outside world. I found out later that no white man had set foot on his remote little key for several years.

He took me to a little thatched hut and waved me to a bamboo chair. It was a pleasant place, with a bed of dried palm leaves, a few withered books, some fishing equipment, and a bright rifle. Darke produced from somewhere a bottle with a greenish heavy liquid in it, and two glasses. "Opono," he said, apologetically. "Made from the sap of the opono tree. Horrible stuff, but kicky." I asked him if he would care for a touch of Bacardi, of which I had a quart on the launch, and he said he would. I went down and got it. . . .

"A newspaperman, eh?" said Darke, with interest, as I filled up the glasses for the third time. "You must meet a lot of interesting people." I really felt that I had met a lot of interesting people and, under slight coaxing, began to tell about them: Gene Tunney, Eddie Rickenbacker, the Grand Duchess Marie, William Gibbs McAdoo. Darke listened to my stories with quick attention, thirsty as he was for news of the colorful civilization which, he told me, he had put behind him twenty years before.

"You must," I said at last, to be polite, "have met some interesting people yourself."

"No," he said. "All of a stripe, until you came along. Last chap that put in here, for example, was a little fellow name of Mark Menafee who turned up one day some three years ago in an outboard motor. He was only a trainer of fugitives from justice." Darke reached for the glass I had filled again.

"I never heard of anyone being that," I said. "What did he do?"

"He coached fugitives from justice," said Darke. "Seems Menafee could spot one instantly. Take the case of Burt Fredericks he told me about. Fredericks was a bank defaulter from Connecticut. Menafee spotted him on a Havana boat— knew him from his pictures in the papers. 'Hello, Burt,' says Menafee, casually. Fredericks whirled around. Then he caught himself and stared blankly at Menafee. 'My name is Charles Brandon,' he says. Menafee won his confidence and for a fee and his expenses engaged to coach Fredericks not to be caught off his guard and answer to the name of Burt. He'd shadow Fredericks from city to city, contriving to come upon him unexpectedly in dining-rooms, men's lounges, bars, and crowded hotel lobbies. 'Why Burt!' Menafee would say, gaily, or 'It's old Fredericks!' like someone meeting an old friend after years. Fredericks got so he never let on—unless he was addressed as Charlie or Brandon. Far as I know he was never caught. Menafee made enough to keep going, coaching fugitives, but it was a dullish kind of job." Darke fell silent. I sat watching him.

"Did you ever meet any other interesting people?" I asked.

Meet Two Professional Humorists: Mr. Twain and Mr. Thurber

21

"There was Harrison Cammery," said Darke, after a moment. "He put in here one night in a storm, dressed in full evening clothes. Came from New York—I don't know how. There never was a sign of a boat or anything to show how he got here. He was always that way while he was here, dully incomprehensible. He had the most uninteresting of manias, which is monomania. He was a goldfish-holder." Darke stopped and seemed inclined to let the story end there.

"What do you mean, a goldfish-holder?" I demanded.

"Cammery had been a professional billiard-player," said Darke. "He told me that the strain of developing absolutely nerveless hands finally told on him. He had trained so that he could balance five BB shot on the back of each of his fingers indefinitely. One night, at a party where the host had a bowl of goldfish, the guests got to trying to catch them with one grab of their hand. Nobody could do it until Cammery tried. He caught up one of the fish and held it lightly in his closed hand. He told me that the wettish fluttering of that fish against the palm of his hand became a thing he couldn't forget. He got to snatching up goldfish and holding them, wherever he went. At length he had to have a bowl of them beside the table when he played his billiard matches, and would hold one between innings the way tennis-players take a mouthful of water. The effect finally was to destroy his muscular precision, so he took to the islands. One day he was gone from here—I don't know how. I was glad enough. A singularly one-track and boring fellow."

"Who else has put in here?" I asked, filling them up again.

"Early in 1913," said Darke, after a pause in which he seemed to make an effort to recall what he was after, "early in 1913 an old fellow with a white beard—must have been seventy-five or eighty—walked into this hut one day. He was dripping wet. Said he swam over from the mainland and he probably did. It's fifty miles. Lots of boats can be had for the taking along the main coast, but this fellow was apparently too stupid to take one. He was as dull about everything as about that. Used to recite short stories word for word—said he wrote them himself. He was a writer like you, but he didn't seem to have met any interesting people. Talked only about himself, where he'd come from, what he'd done. I didn't pay any attention to him. I was glad when, one night, he disappeared. His name was . . ." Darke put his head back and stared at the roof of his hut, striving to remember. "Oh, yes," he said. "His name was Bierce. Ambrose Bierce."[1]

"You say that was in 1913, early in 1913?" I asked, excitedly.

"Yes, I'm sure of it," said Darke, "because it was the same year C-18769 showed up here."

"Who was C-18769?" I asked.

"It was a carrier pigeon," said Darke. "Flew in here one night tuckered by the trip from the mainland, and flopped down on that bed with its beak open, panting hard. It was red-eyed and dishevelled. I noticed it had something sizable strapped under its belly and I saw its registration number, on a silver band fastened to its leg: C-18769. When it got rested up it hung around here for quite a while. I didn't pay much attention to it. In those days I used to get the New York papers about once a month off a supply boat that used to put in at an island ten miles from here. I'd row over. One day I

Meet Two Professional Humorists: Mr. Twain and Mr. Thurber

[1] *Ambrose Bierce:* American satirist, storyteller, and poet (1842–1914?).

saw a notice in one of the papers about this bird. Some concern or other, for a publicity stunt, had arranged to have this bird carry a thousand dollars in hundred-dollar bills from the concern's offices to the place where the bird homed, some five hundred miles away. The bird never got there. The papers had all kinds of theories: the bird had been shot and robbed, it had fallen in the water and drowned, or it had got lost."

"The last was right," I said. "It must have got lost."

"Lost, hell," said Darke. "After I read the stories I caught it up one day, suddenly, and examined the packet strapped to it. It only had four hundred and sixty-five dollars left."

I felt a little weak. Finally, in a small voice, I asked: "Did you turn it over to the authorities?"

"Certainly not," said Darrell Darke. "A man or a bird's life is his own to lead, down here. I simply figured this pigeon for a fool, and let him go. What could he do, after the money was gone? Nothing." Darke rolled and lighted a cigarette and smoked a while, silently. "That's the kind of beings you meet with down here," he said. "Stupid, dullish, lacking in common sense, fiddling along aimlessly. Menafee, Cammery, Bierce, C-18769—all the same. It gets monotonous. Tell me more about this Grand Duchess Marie. She must be a most interesting person."

For Writing and Discussion

1. What clues in the first paragraph reveal that this story is a parody? Do you know of any story that it might be imitating, or do you know of any films in which the settings, characters, or situations are similar?

2. How does Thurber's use of adjectives in the first two paragraphs contribute to the humor of this passage?

3. What examples of exaggeration do you see in each of the incidents related by Darke?

4. Is the basic device of the story understatement or exaggeration? Support your answer by referring to specific statements or incidents from the story.

5. Which of these repetitive linking devices or words do you consider most effective: the use of the words *interesting, uninteresting, stupid;* Darke's pauses; or, the refilling of the glasses as the story proceeds? Give reasons for your answers.

6. Suppose Darke had found his visitors "interesting." Would the story have seemed more or less comic? Why? Why does Darke consider his visitors dull?

7. What instances of obsessive or repetitive behavior occur in this story? Which of them seem believable to you? In which could you yourself become obsessively interested? Have you ever been hooked on a lucky charm, or stayed up all night trying to remember the title of a song?

8. Would the story be more or less humorous if the various incidents were presented in a different order? If so, what order would you suggest? What is "climactic" about the order Thurber chose?

9. What is the basic difference in personality between Darke and the secretary of Twain's story? How are they alike in their manner of delivery or in their reaction to their own letters or stories?

10. The author's choice of names adds to the humor of the story. What is funny about the names Thurber uses? Why do you think he chose not to make up a name for Ambrose Bierce?

11. What difference would it make if you substituted the following names for the narrator's roster of the famous people he had met?

Gene Tunney:	Joe DiMaggio	Joe Namath
Grand Duchess Maria:	Duchess of Windsor	Rose Kennedy
Eddie Rickenbacker:	Howard Hughes	Neil Armstrong
William Gibbs McAdoo:	J. William Fulbright	John Mitchell

12. A characteristic of the comic hero is rigidity, inflexibility. How flexible is Darke in adjusting to society in general? How flexible is he in adjusting to the particular situation in which he finds himself—in his response to each island visitor, for instance?

FROM *The Adventures of Huckleberry Finn*

MARK TWAIN

The quiet humor of this excerpt from *The Adventures of Huckleberry Finn* might seem more characteristic of Thurber than of the usually robustious Twain. Huck Finn's description of the wonders of a circus performance stands as a gem of gentle satire. The comic aspects of the selection stem from Twain's placing the narrator in a world unfamiliar to him. The reader's ability to see through the curtain that blinds Huck enables him to enjoy Huck's completely unconscious humor.

FROM
The Adventures
of Huckleberry Finn   It was a real bully circus. It was the splendidest sight that ever was when they all come riding in, two

Meet Two
Professional
Humorists:
Mr. Twain
and Mr. Thurber

and two, and gentleman and lady, side by side, the men just
in their drawers and undershirts, and no shoes nor stirrups,
and resting their hands on their thighs easy and comfortable
—there must 'a' been twenty of them—and every lady with a
lovely complexion, and perfectly beautiful, and looking just
like a gang of real sure-enough queens, and dressed in
clothes that cost millions of dollars, and just littered with
diamonds. It was a powerful fine sight; I never see anything
so lovely. And then one by one they got up and stood, and
went a-weaving around the ring so gentle and wavy and
graceful, the men looking ever so tall and airy and straight,
with their heads bobbing and skimming along away up there
under the tent roof, and every lady's rose-leafy dress flapping
soft and silky around her hips, and she looking like the most
loveliest parasol.

And then faster and faster they went, all of them dancing,
first one foot stuck out in the air and then the other, the
horses leaning more and more, and the ringmaster going
round and round the center pole, cracking his whip and
shouting "Hi!—hi!" and the clown cracking jokes behind
him; and by and by all hands dropped the reins and every
lady put her knuckles on her hips and every gentleman
folded his arms, and then how the horses did lean over and
hump themselves! And so one after the other they all skipped
off into the ring and made the sweetest bow I ever see and
then scampered out, and everybody clapped their hands
and went just about wild.

Well, all through the circus they done the most astonish-
ing things, and all the time that clown carried on so it most
killed the people. The ringmaster couldn't ever say a word
to him but he was back at him quick as a wink with the funniest things a body ever said, and how he ever *could* think
of so many of them, and so sudden and so pat, was what I
couldn't no way understand. Why, I couldn't 'a' thought of
them in a year. And by and by a drunk man tried to get into
the ring—said he wanted to ride, said he could ride as well
as anybody that ever was. They argued and tried to keep him
out but he wouldn't listen, and the whole show came to a
standstill. Then the people begun to holler at him and make
fun of him, and that made him mad and he begun to rip and
tear; so that stirred up the people, and a lot of men begun
to pile down off of the benches and swarm towards the ring,
saying, "Knock him down! throw him out!" and one or two
women begun to scream. So, then, the ringmaster he made
a little speech and said he hoped there wouldn't be no dis-

turbance, and if the man would promise he wouldn't make no more trouble he would let him ride if he thought he could stay on the horse. So everybody laughed and said all right, and the man got on. The minute he was on, the horse begun to rip and tear and jump and cavort around, with two circus men hanging on to his bridle trying to hold him, and the drunk man hanging on to his neck and his heels flying in the air every jump, and the whole crowd of people standing up shouting and laughing till the tears rolled down. And at last, sure enough, all the circus men could do, the horse broke loose and away he went like the very nation, round and round the ring, with that sot laying down on him and hanging to his neck, with first one leg hanging most to the ground on one side and then t'other one on t'other side, and the people just crazy. It warn't funny to me, though; I was all of a tremble to see his danger. But pretty soon he struggled up astraddle and grabbed the bridle, a-reeling this way and that, and the next minute he sprung up and dropped the bridle and stood! and the horse a-going like a house afire, too. He just stood up there, a-sailing around as easy and comfortable as if he warn't ever drunk in his life—and then he begun to pull off his clothes and sling them. He shed them so thick they kind of clogged up the air, and altogether he shed seventeen suits. And, then, there he was, slim and handsome and dressed the gaudiest and prettiest you ever saw, and he lit into that horse with his whip and made him fairly hum—and finally skipped off, and made his bow and danced off to the dressingroom, and everybody just a-howling with pleasure and astonishment.

Then the ringmaster he see how he had been fooled, and he *was* the sickest ringmaster you ever see, I reckon. Why, it was one of his own men! He had got up that joke all out of his own head and never let on to nobody. Well, I felt sheepish enough to be took in so, but I wouldn't 'a' been in that ringmaster's place, not for a thousand dollars. I don't know; there may be bullier circuses than what that one was but I never struck them yet. Anyways, it was plenty good enough for *me;* and wherever I run across it, it can have all of *my* custom[1] every time.

[1] *Custom:* patronage, business.

For Writing and Discussion

1. What does this passage reveal about Huck's age and experience? How would you characterize Huck in one word only? This type of

narrator is a stereotype in literature. What other stories or novels have you read in which the narrator is the same kind of person as Huck?

2. Characterizing Huck with one word only would give an incomplete impression of him. What other dimension of Huck is revealed in the following statement, as he speaks of the drunk on the horse? "It warn't funny to me, though; I was all of a tremble to see his danger."

3. Contrast Twain's narrators: Huck and the senator's secretary.

4. What is the effect of the following phrases:

> "the men just in their drawers and undershirts"
> "clothes . . . just littered with diamonds"
> "all of them dancing, first one foot stuck out
>   in the air and then the other"

What effect was intended? How do you account for the discrepancy?

5. Does Twain's use of dialect add to the humor? What is the effect of the following statement, for example?

> "He (the make-believe drunk) had got up that joke
> all out of his own head and never let on to nobody."

Does humorous dialect of this type give the reader a feeling of superiority? Does the reader tend to laugh at or with the speaker?

6. Taking into account the reasons for Huck's own reaction, how do you think another spectator at this circus scene would describe "the splendidest sight that ever was"?

7. Humor aside, this passage is an example of excellent description. What are some of the most significant details used by Twain in order to convey movement and a mood of excitement and danger?

8. Twain does not appeal to all of the senses in this passage. Which sensory appeals are missing? Would they generally be significant in describing a circus? What could account for Twain's not using them?

Mr. Preble Gets Rid of His Wife

JAMES THURBER

"Mr. Preble Gets Rid of His Wife" is one of Thurber's cold-eyed views of men, women, and the state of marriage. In this story Thurber approaches Twain's forte, the bitterly ironic, even though

Thurber's protagonist softens his bitterness in an absurd wish-fulfillment dream. It is in the great tradition of comedy to take on the commonplaceness of the aggravations of marriage. What makes Thurber different? First of all, though his characters are stereotypes, they are stereotypes with a twist. His manner of treating the characters and the situation is everything; the story moves straight into absurdity, with much of the humor coming from Mrs. Preble's gradually working herself into a zanily incongruous position.

Mr. Preble Gets Rid of His Wife

Mr. Preble was a plump middle-aged lawyer in Scarsdale. He used to kid with his stenographer about running away with him. "Let's run away together," he would say, during a pause in dictation. "All righty," she would say.

One rainy Monday afternoon, Mr. Preble was more serious about it than usual.

"Let's run away together," said Mr. Preble.

"All righty," said his stenographer. Mr. Preble jingled the keys in his pocket and looked out the window.

"My wife would be glad to get rid of me," he said.

"Would she give you a divorce?" asked the stenographer.

"I don't suppose so," he said. The stenographer laughed.

"You'd have to get rid of your wife," she said.

Mr. Preble was unusually silent at dinner that night. About half an hour after coffee, he spoke without looking up from his paper.

"Let's go down in the cellar," Mr. Preble said to his wife.

"What for?" she said, not looking up from her book.

"Oh, I don't know," he said. "We never go down in the cellar any more. The way we used to."

"We never did go down in the cellar that I remember," said Mrs. Preble. "I could rest easy the balance of my life if I never went down in the cellar." Mr. Preble was silent for several minutes.

"Supposing I said it meant a whole lot to me," began Mr. Preble.

"What's come over you?" his wife demanded. "It's cold down there and there is absolutely nothing to do."

"We could pick up pieces of coal," said Mr. Preble. "We might get up some kind of a game with pieces of coal."

"I don't want to," said his wife. "Anyway, I'm reading."

"Listen," said Mr. Preble, rising and walking up and down. "Why don't you come down in the cellar? You can read down there, as far as that goes."

"There isn't a good enough light down there," she said, "and anyway, I'm not going to go down in the cellar. You may as well make up your mind to that."

"Gee whiz!" said Mr. Preble, kicking at the edge of a rug. "Other people's wives go down in the cellar. Why is it you never want to do anything? I come home worn out from the office and you won't even go down in the cellar with me. God knows it isn't very far—it isn't as if I was asking you to go to the movies or some place."

"I don't want to *go!*" shouted Mrs. Preble. Mr. Preble sat down on the edge of a davenport.

"All right, all *right,*" he said. He picked up the newspaper again. "I wish you'd let me tell you more about it. It's—kind of a surprise."

"Will you quit harping on that subject?" asked Mrs. Preble.

"Listen," said Mr. Preble, leaping to his feet. "I might as well tell you the truth instead of beating around the bush. I want to get rid of you so I can marry my stenographer. Is there anything especially wrong about that? People do it every day. Love is something you can't control ——"

"We've been all over that," said Mrs. Preble. "I'm not going to go all over that again."

"I just wanted you to know how things are," said Mr. Preble. "But you have to take everything so literally. Good Lord, do you suppose I really wanted to go down in the cellar and make up some silly game with pieces of coal?"

"I never believed that for a minute," said Mrs. Preble. "I knew all along you wanted to get me down there and bury me."

"You can say that now—after I told you," said Mr. Preble. "But it would never have occurred to you if I hadn't."

"You didn't tell me; I got it out of you," said Mrs. Preble. "Anyway, I'm always two steps ahead of what you're thinking."

"You're never within a mile of what I'm thinking," said Mr. Preble.

"Is that so? I knew you wanted to bury me the minute you set foot in this house tonight." Mrs. Preble held him with a glare.

The
Comic
Spirit

———

30

"Now that's just plain damn exaggeration," said Mr. Preble, considerably annoyed. "You knew nothing of the sort. As a matter of fact, I never thought of it till just a few minutes ago."

"It was in the back of your mind," said Mrs. Preble. "I suppose this filing woman put you up to it."

"You needn't get sarcastic," said Mr. Preble. "I have plenty of people to file without having her file. She doesn't know anything about this. She isn't in on it. I was going to tell her you had gone to visit some friends and fell over a cliff. She wants me to get a divorce."

Meet Two
Professional
Humorists:
Mr. Twain
and Mr. Thurber

"That's a laugh," said Mrs. Preble. *"That's* a laugh. You may bury me, but you'll never get a divorce."

"She knows that! I told her that," said Mr. Preble. "I mean —I told her I'd never get a divorce."

"Oh, you probably told her about burying me, too," said Mrs. Preble.

"That's not true," said Mr. Preble, with dignity. "That's between you and me. I was never going to tell a soul."

"You'd blab it to the whole world; don't tell me," said Mrs. Preble. "I know you." Mr. Preble puffed at his cigar.

"I wish you were buried now and it was all over with," he said.

"Don't you suppose you would get caught, you crazy thing?" she said. "They always get caught. Why don't you go to bed? You're just getting yourself all worked up over nothing."

"I'm not going to bed," said Mr. Preble. "I'm going to bury you in the cellar. I've got my mind made up to it. I don't know how I could make it any plainer."

"Listen," cried Mrs. Preble, throwing her book down, "will you be satisfied and shut up if I go down in the cellar? Can I have a little peace if I go down in the cellar? Will you let me alone then?"

"Yes," said Mr. Preble. "But you spoil it by taking that attitude."

"Sure, sure, I always spoil everything. I stop reading right in the middle of a chapter. I'll never know how the story comes out—but that's nothing to you."

"Did I make you start reading the book?" asked Mr. Preble. He opened the cellar door. "Here, you go first."

"Brrr," said Mrs. Preble, starting down the steps. "It's *cold* down here! You *would* think of this, at this time of year! Any other husband would have buried his wife in the summer."

"You can't arrange those things just whenever you want to," said Mr. Preble. "I didn't fall in love with this girl till late fall."

"Anybody else would have fallen in love with her long before that. She's been around for years. Why is it you always let other men get in ahead of you? Mercy, but it's dirty down here! What have you got there?"

"I was going to hit you over the head with this shovel," said Mr. Preble.

"You were, huh?" said Mrs. Preble. "Well, get that out of your mind. Do you want to leave a great big clue right here in the middle of everything where the first detective that comes snooping around will find it? Go out in the street and find some piece of iron or something—something that doesn't belong to you."

"Oh, all right," said Mr. Preble. "But there won't be any piece of iron in the street. Women always expect to pick up a piece of iron anywhere."

"If you look in the right place you'll find it," said Mrs. Preble. "And don't be gone long. Don't you dare stop in at the cigarstore. I'm not going to stand down here in this cold cellar all night and freeze."

"All right," said Mr. Preble. "I'll hurry."

"And shut that *door* behind you!" she screamed after him. "Where were you born—in a barn?"

For Writing and Discussion

1. Does the introductory paragraph of this story prepare you in any way for the conversation that follows? How? If not, why not?

2. The husband-wife-stenographer situation sounds like a stereotyped marital triangle. How serious do you think Mr. Preble is about his stenographer?

3. One of the devices of humor is the topsy-turvy situation. How does Mr. Preble's conversation with his wife differ from the stereotyped husband-wife evening conversation?

4. What is the first absurd suggestion that Mr. Preble makes? Why is it absurd?

5. What statement gives the first hint that Mrs. Preble will fall into the game? What is the process by which Thurber brings about Mrs. Preble's reversal of position? What would be a more commonplace illustration of the man-wife relationship parodied by Thurber in which this type of reversal occurs?

6. How, in general, does the dialogue in this story keep you off balance? What is the blend of the real and the unreal, the familiar and the unexpected, the commonplace and the absurd that is the basis for the unbalanced effect? For example, examine Mrs. Preble's scorn for her husband. What is the tenor of her remarks? How does this contribute to the humor of the story?

7. Do you think Mr. Preble will return with a weapon and clobber his wife? Or will he wake up, and having purged himself through his dream, accept his wife as one of his life's bad jokes?

8. If Mr. Preble returns to the cellar, let's say with a piece of iron, what do you think Mrs. Preble's comments will be?

Meet Two Professional Humorists: Mr. Twain and Mr. Thurber

9. How does Thurber treat marriage in this story? How serious do you think Thurber is? Might this story be an attempt to reform the institution of marriage? Is the reader concerned with the actual morality of the situation? Explain your answer.

10. Is the conversation between the Prebles truly absurd? What is the relationship of their conversation to fantasy? to dream? Which does the conversation resemble more? Have you ever gone through a period when you were upset over, let's say, a broken romance? Can you recall the absolutely unrealistic expectations you had about revenge or a new start? Does the Prebles' conversation sound like a replay of some of the inner dialogues you had at the time? Explain.

3

Trying Your Hand at Humor: A Preview of Techniques and Devices

In "The Case for Comedy," James Thurber remarked that "As brevity is the soul of wit, form . . . is the heart of humor and the salvation of comedy." Form is not formula, however, as Thurber points out in the short selection that follows, in which he gives advice to writers on their way to becoming humorists. Do you think Thurber intends this advice to be taken seriously, or does he present it "tongue-in-cheek"?

What's So Funny?

JAMES THURBER

A young lady, Miss E. H., of Oklahoma City, has written me asking if there are any standing rules for writing humor. I am naturally flattered to have been selected as an official spokesman in this matter, and I hope I will not intone as I go along, or become too pontifical, or turn surly.

Perhaps we might begin with a caption for a drawing I have had around for years: "Where were you all night, Chastity?" This is known to the trade as a Formula Caption, or one that is subject to endless variations: "Quit messing around with that loaded pistol, Prudence," and "For Heaven's sake, Patience, will you please give me a chance to explain?" There are many formula situations with which every magazine reader is familiar: the man falling from a building and saying something to a girl in an office on his way down; the man and the girl cast away on a raft in the ocean; the two artisans working on the face of a gigantic clock; and the two beachcombers on the beach discussing what they have come there to forget. This last, by the way, was best done nearly forty years ago in what must have been its original version: the First Beachcomber says, "What did you come here to forget?" and the Second Beachcomber says, "I've forgotten." So much for formulas in comic art.

I have established a few standing rules of my own about humor, after receiving dozens of humorous essays and stories from strangers over a period of twenty years. 1) The reader should be able to find out what the story is about. 2) Some inkling of the general idea should be apparent in the first five hundred words. 3) If the writer has decided to change the name of his protagonist from Ketcham to McTavish, Ketcham should not keep bobbing up in the last five pages. A good way to eliminate this confusion is to read the piece over before sending it out, and remove Ketcham completely. He is a nuisance. 4) The word "I'll" should not be divided so that the "I" is on one line and " 'll" on the next. The reader's attention, after the breaking up of "I'll," can never be successfully recaptured. 5) It also never recovers from such names as Ann S. Thetic, Maud Lynn, Sally Forth, Bertha Twins, and the like. 6) Avoid comic stories about plumbers who are mistaken for surgeons, sheriffs who are terrified by gunfire, psychiatrists who are driven crazy by women patients, doctors who faint at the sight of blood, adolescent girls who know more about sex than their fathers do, and midgets who turn out to be the parents of a two-hundred-pound wrestler.

I have a special wariness of people who write opening sentences with nothing in mind, and then try to create a story around them. These sentences, usually easy to detect, go like this: "Mrs. Ponsonby had never put the dog in the oven before," " 'I have a wine tree, if you would care to see it,' said Mr. Dillingworth," and "Jackson decided suddenly, for no reason, really, to buy his wife a tricycle." I have never traced the fortunes of such characters in the stories I receive beyond the opening sentence, but, like you, I have a fair notion of what happens, or doesn't happen, in "The Barking Oven," "The Burgundy Tree," and "A Tricycle for Mama."

An aging author who receives, but never has the time or strength to read, humorous stories written by women that invariably run to 8,500 words, can usually get a pretty good idea of the material from the accompanying letters, many of which contain snapshots of the writer's husband, baby, and beach cottage. These pieces have usually been written in a gay, carefree vacation mood, and it is a sound rule to avoid self-expression at such a time, since it leads to over-emphasis, underlining, unnecessary quotation marks, and the odd notion that everything that happens is funny. The American housewife, possibly as the result of what might be called the "Blandings Influence," also seems to believe that amusement is inherent in everything that goes wrong about the house and in everybody that comes in to fix it. My own experience has not been that fortunate. In my view, a carpenter named Twippley is likely to be as dull as a professor named Tweedle, and I think we are safe in setting this up as a standing rule.

Another reliable rule, Miss E. H., is that nocturnal urges to get out of bed and write something humorous should be strongly resisted. The woman who springs up, lights the light, wakes her husband, and starts "writing it out" is not only a nuisance, but is almost certainly laboring under the common illusion of the sleepy that the commonplace is remarkable. These night pieces are usually dashed off in less than twenty minutes, and when written by the female, seem to grow out of the conviction that writing late at night lends a special magic to prose, like writing in a rose arbor or on a houseboat. The magic, alas, rarely survives the cynical light of day. Tender is the night, but it has neither literary style nor creative talent, and no more enhances the quality of a lady's output than does the assumption of such cute and booksy *noms de plume* as Suzanna Prynne or Priscilla Winkle.

Since I was twelve, I have had an antipathy to ladies or gentlemen who write comic stories in baby talk, Deep Southern dialect, or other exasperating lingos, or whose characters lisp, or stammer, or talk like Red Skelton. I am also distinctly cool to writers who try to interest me in tribal dialect, African, Mayan, or American Indian. My worst personal experience in that field was when I read, or tried to read, a manuscript dealing with the confused whimsies of the Sho-shone Indians. Its author sent a letter with it that began: "I have lived among the Shoshones for twenty years, and have thought for some time that their humor, which consists mainly of heavy banter, would be a valuable contribution to American folklore. In some instances, as in the case of *ogla wahgu,* which is not easily rendered into English, I have made no attempt at translation. *Ogla wahgu* means, variously, 'not for me,' and 'I am going,' and, more rarely, 'strook him.' " My secretary returned the manuscript with a polite letter saying that I had died.

There ought to be a law, Miss E.H., and not merely a rule, against the sort of thing that emerges when an authoress— she is usually either very young or in her treacherous fifties —"invents" what she calls a new kind of humor. This stuff, out of "Tender Buttons" by "Jabberwocky," is even less clear than the kidding around of the Shoshones. One example be-gan: "He was in bad, but she knew he was not a sloop." Another exhibit, as hard to believe as it was tedious to de-cipher, started off like this: " 'Where have you asked?' Sylvia been. 'No answer in particular,' Roger whered." It is possible that a new and valid kind of humor may be invented some day, but I hope the inventor will send it to someone else, not me.

My final standing rule, Miss E. H., is that the young wife and mother should sedulously avoid the cowsie-wowsie type of humor. This genus invariably begins something like this: "Now that she had become a humming bird she wondered what George had become and *where* he was! Then she *knew!* Of course, how silly of her! George would be a flower with a bell much too deep for her to reach into. Wasn't that *just* like spiteful, inconsiderate George! She hoped suddenly that he would be eaten by a cow. It would serve him. . . ." I do not know what in the name of God causes this, but there is a lot of it, and most of it is sent to me. From the snapshots the authoresses enclose of themselves, their husbands, and their babies, I gather that they are healthy, reasonably sane, well-mated, and happy. I hate to think that humor is not compatible with a successful marriage, but what else am I to think?

We now come to the perennial parody of Noel Coward of which the ladies are so fond, and there is, in my house, a standing rule about that, too. And, if, after your marriage, you ever send me a burlesque of "Private Lives," Miss E. H., signed with the name "Knowall Coward," I will burn the snapshot of you and your husband and the beach cottage. As for your poor baby—but I am getting surly now and will close, with best wishes, love and kisses, and a friendly warning that humor can be a headache, dear Miss E. H. Why don't you become a bacteriologist, or a Red Cross nurse, or a Wave, like all the other girls?

Cordially yours.

In spite of Thurber's counsel to the budding humorist against reliance on formulas, he himself has used, with decided humorous effect, every one of the tricks he decries. Anyone who has followed his favorite television comic, or who eagerly searches out columns and articles by a particular humorist, knows that there *are* a number of devices that are used over and over again to create comic effects. These devices are used in different combinations and for different purposes and with slightly different "twists" that reflect the author's peculiar genius. Certain writers seem to favor some devices over others, and to combine these in ways that relate in some manner to their style. Style is not, of course, merely the unique way that a particular comic or humorist uses techniques of comedy. It is a great deal more than that, for it also includes his typical subjects, his favorite tones, his point of view—all the things that help you recognize a particular sketch as having been written by him and him alone.

Think back over the stories you read in Chapters 1 and 2, for instance. Which of the two writers seems most adept at extravagant, overstated, "broad" comedy? Who tends to dwell on the absurd interconnections between an individual's outer real world and his inner fantasy world? Who is boisterous and down-to-earth, and who is understated, subtle, and quietly funny? It's obvious right from the first acquaintance with Twain and Thurber that though they are both comic geniuses, they are also quite different kinds of humorists. And yet they both use the same "formulas" and devices that are stock in trade for all comic figures. Actually, most of these techniques are used by any competent writer. In this book, however, we shall be especially interested in how they can be used to create comic effects.

PUTTING YOURSELF IN THE HUMORIST'S PLACE

The rest of this chapter will provide an overview of some of the main devices all humorists use to achieve comic results. You will have a chance in this chapter to try your hand at some of them. Many more extended suggestions and aids for creating your own humor will be found throughout the rest of the book. The sampling offered here may whet your appetite for seeing what you can do with some tried-and-true formulas that you will have to develop more completely when you write or prepare for oral delivery extended assignments in comic modes.

It is just as difficult to categorize humorous techniques as it is to define and differentiate comedy from other modes of literature, or to separate various types of comic writing from each other. So the classifications of techniques that follow are somewhat arbitrary and overlapping and are necessarily incomplete in scope. They are supplied to provide a framework for your preliminary practice and understanding.

Surprise: Incompatible Mixtures and Disappointed Expectations

Henri Bergson emphasized the childlike quality of much humor, especially the child's delight in games or toys that combine elements of repetition with the anticipation of either rediscovery or surprise. Think of the game of hide-and-go-seek, for instance. Here we have a repeated act of hiding, combined with the anticipation of sure discovery, but with the surprise of the repeated change in location of the hiding place. The surprise, incidentally, may be that the hiding place is in fact quite unexpected or that it is so obvious that the seeker will overlook it. The elements of surprise and discovery are central to most tricks and games.

The humor that is aimed at creating the spontaneous laughter of pure play or amusement uses devices that put the reader or audience in the place of the seeker after the hidden jokes that the narrator has provided either for the audience or for his character-participants. We expect one sort of outcome as a result of conventions we are accustomed to, but we are duped into looking in the wrong places for their application; or else we automatically go on seeking the hidden meaning when it is right there in front of our very eyes. Thurber's sketch "What's So Funny?" is that sort of joke. He leads us to believe that he is going to demolish rules and formulas, but he has actually either hidden these rules in his own writing or displayed them so obviously that we almost miss them. The joke is on us because we laugh at formulas that the author suggests are not funny.

When we ask how Thurber hides his little jokes from the

reader until the surprises tell him he has been tricked, we find several recurring devices—all of them involving departures from the reader's expectations: (1) inserting the unexpected into an expected or usual pattern; (2) leading the reader to expect something unusual, and then providing instead something obviously trite or literal; (3) juxtaposing incongruous or unrelated items to create novel or surprising relationships. Thurber's six rules for writing humor, for instance, are arranged in a pattern familiar to all students of English who have suffered through countless "rules" in grammar and composition texts. We expect the rules to deal seriously with the processes of determining appropriate usage or of composing particular forms of discourse. But Thurber's first rule for writing humor is so trite that it is absurd: "The reader should be able to find out what the story is about." (The remark is also satiric if the reader happens to have been mystified by some currently fashionable stories with more symbolic weight than the narrative can carry.) Thurber also sprinkles in redundancies, which are listed as separate items instead of being grouped together. His third "rule," using specific names, illustrates the device of inserting irrelevant or trivial material into a pattern that is general and purportedly concerned with major principles. His fourth item is similar to the third in its insistence on picayune detail in the context of general principles, but it also satirizes the kinds of trivial punctuation rules that appear in style manuals and textbooks. It is also an absurd example because scarcely anyone would consider dividing "I'll" in the first place. His fifth admonition he himself proceeds to negate by surprising us with examples that most of us would consider humorous. And the plots he tells us to avoid have indeed been used with humorous intent, especially in movies and in Thurber's and Twain's own stories—in spite of Thurber's warning to avoid these stereotyped situations.

The irrelevancies and incongruities inserted in humor that is purely entertaining are like the deliberately misleading clues the hider plants to throw the seeker off his track. A perfect example of this kind of surprise technique is that used by the senator's secretary in Twain's story, "My Late Senatorial Secretaryship." The correspondents who request favors or information are in the position of the seeker, and the secretary is supposed to hide the unpleasant answers the senator wishes to conceal, or at least make them more palatable. The letters contain most of the devices Thurber used in "What's So Funny?"—irrelevant responses that are completely unrelated to the question or problem; deliberately ambiguous or misleading material; and the added surprise of violating the reader's expectation that letters should above all be courteous. And Twain uses the trick of placing the literal, most obvious answers under the guise of the secretary's statement that he intended only to follow directions, when he actually is trying to show up the senator.

Other examples of incongruities in "What's So Funny?" are the linking of proper names like "Prudence" with actions that are at odds with the general meaning of the name: "Quit messing around with that loaded pistol, Prudence." The titles and opening sentences Thurber warns against are incongruous mixtures also. The humor in an opening sentence like "Mrs. Ponsonby had never put the dog in the oven before" is the incongruity of the very idea of ever putting a dog (alive or dead) in an oven, with the surprising and unexpected implication that there is actually nothing unusual about having done so. The same type of surprise occurs in the title "The Barking Oven." Thurber provides another type of surprise in his story "Casuals of the Keys," where the "uninteresting" guests really do quite unusual and surprising things.

Thurber does warn us, however, against using a surprise formula alone, with no relationship to a total humorous intent that can maintain itself beyond the initial shock of the formula. His illustrations, where one word in a very conventional kind of statement is simply exchanged for another (" 'Where have you asked?' Sylvia been. 'No answer in particular,' Roger whered.") actually doesn't strike us funny, even though the word order is indeed surprising. Humor must surprise us quickly, in a flash of insight. Anything we have to think about too long—figure out in a kind of detour from the main joke—destroys the split-second timing that we aim for in surprises. That's the reason, too, that the humor of the Shoshone Indians—whose language is a barrier to us, something that slows down the flow of the story—bores us rather than makes us laugh.

Practicing the Art of Surprise

1. Locate in a handbook of grammar and composition a short summary or list of principles for using a particular mark of punctuation, such as the colon, or for writing a particular type of paragraph, such as a paragraph of explanation or contrast. Rewrite the "formula" in

a list similar to that of Thurber's six rules for writing humor. Use at least one device that surprises the reader by (a) placing the unexpected in an expected context; (b) placing the obvious where the reader would anticipate novelty; (c) placing incongruous words or things in juxtapositions in order to create surprising relationships.

2. Evidently Thurber's imaginary correspondents think certain proper names are naturally "funny." Think of some names you consider humorous because of the incongruity of sound and meaning. Other names may be incongruous with an action the person is engaged in or with the character of the person who bears the name. (You might try names like Mr. Saint, Miss Joyner, Mrs. Fly, Mr. Meany.)

3. Thurber's cartoons often illustrate an incongruity between the visual impression the viewer has and the mental impression he receives from the verbal caption that accompanies the cartoon. When this happens, the picture and its caption are incongruous. The cartoons that follow illustrate this technique of surprise. What is the incongruity between the girl's prayer and the way she is pictured? How does the physical appearance of the little man in the second cartoon contrast with the caption?

"... and keep me a normal, healthy, American girl."

"I don't want him to be comfortable if he's going to look too funny."

Draw your own cartoon and supply a caption that is incongruous.
Or develop a caption for an illustration that you found in a magazine or newspaper.

The Humor of Character: Departures from the Norm

The English writers William Hazlitt and Samuel Coleridge emphasize natural humor as being inherent in certain kinds of situations, but they see it especially in the "peculiarity of individual temperament and character." A person who in habit or mannerism reveals a slight departure from our normal expectations of sensible conduct or thought is said to have an *idiosyncrasy,* a word formed from the Greek roots meaning "a peculiar mixing-together." If his behavior reveals unusual departures from the norm, he is usually considered *eccentric.* The humor arises, as does all humor, from the surprise of the unexpected—in this case, the unexpected human response. Among the techniques for creating the humor of idiosyncrasy are those described in the preceding section on the techniques for surprise; that is, the humorous character may be pictured as physically quite ordinary but involved in actions one would expect of a quite extraordinary person, or vice versa.

There are, however, two techniques for creating the humor of eccentric character and situation that are peculiarly suited for this kind of comedy. These devices are *distortion* and *repetition.* Bergson, the same French philosopher who stressed the element of childlike games or fun in the surprise of humor, describes in great detail how humor arises when a human being develops a response that is so repetitive that he resembles a mechanism wound up for robotlike responses, regardless of the situation that stimulates such responses. In a sense, this is a sort of "distorted" repetition, since, in doing our daily jobs, we all develop repetitive routines that are normal or expected habits. The simplest way to use repetition in association with situation and character is to have the character repeat the same word over and over, preferably in unsuitable contexts, as Darke keeps using the word "uninteresting" or "interesting." Or the character may engage in a repetitive act, as when the senator's secretary repeatedly and deliberately takes the senator too literally. Mrs. Preble's repetitive attempts to get her husband to go out and find a suitable weapon for her demise are extremely eccentric illustrations of this device. Bergson stresses the fact, however, that the most comic effect is created precisely by the most idiosyncratic and unusual compulsions; for example, the goldfish-holder's compulsion to grab any goldfish he sees, or Mr. Preble's compulsion to kill his wife, or compulsion of the

Trying Your Hand at Humor: A Preview of Techniques and Devices

45

would-be writer of humor, described in "What's So Funny?", to rise from her bed at night to dash off her comic scribblings. The humor arises from the inappropriateness of the repetitive action to the situation in which it is practiced; and the greater the disparity between the situation and the invariable response, the greater the comic effect.

Another, related, way to create a humorous character is to distort the mixture of traits we all expect in real life, so that one trait dominates the entire personality. This device, a form of exaggeration, can be used in creating tragic characters also. Think of the tragic flaw in the Greek and Elizabethan heroes, the trait responsible—along with fate—for their downfalls. The same trait that may result in tragic consequences, however, can be put to humorous use by placing the character in a situation, or using him as a foil to a particular person, so that his pride, or his stinginess, or his greed, makes him the subject of ridicule or laughter rather than of fear or pity. One of the reasons the senator in Twain's story is funny is that he is invariably pompous in his choice of words and invariably hypocritical in his dealings with his constituents. And Twain pits him against another character who is invariably literal-minded and tongue-in-cheek.

You will meet a number of characters in succeeding sections of this book whose comic effect on the reader is created in large measure by an overplaying or distorting of one particular character trait. But meanwhile, think of the quality that comes to mind when you consider comedians such as Jack Benny, Bill Cosby, Goldie Hawn, Flip Wilson, or whoever you yourself consider funny because they have a cultivated quirk of some kind. Or think of the comic strips and movies that have gotten a laugh for their distorted stereotypes of the tightwad, the henpecked husband, the overliberated woman, the student radical or longhair, the dumb blonde, the girl-chaser. You'll be reading tall tales in the next chapter, but you already know a number of these; so you will recall that the hero of the tall tale is either exaggeratedly strong or adventurous or daring or . . . and his adversary is exaggeratedly stupid, cowardly, or dull.

You will also find extended suggestions for creating a comic human machine in Chapter 7, "Making Trouble Pay." But meanwhile, here are a few warmup exercises to let you try your hand at doing what you're usually trying *not* to—repeating and distorting.

Repetition and Distortion

1. Think of actions or habits that someone close to you performs so repeatedly that you are conscious of them. Do these actions annoy you, or have you become so accustomed to them that they go unnoticed? How could you use any one of these repetitious actions or gestures as the basis for a humorous character sketch or anecdote?

2. Ask a friend to tell you of your own repeated expressions, or of a repeated gesture of which you yourself may be unaware. Try thinking of yourself as a character in a story. How could you repeat your own remarks or gestures to create a humorous effect?

3. Some jobs *require* constant, routine repetitions. A worker in a cannery, for instance, might spend all day doing one operation. A file clerk spends most of his time arranging papers alphabetically. Think of some other routine jobs, some you do yourself, or some friends or members of your family do. Let your mind wander over the possibilities for humor if the person continues the repetition of the routine in places where it is inappropriate. Draw a cartoon or give a short summary of your idea to friends.

4. Think of a person you know or of a television personality you particularly like or dislike who has a dominant habit or characteristic that is a kind of "tag" or trademark. Make up some situations in which this characteristic would be grossly exaggerated or noticeable. Consider ways in which a nickname you invent, or a particular type of clothing, could reinforce the exaggeration.

Departures from Logic: The "Topsy-Turvy" Technique

Mr. Preble is comic, in part at least, because of his repetitive acts and thoughts; and Mrs. Preble "surprises" us by her sudden switch from resistance to a seeming acquiescence in Mr. Preble's plan of going down into the cellar. But more fundamental to the humor of this particular story than the devices of repetition and unexpected switches of normal behavior is the underlying feeling the reader has that Mr. Preble's logic is completely counter to everyday common sense. We really don't *believe* in Mr. Preble's intentions, and we actually never know if Mrs. Preble is playing a role in order to divert a lunatic, or whether she is just as "crazy" as her husband seems to be. Both of them are decidedly unrealistic, since they seem to be imposing their own fantasies on the everyday world. In a similar, though less grim way, Huck imposes *his* "practical" logic onto the fantasy world of the circus and comes up with a topsy-turvy view. In "What's So Funny?", one of the formulas Thurber suggests we avoid is that of a "man falling from a building and saying something to a girl in an office on his way down . . . "—an equally absurd expectation on the part of the man.

The humorous technique illustrated in each of these examples is a special variation of the "departure from the norm," a departure from the common-sense principles of logic. The departures are not merely unexpected switches placed in the path of the reader to throw him off his guard before the comic "surprise" the author has hidden from him; nor are they simply exaggerated or slightly distorted thought processes or quirks of character. They are examples of what Bergson called "dream logic." Bergson pointed out that whenever a character begins to act as if his own peculiar fantasies are universally recognizable as "sensible," he becomes comic to us because we recognize his actions as in fact "absurd." People who act irrationally, as if they were in a dream world instead of in an objectively "real" world, are not merely eccentric; they are, at least temporarily, and in the opinion of the average observer, "off their rockers."

The device used to create the humor of absurd or irrational behavior has been called the "upside-down" or "topsy-turvy" technique. It involves portraying a character whose actions are completely counter to reasonable behavior. Two conditions must prevail to create the humor of this character: (1) he must be acting out his fantasy in a very commonplace way, as if he himself believed his conduct completely sensible; and (2) the situation in which he finds himself must be a conventional one, where the reader has definite and commonly accepted ideas of what would in fact be considered "sensible."

This device can also be used in reverse; that is, by presenting a fantastic situation in which the character responds in a matter-of-fact way. Mr. Preble illustrates the first type of "topsy-turvy" conduct, and the man falling from the office building and talking on his way down—or Huck interpreting an artificial world in terms of his practical one—are illustrations of the reversed type.

See if the following exercises can help you get the "feel" of this kind of humorous technique.

The Topsy-Turvy Technique

1. Recall a dream that seemed perfectly reasonable at the time you were dreaming it, but that was actually fantastic or impossible.

Develop the plot of your dream into a short anecdote which you write or tell in factual style, as for a newspaper report, as if it actually happened.

2. One of the most frequent ways of creating the humor of the absurd is by starting with a perfectly conventional situation or remark, one that is perhaps joking (as Mr. Preble's remarks about running off with his secretary would seem to be) or merely courteous (as in, "Well, *anything* we can do to help would be our pleasure"). Work out a situation that might develop humorously because any of the following remarks were taken seriously or were related to a fantasy-wish of the person to whom the remarks were addressed. Be sure your character responds in a completely illogical or impractical way, but that *he* considers his behavior perfectly normal.

   a. "Hello, Joe. Haven't seen you, the wife, and kids for ages. How about dropping around sometime. Any time. . . . Sure, all eleven kids . . ."
   b. "How are you?" "O.K. Never felt better. Feel so strong I could lift a piano with one hand."
   c. "I'm sick and tired of your nagging about my (weight, smoking, homework, cooking . . . or whatever). One of these days I'm going to run off to a desert island and never come home."
   d. "Jane's parents don't give her such a hard time, Mom." "Then why don't you go to live with Jane's parents?"

3. Provide, as caption for this famous Thurber cartoon, a verbal statement that is a reversal of the kind of logic illustrated in the drawing.

Thurber's caption for this cartoon is: "That's my first wife up there, and this is the present Mrs. Harris." What other captions would suit this situation?

Find an advertisement or magazine illustration that portrays an unusual situation. Write a caption for it to demonstrate the "topsy-turvy" technique.

4. Another "topsy-turvy" version of logic is to present an absurd or highly improbable action (such as those presented in myths, fairy tales, dreams) as the "reality," and at the same time to present the practical comment, the view we would consider more realistic, as the incorrect or "absurd" element. The two cartoons below illustrate this technique.

"You and your premonitions!"

"All right, have it your way—you heard a seal bark."

*Trying Your Hand
at Humor:
A Preview
of Techniques
and Devices*

Unmasking Sham and Hypocrisy:
Exposure by Comparison and Contrast

Most of the critics and scholars who have tried to define comedy have commented on its function of unmasking pretense. George Meredith associates the comic revelation of hypocrisies not merely with individuals but with social groups, whose collective vanities or self-deceptions are related to social problems or to social customs and conventions. Meredith was especially concerned with the kind of stage play called a "comedy of manners," in which comic devices are used to expose social pretensions. This particular function of comedy is dealt with at length in the chapters on satire and bitter irony.

All comic writing, though, tends to portray man as a fallible, weak creature, subject to vain aspirations and conceits. The technique used most frequently to expose man's weakness, whether it be destructive or merely laughable, is contrast. It is perhaps inaccurate to speak of contrast as a technique, and particularly to use it in the singular form; for contrast is such a fundamental rhetorical device that it can scarcely be called "a device" at all. There are many kinds of comic comparison and contrast: among them, the contrast between logic of the everyday world, and the fantasy-logic of absurdity; the contrast between the norms of behavior and the eccentric departures from these norms; the contrast and similarity between sounds of words and their meanings, between meanings of words and their referents, and so forth.

The comparisons and contrasts that are used to reveal hypocrisies and evil, however, are of a special kind because they have a special purpose—to expose sham to ridicule and thereby to reduce the stature of the individual or group hiding behind its front.

The most generally used technique for the humorous revelation of pretense is the establishment of a contrast between one or more of the methods used to develop characterizations—the character's behavior, words, appearance, mannerisms, and name, and the description of other characters' reactions to him. The senator in Twain's story is consistently pompous in language and manner; but his directions to the secretary are a contrast to his real intention, which is to deceive his constituents into thinking they have been helped.

The secretary's words contrast sharply with his actions. Both characters are deceitful, but our sympathies lie with the "unconscious" hypocrite precisely because the senator is unwilling to acknowledge his duplicity and because Twain wishes to expose him and hold him up to ridicule. You will read much less laughable exposures of political frauds in Sections Four and Five of this book; but the technique of contrast is similar except that in satire and irony it is coupled with a biting tone rather than a light-hearted one.

If the humorist is pointing out social or group ills, he may have one character typify the entire group and then develop the contrasts we have mentioned. No doubt Twain's senator represents a particular type of politician. Alternatively, the humorist may describe the contrasts between actions and statements of the group when its members are together, safe from general scrutiny, and the actions and words of these same people when they are dealing with those they wish to deceive.

These kinds of comparisons are part of the humorist's narrative technique and are built into the fabric of his story. There are, in addition, some rhetorical devices when the comparison and contrast are related to language choices open to the writer. The most useful for the exposure of hypocrisies—that is, for satiric purposes—are forms of verbal irony, in which the true feelings or beliefs of the speaker are contrasted with his actual utterances about these emotions or ideas. Sarcasm and understatement are probably the most common forms of verbal irony. We have all made sarcastic remarks intended to reduce our antagonist's stature in other people's eyes or to expose what we, at least, consider his weaknesses. Understatement is a little more subtle and often more effective than sarcasm. Sarcasm depends on contrast between what is said and what is believed or intended: substituting "That was a brilliant idea" for "I think that was pretty stupid." Understatement involves the deliberate weakening of an otherwise positive statement: substituting, for example, "He's pretty economical" for "He's a perfect miser."

There are numerous other kinds of techniques available to the humorist, as we have said, but it is important to remember that the selection of one kind over another must be related to the writer's purpose. In the two short exercises that follow, you are asked to use contrasts and comparisons to expose a truth that has been hidden under a cloak of pretense.

1. Make a sarcastic statement about the following types of people: "dumb" blondes; overcute children; self-con-

Trying Your Hand at Humor: A Preview of Techniques and Devices

sciously well-dressed men or women; overcritical teachers.

2. Write a sentence containing an understatement about (1) George Washington's honesty, (2) the size of a miniature poodle or a Pekingese, (3) the florid oratory of a Fourth of July speaker, (4) the charitable intentions of a "friend" who gossips behind one's back.

Playing With Words

If you are a writer, rather than a television or stage comic or a cartoonist, language, with its special possibilities and limitations, is the medium with which you must create your comic effects. There is a special kind of humorous effect that depends almost solely on language. For example, all of the following excerpts from "What's So Funny?" illustrate the kind of humor that results from playing with words:

a. "In my own view, a carpenter named Twippley is likely to be as dull as a professor named Tweedle . . ."

b. " . . . such names as Ann S. Thetic, Maud Lynn, Sally Forth, Bertha Twins, and the like."

c. *Ogla wahgu* means, variously, 'not for me,' and 'I am going,' and, more rarely, 'strook him.' "

d. "Tender is the night, but it has neither literary style nor creative talent . . ."

e. ". . . a burlesque of 'Private Lives' . . . signed with the name 'Knowall Coward'."

The first example takes us back to the kind of verbal play that children engage in, laughing at certain sounds and names that seem either pleasant or "funny." Adults seem to retain this same propensity. Think of some of the words that strike you as being funny, some names you might use for a certain type of comic character. Though we might differ widely in our candidates for naturally funny terms, probably we would make our choices because the sounds of the words strike us as un-English or unfamiliar or because the word is associated in our mind with an experience or similar sounding word that actually does have a humorous association. For example, what names would you consider believable or "realistic" for a plumber? a policeman? a motorcyclist? an interior decorator? How would you adjust these names for a humorous effect?

The second example produces names that, if read aloud

quickly, sound as if they were adjectives ("maudlin") or reports of events ("Bertha Twins"). Try a few of your own, before moving on to the third example of verbal play, in which the writer uses foreign phrases that are either vaguely familiar or totally unfamiliar to the reader. In the example given here, the term itself sounds unusual to our ears, and one of the translations is a nonsense form ("strook") that sounds as if it might be a verb form such as "took." Another variation of the same technique is to use well-known foreign terms in inappropriate places. In "The Dog That Bit People," a Thurber story that appears later in this book, a dog who has bitten just about everybody within biting distance but who is nevertheless dearly loved by the mother of the family, is buried by a son: "On the board I wrote with an indelible pencil 'Cave Canem.' Mother was quite pleased with the simple classic dignity of the old Latin epitaph." Thurber here is counting on the reader's ability to translate the inscription, which must be more accurate than the mother's. She is unaware that it means "Beware of the dog." No doubt you can think of some humorous ways to use expressions like "E pluribus unum" or "hors d'oeuvre" or "table d'hôte" or "carpe diem."

The fourth example from "What's So Funny?" illustrates the insertion into an inappropriate context of an allusion to literature or to some familiar or proverbial expression. Not strictly a linguistic or verbal device, it is nevertheless a form of humor that depends upon the reader's knowledge of the exact words and origin of an allusion. The classic example of a misquoted or misinterpreted allusion is that of the child who repeats the Lord's Prayer, beginning with "Our Father Who art in heaven, Harold be thy name." Twain uses this device in the beginning of "My Late Senatorial Secretaryship" when in the role of the narrator, he says: "My bread began to return from over the waters . . . " *Tender Is the Night* is the title of a serious novel by F. Scott Fitzgerald, and Thurber's use of the title in connection with the night-scribbler's compulsions places it in a humorous context not appropriate to Fitzgerald's work. Thurber also uses allusions as a source of humor by garbling them or misquoting them: for example, in "Here Come the Dolphins" (page 260), he writes "How sharper than a sermon's truth . . ." for "How sharper than a serpent's tooth."

Think of ways you could garble such sayings as: "A stitch in time saves nine"; "All's well that ends well"; "Life is just a bowl of cherries." Or select any other well-known saying, and twist it for comic effect.

The fifth device is one that has been called the "lowest form of humor": the pun. A pun is formed by deliberately confusing words or phrases that sound alike but have different meanings. Think of authors, television personalities, or other well-known people, whose names you can pun on. Try your puns out on friends to see who can make up the "worst," which is often the "best," pun.

The Indispensable Technique: Assuming the Guise of Detachment

If the elements of comedy are what critics have observed them to be, and if humor arises from certain situations, characters, and word plays, then the humorist must use techniques that capture the childlike pleasure in surprise and repetition-with-variations. He must also use techniques that reveal the humor in repetitive thoughts or actions or in words *without* variations, the sort of phenomena we notice in human beings who become such slaves to routines or taboos that they are more like wound-up toys or machines than like rational human beings. Humorists must capitalize on our liking to be "in" on the joke that the "fall guy" is unaware of.

The creator of comedy must learn what devices best reveal the ridiculous or absurd elements in individuals and situations. He must master how to reveal hypocrisies and vanities in a humorous rather than a didactic or sermonizing way. He must know how to help us make light of troubles that are more irritating or temporarily frustrating than tragic, but he must also use techniques that bare ugliness and brutality. And, most difficult of all, he must be able to let us laugh at someone else first, and then have us suddenly realize that in many cases *we* are equally laughable, vain, or weak. The humorist must do all these things without seeming to be involved deeply personally, except perhaps in the case of bitter humor, when his anger may often erupt through the mask of ironic detachment. For the key technique of the humorist is that of detachment, real or simulated.

Distance from the narrative action is not achieved by what we may accurately call techniques or devices. Rather it results from a combination of two basic elements of narration—point of view and tone. Every succeeding section of this book will consider these two elements in their particular relation to each of the four types of comedy we will deal with. We can, at this time, speak very generally of some of the typical narrative points of view and stylistic tones most useful to humorous writers. The author can, for instance, assume the role of an impersonal narrator, writing as a first-person observer or third-person reporter of events. In either case, he must adopt the role of the uninvolved, or at least not centrally involved, spectator or participant. Or, he may write as a first-person narrator who is actively involved but who describes the action from a limited or prejudiced viewpoint.

The stories you have read illustrate these varying points of view. Thurber's first-person narrator who visits Darrell Darke on his little island is uninvolved in the events he describes; Thurber's third-person impersonal narrator relates the story of Mr. Preble and his wife. The senator's secretary is quite enmeshed in the action, but he tells his story in a completely matter-of-fact way and from a prejudiced point of view. And Huck, an involved spectator at the circus, tells us his story from the limitations of his own experience with circuses and in the straightforward way he usually uses when he describes physical aspects of setting or character.

It is important to notice that when the narrator is either playing a key role in the action (as the secretary is) or is keenly interested in the action (as Huck is), the *tone* rather than the narrative point of view must convey the detachment of humor. It is, in fact, the interrelationship of tone and viewpoint that creates the humorous effect in these two instances. The tone necessarily changes to counter the point of view or to complement and support it. If the first-person narrator has a stake in the action he describes, then he must either exaggerate his responses or understate them. Huck's tone is one of excited response, but here the reader corrects Huck's vision with his own knowledge of the circus. The secretary's tone is the more usual tone adopted by humorists— very deadpan, literal, seemingly direct and down-to-earth. It is obviously a tongue-in-cheek device. An uninvolved narrator, whether first or third person, usually adopts a matter-of-fact tone, reporting the most unusual events or character traits as if they were quite ordinary. This kind of narrator, exemplified by Darke's guest and the anonymous narrator of Mr. Preble's compulsions, relies more heavily on understatement than on tongue-in-cheek innocence or simulated literalness.

As Mark Twain will tell you in the final section of this chapter, deadpan delivery is indispensable to oral humor or to oral readings.

But for the present, to practice the art of detached narration and/or matter-of-fact tone, you might try your hand at the following exercises.

Detached Narration and Tone

1. Write a short paragraph following these directions from an English teacher bent on helping you "make your writing more interesting." Create humor by taking the directions at face value and by assuming a first person, innocent, literal narrator.

   a. Write a vivid description of some activity you particularly enjoy, like gardening or playing a guitar. Use as many colorful verbs as possible! Make your description come alive!

   b. Develop a comparison of spring and winter. Try for originality and unique, "never-before" figures of speech, such as personification and similes.

2. Make a collection of directions in the form of short commands that you have seen or read in public places or in advertisements. The pointing finger of Uncle Sam on posters for military recruitment, with the caption, "Your country wants you. Enlist now!" is an example of a command which, if taken literally by every eligible male and female, would produce ludicrous results. Select one from your collection of commands and imagine yourself as a third-person observer or a first-person involved narrator. Describe briefly the kinds of situations you might create if you were to develop this idea into a humorous sketch.

3. Understatement is frequently used to establish a matter-of-fact tone. Twain's secretary, who, after disastrous conflicts with his superior, says "I judged it best to resign" is understating, as he is when he remarks that one of his letters "appears to me to dodge the water-lot question" when, in actuality, it was not mentioned at all. And the word "uninteresting" in "Casuals of the Keys" is an understatement. Understatement is a most effective device by which to reduce to everyday dimensions an event that is extravagant. One of Thurber's most famous drawings illustrates this coupling of understatement with extravagant or outlandish action.

"Touché!"

Select a picture or illustration of a violent or exaggerated action (from a sports magazine, for example) and devise an understated caption. Try to limit your caption to a short sentence or, if possible, a single word.

Techniques of "Talking" a Story

All the devices for achieving comic effects that have been discussed or tried out in this chapter are the customary resources of any good humorist. But as Mark Twain pointed out on a number of occasions, "Written things are not for speech; their form is literary . . . " Twain did not imply that written pieces cannot be made funny when adapted for oral presentation. He was simply applying his awareness of the fact that spoken language—the "primary" or fundamental language—has a number of advantages over its graphic counterpart because the built-in intonational systems of speech and its greater range of options among linguistic usages and styles give it more flexibility and versatility than writing. The speaker has the advantage, too, of a "live" audience whose responses give him clues to the need for changes in his delivery as he goes along. The writer's audience, on the other hand, is usually one anonymous reader who "translates" the author's meaning in private, in terms of his own experience and his personal interpretation of the relationships between such written devices as italicized words and punctuation marks and the stresses, pitches, and pauses they may or may not represent. Twain knew that reading aloud from a printed text, no matter how competent the interpretation, is not as effective as telling a story as though talking spontaneously to one's listeners. Indeed, Twain's writing style—informal and colloquial—reflects the oral tradition better than that of any other American writer.

Twain spent a considerable part of his life on the public platforms of the then popular lecture circuits, giving what were called "public readings." He describes in his *Autobiography* his own reactions to the best-known public reader of his day, the novelist Charles Dickens, whom Twain first heard in Steinway Hall in New York City in January, 1868. Dickens read aloud from his own works, "with great force and animation, in the lively passages, and with stirring effect. It will be understood that he did not merely read but also acted . . . "

But when Twain tried his own hand at reading directly from the text, he was not pleased with the results:

> I had never tried reading as a trade, and I wanted to try it. . . . It was ghastly! At least in the beginning. I had selected my readings well enough but had not studied them. I supposed it would only be necessary to do like Dickens—get out on the platform and read from the book. I did that and made a botch of it. Written things are not for speech; their form is literary; they are stiff, inflexible, and will not lend themselves to happy and effective delivery with the tongue— where their purpose is to merely entertain, not instruct; they have to be limbered up, broken up, colloquialized, and turned into the common forms of unpremeditated talk— otherwise they will bore the house, not entertain it. After a week's experience with the book, I laid it aside and never carried it to the platform again; but meantime I had memorized those pieces, and in delivering them from the platform they soon transformed themselves into flexible talk, with all their obstructing preciseness and formalities gone out of them for good.

One of the readings which I used was part of an extravagant chapter in dialect from *Roughing It* which I entitled "His Grandfather's Old Ram." After I had memorized it, it began to undergo changes on the platform, and it continued to edit and revise itself night after night until, by and by, from dreading to begin on it before an audience, I came to like it and enjoy it. I never knew how considerable the changes had been when I finished the season's work; I never knew until ten or eleven years later, when I took up that book in a parlor in New York one night to read that chapter to a dozen friends, of the two sexes, who had asked for it. It *wouldn't read*—that is, it wouldn't read aloud. I struggled along with it for five minutes and then gave it up and said I should have to tell the tale as best I might from memory. It turned out that my memory was equal to the emergency; it reproduced the platform form of the story pretty faithfully after that interval of years.

I find myself unable to clearly and definitely explain why the one can be effectively *recited* before an audience and the other can't; there is a reason, but it is too subtle for adequate conveyance by the lumbering vehicle of words; I sense it but cannot express it; it is as elusive as an odor, pungent, pervasive, but defying analysis. I give it up. I merely know that the one version will recite, and the other won't.

By reciting I mean, of course, delivery from memory; neither version can be read effectively from the book. There are plenty of good reasons why this should be so, but there is one reason which is sufficient by itself, perhaps: in reading from the book you are telling another person's tale at second hand; you are a mimic and not the person involved; you are an artificiality, not a reality; whereas in telling the tale without the book, you absorb the character and presently become the man himself, just as is the case with the actor.

The greatest actor would not be able to carry his audience by storm with a book in his hand; reading from the book renders the nicest shadings of delivery impossible. I mean those studied fictions which seem to be the impulse of the moment and which are so effective; such as, for instance, fictitious hesitancies for the right word, fictitious unconscious pauses, fictitious unconscious side remarks, fictitious unconscious embarrassments, fictitious unconscious emphases placed upon the wrong word with a deep intention back of it—these and all the other artful fictive shades which give to a recited tale the captivating naturalness of an impromptu narration can be attempted by a book reader and are at-

Trying Your Hand at Humor: A Preview of Techniques and Devices

tempted, but they are easily detectable as artifice, and although the audience may admire their cleverness and their ingenuity as artifice, they only get at the intellect of the house, they don't get at its heart; and so the reader's success lacks a good deal of being complete.

When a man is reading from a book on the platform, he soon realizes that there is one powerful gun in his battery of artifice that he can't work with an effect proportionate to its caliber: that is the *pause*—that impressive silence, that eloquent silence, that geometrically progressive silence which often achieves a desired effect where no combination of words howsoever felicitous could accomplish it. The pause is not of much use to the man who is reading from a book because he cannot know what the exact length of it ought to be; he is not the one to determine the measurement—the audience must do that for him. He must perceive by their faces when the pause has reached the proper length, but his eyes are not on the faces, they are on the book; therefore he must determine the proper length of the pause by guess; he cannot guess with exactness, and nothing but exactness, absolute exactness, will answer.

The man who recites without the book has all the advantage; when he comes to an old familiar remark in his tale which he has uttered nightly for a hundred nights—a remark preceded or followed by a pause—the faces of the audience tell him when to end the pause. For one audience the pause will be short, for another a little longer, for another a shade longer still; the performer must vary the length of the pause to suit the shades of difference between audiences. These variations of measurement are so slight, so delicate, that they may almost be compared with the shadings achieved by Pratt and Whitney's ingenious machine which measures the five-millionth part of an inch. An audience is that machine's twin; it can measure a pause down to that vanishing fraction.

Much later in his life, in 1895 to be precise, in a piece entitled "How to Tell a Story," Twain gave more definite directions for telling particular types of humorous tales. It was these kinds of tales that Twain himself was adept at both writing and telling—the rambling, discursive story he referred to in the preceding excerpt from his autobiography, and also the kind of story, often in the form of an exaggerated joke or tall tale, where the narrator is portrayed as a deadpan, straight-faced rube who is actually making a fool of his more urbane and pretentious antagonist.

I do not claim that I can tell a story as it ought to be told. I only claim to know how a story ought to be told, for I have been almost daily in the company of the most expert story-tellers for many years.

There are several kinds of stories, but only one difficult kind—the humorous. . . .

The humorous story is told gravely; the teller does his best to conceal the fact that he even dimly suspects that there is anything funny about it; but the teller of the comic story tells you beforehand that it is one of the funniest things he has ever heard, then tells it with eager delight, and is the first person to laugh when he gets through. And sometimes, if he has had good success, he is so glad and happy that he will repeat the "nub" of it and glance around from face to face, collecting applause, and then repeat it again. It is a pathetic thing to see.

Very often, of course, the rambling and disjointed humorous story finishes with a nub, point, snapper, or whatever you like to call it. Then the listener must be alert, for in many cases the teller will divert attention from that nub by dropping it in a carefully casual and indifferent way, with the pretense that he does not know it is a nub.

Artemus Ward[1] used that trick a good deal; then when the belated audience presently caught the joke he would look up with innocent surprise, as if wondering what they had found to laugh at. . . .

To string incongruities and absurdities together in a wandering and sometimes purposeless way, and seem innocently unaware that they are absurdities, is the basis of the American art, if my position is correct. Another feature is the slurring of the point. A third is the dropping of a studied remark apparently without knowing it, as if one were thinking aloud. The fourth and last is the pause.

Artemus Ward dealt in numbers three and four a good deal. He would begin to tell with great animation something which he seemed to think was wonderful; then lose confidence, and after an apparently absent-minded pause add an incongruous remark in a soliloquizing way; and that was the remark intended to explode the mine—and it did.

For instance, he would say eagerly, excitedly, "I once knew a man in New Zealand who hadn't a tooth in his head" —here his animation would die out; a silent, reflective pause

[1] *Artemus Ward:* pseudonym of Charles Farrar Browne (1834-67), newspaper humorist and lecturer.

Trying Your Hand at Humor: A Preview of Techniques and Devices

63

would follow, then he would say dreamily, and as if to himself, "and yet that man could beat a drum better than any man I ever saw."

The pause is an exceedingly important feature in any kind of story, and a frequently recurring feature, too. It is a dainty thing, and delicate, and also uncertain and treacherous; for it must be exactly the right length—no more and no less— or it fails of its purpose and makes trouble. If the pause is too short [long?] the impressive point is passed, and the audience have had time to divine that a surprise is intended —and then you can't surprise them, of course.

And finally: to close our preview of techniques, put yourself in Twain's place on whatever "public" platform is available to you, and retell a part of "My Late Senatorial Secretaryship" or any other excerpt from one of the sketches you have read so far. Or you might even skim ahead and find a short selection to deliver (as a kind of preview of things to come) to others who are reading this book.

PART TWO

The
Release
of
Laughter

4

Jokes,
Jests,
and Tall Tales

Although some of the spirit of vaudeville has been preserved on television variety shows, especially those with spots for acrobats, mimes, stand-up comedians, and clowns like Red Skelton, many people today may never have had the experience of seeing real, old-time vaudeville shows. Most people, however, have probably been to a circus, where aerialists vie with lion tamers to prove raw courage and skill in breathtaking demonstrations of the thin line between safety and danger, drama and tragedy, life and death. The circus ring is also the place where the zaniness of the human clown is counterpointed by the clownish antics of monkeys and bears, often in human dress. One moment you're clutching your seat in a mood compounded of fear for the safety of the aerialist and admiration for his cool disregard of danger. Five minutes later, your tenseness is dispelled by the clown's doleful imitation of the same stunts, this time carried out on a plank only a few inches from the sawdust and culminated by his inevitable pratfall, accompanied by roars of laughter from the stands.

Did you ever wonder why you don't laugh when an aerialist occasionally slips from the taut line into the net beneath? and why the clown's misfortunes—his tears, his falls from moving horses, the rebuffs he suffers from the beautiful bareback rider—all promote hilarity? If the lion tamer were suddenly to find his cracking whip powerless to fend off the rush of ferocious beasts, you would gasp in horror. Yet the bear's and the gorilla's pursuit of the fleeing clown—who trips over his own extended shoe soles and often ends in being overtaken and carried off in a viselike grip—provokes laughter.

"But the clown's danger isn't real," you say. Or "The gorilla is trained."

"But so are the lions. . . . ", I respond. "Anyway, don't you think there's some danger of the clown's falling from the moving automobile, or being trampled under the horses' hooves?"

"Yes, but as soon as the people realize the clown might be hurt, their laughter would change to apprehension, to dismay."

You would be aware that part of the essence of the comic reaction is the *expectation* of laughter aroused by the situation itself. We expect that clowns will be funny and that they will not get hurt; we expect aerialists—even the clowning ones who perform on the wires—to be adept and death-defying.

How, though, would you explain the laughter that explodes when you see someone—not in a circus—fall down, or slip on ice and zigzag crazily from side to side, or get caught in an embarrassing or humiliating situation either by chance or as the result of falling for a practical joke or a trick?

The reasons we often laugh at the same situation that makes us fearful in other circumstances are not as simple to discover as you might suppose. Some very intelligent philosophers and psychologists who have looked into this question have come up with a number of different answers. One theory is that people laugh at the physical discomforts or embarrassments of others out of spontaneous relief upon realizing that they themselves are not the victims. Another explanation is that people demonstrate their feelings of superiority over others and satisfy their competitive feelings—even aggressions and hostilities—by perpetrating practical jokes or by sharing the trickster's triumph by laughing at his dupe.

A third explanation of the loud laugh aroused by slapstick or "low" comedy and practical jokes assumes a more complimentary view of human nature. It regards laughter at low comedy as a retention of the child's natural love of play. Jokes and tricks are kinds of games that satisfy a childlike delight in the unexpected, a love of surprise—provided the surprise is not a threatening one. There is probably some truth in all three points of view, though quite obviously the combination of aggressiveness, competitiveness, relief of tension, or well-meaning playfulness varies with different kinds of jokes or with the personality of the trickster and the guffawing observer.

The kinds of comic situations we have been discussing are mainly those we see acted out before our very eyes, often without verbal accompaniment. The clown's grotesque costume and violent exertions carry the joke, as do the distorted faces and awkward falls of the practical joker's quarry. Actually, words often spoil these jokes by adding a comment that diminishes the shock value of the comic event. The writing of low comedy, then, using practical jokes and slapstick or absurd situations as material for stories and sketches, presents problems. What devices of language, what kinds of plots and characters does the writer use to make the reader *see* the embarrassment and *hear* the crashing falls? How can he duplicate the split-second shock of surprise that evokes a spontaneous explosion of mirth from a reader?

Both Twain and Thurber handled low comedy well. Of the two, Twain tended toward *extremes* of humor—slapstick, burlesques, jokes and tricks at one end of the spectrum of comedy, and grim, ironic "black" humor at the other. Perhaps because he inherited the Western tradition of the broad joke, the admiration for a well carried-off hoax, Twain is a master of written "low" comedy. But Thurber, despite his natural talent for the subtler joke and the quieter satire, can match Twain when he deals with characters like Birdey Doggett, the practical joker *par excellence*. Thurber's attitude toward his protagonist is not as ungrudgingly admiring as Twain's is toward his senator's secretary (presumably one Sam Clemens), but try to keep from laughing as you work your way into the story.

Shake Hands with Birdey Doggett

JAMES THURBER

John Birdey Doggett, known as Birdey to the few people who speak to him, must be fifty-three now, but he wears his years with a smirk and he is as bad a practical joker as ever. Other American cutups in the grand tradition began

Jokes, Jests, and Tall Tales

to disappear in October, 1929, and they are as hard to find now as a bison, but Doggett's waggishness has no calendar. You must have run into him at some party or other—he's the man whose right hand comes off when you try to shake it. The late George Bancroft once pulled that gag in a movie, but that was so long ago the picture must be a cherished item in the Museum of Modern Art's film library.

Even now, when everybody else was running the gamut of bomb fear, from A to H, Birdey Doggett was at Grand Central with one rollerskate, which he managed to attach to the shoe of a man sleeping on a bench. When the fellow woke and stood up, he described a brief, desperate semi-circle, clutched a woman shopper about the knees, dragged her and her bundles to the cold floor, and was attacked by her muzzled Scotty. Doggett, as always, was the first to lend a hand, helping the woman to her feet and then turning to the man. "Where the hell's your other skate?" he demanded sharply. "That's what's caused all this trouble." He took his skate off the victim's foot and disappeared into the crowd that had begun to gather. "What's the matter over there?" a small man asked him apprehensively. Doggett shrugged. "Oh, they found a woman with a ticking package," he said. The other man turned and left the station, missing the train he had told his wife he would take. Doggett's pranks usually have the effect of involving people on their far edges, one or two of whom have been divorced as a result.

A publisher I know thinks Doggett would make a good story. I disagree, because I don't think there's anything good about the fellow, but I have done some checking up on him out of force of habit. His father, the late Carrol Lamb Doggett, was a Methodist minister and his mother was a witch, born Etta June Birdey. When her son was only ten she taught him how to set strangers' umbrellas on fire. After an April shower she would sally forth with the little hellion—they lived in Dayton—in search of a citizen with a floppy umbrella. After an April shower, Dayton men lower their umbrellas without bothering to roll them. Mrs. Doggett would hunt until she found a man waiting for a streetcar, his umbrella sagging open at his side. She would then surreptitiously fill the umbrella with paper, several dozen kitchen matches, and perhaps one or two pingpong balls. As the streetcar approached she would drop a lighted match into the umbrella. Now, Hell hath no dismay like that of a gentleman whose wet umbrella suddenly bursts into flame. Instead of rolling the thing to smother the blaze, or simply throwing it away, nine out of ten men, according to Doggett's statistics, will flail it around in the air, thus increasing the conflagration. Many of Mrs. Doggett's victims were arrested for disturbing the peace or for arson.

Birdey Doggett has never been much interested in the exasperating paraphernalia of the trick and puzzle shops. Oh, he still uses the wax hand, and he has tried out dribble glasses, whoopee cushions, the foul smelling stuff you put on chair bottoms to make people think they have sat on a lighted cigarette, and other such juvenile props, but they never got a real hold on his fancy. He likes the elaborate rib involving a lot of people, the more the better. He will take a sackful of cold poached eggs to some crowded Fifth Avenue store at Christmas time and slip them, one at a time, into the pockets of shoppers' husbands, and he dreams of bumping into a woman visitor in the Ancient Glass and

Crystal Room of some museum, dropping an ordinary table tumbler on the tile floor, sobbing, "Sweet God, lady, you have broken the sacred chalice of King Alexander!" and making her believe it. He has pulled this gag over and over since 1924, but never successfully, with the result that he has appeared sixteen times in Jefferson Market Court alone on charges of disturbing the peace, jostling, and attempted rape.

What Doggett probably enjoys more than anything else is following a couple of women along Fifth Avenue or Madison, keeping discreetly out of sight, but well within earshot, until he hears one of the two ladies call the other by name. He says that women are fond of using each other's full name, as in "Why, Miriam Shertle, I never heard of such a thing in all my born days!" As soon as Miss Shertle, let us say, has been thus fully identified, Doggett will walk briskly ahead for several blocks, and then retrace his steps. This soon brings him face to face with his quarry, upon whom he will pounce with a delighted, "Why, Miriam Shertle, fancy meeting you here! Uncross those lovely eyes, and tell me how you've been!" A young woman he once accosted like this in Harrisburg asked him to her house for cocktails, in the hope that some member of her family would know who he was, but nobody was home. His hostess turned out to be a bore, so Birdey put knockout drops in her second martini, and after she had passed out, he stole a marble plaque of Kitchener from her mother's room and went away. The next day it arrived at the Shertle's, beautifully wrapped and bearing a card with the simple legend: "Merry Christmas from the President of the United States."

John Birdey Doggett married a tapioca brain one afternoon twenty years ago, possibly because he had lost a bet. Nobody knows. He took her to his house and told her to wait in the living room while he went upstairs and quieted his two Great Danes. He put a record of a dogfight on a phonograph he kept in his bedroom and slipped quietly out the back door. At three in the morning, he showed up in the living room with two match players, Lew Getling and Vic Talbot.

"Who is this disconsolate female," Talbot demanded, "fairly oozing an incurable antipathy to games of chance and cunning?"

The bride drew herself up stiffly. "I am Mrs. John Birdey Doggett," she said, striving for a hauteur the name will not sustain.

"I forgot about her," whined Doggett. "After all, we

haven't been married twenty or thirty years. We've only been married eleven hours."

Mrs. Doggett, the former Ann Queely, went home to her mother, Mrs. Paul W. Queely, and never saw Birdey again. I join her in the fervent hope that he may some day choke on his candied dice and pass forever out of our consciousness. He's a hard man to forget, though. I never start to get out of a chair, no matter where I am, without glancing at my shoes to see if I am wearing one rollerskate, and feeling in my pockets for old cold eggs.

For Writing and Discussion

1. Look up the derivation of the word *joke*. Would you prefer the word *trick* to *joke* in speaking of Birdey's peculiar brand of humor? Explain.

2. Clowns are often the butts of their own jokes, but Birdey's jokes are intended to victimize others—that is, they are "practical" jokes. What is "practical" about this particular type of joke? (In answering, consider the difference between *practice* and *theory*.)

3. A practical joke is a form of "low comedy." What do you think is "low" about Birdey's jokes? What saves many of them from being sadistic?

4. Try to imagine that you are watching Birdey instead of reading about him. How do you picture him? Visualize some of his jokes. Which do you think might get most laughter from a "seeing" audience? Why? How does Thurber go about creating a picture of Birdey's situations in words?

5. Which of Birdey's jokes seem to support the theory that low comedy is a form of aggressiveness? Which seem to support the idea that joking is a holdover from childish playing and games?

6. If you hear yourself laughing aloud (or silently) at Birdey's jokes, are you laughing with Birdey or at his victims? What does your reaction to the jokes tell you about your own sense of humor?

7. What is Thurber's stated opinion of Birdey? Do you think Thurber means this statement to be taken literally, or is he joking with his readers in somewhat the same way Birdey jokes with his victims? Why, for example, is the title of the story a kind of joke on Thurber's part?

8. Birdey's preparations for tricking his victims are quite elaborate. Why does he disdain purchasing paraphernalia for practical jokes? What does this reveal about his motives? Does he want simply to get the best of someone else, or do you think he is interested in

Jokes,
Jests,
and Tall Tales

73

going himself one better each time? Which of his jokes did not come off? Why not?

9. How does Thurber's use of proper names contribute to the humor of the story? Does Birdey Doggett have any of the traits of a bird dog?

10. Which of the three main sources of humor—character, situation, or language—is prominent in practical jokes? Cite some examples of Thurber's language and his asides to the reader that contribute to the humor in this story without advancing the plot or description of the action. Is Birdey's character developed, or is he a static, one-dimensional figure? Why is the character who perpetrates jokes of this type a kind of "stock" character—that is, a type of character which recurs so frequently in literature and life that it becomes a convention?

11. What major devices of humor—repetition, exaggeration, understatement, contrast, surprise—are used in this story? Cite examples of each and show how Thurber uses them.

12. "April Fool's Day is a psychologically needed holiday. Everyone needs an excuse to play a trick on someone else, with no penalties attached." Comment on this remark in light of "Shake Hands with Birdey Doggett."

13. The essence of low comedy is the contrived situation, the absurd coincidence, the extreme reactions of characters. Cite ways in which Birdey Doggett illustrates these characteristics of low comedy.

The Invalid's Story

MARK TWAIN

Some of the best jokes are unintentional, the result of uncalculated coincidence. The situation in the following story is one Birdey Doggett would have been proud to have arranged. Mark Twain, however, evidently preferred the kind of trick that backfires on the narrator.

The Invalid's Story I seem sixty and married, but these effects are due to my condition and sufferings, for I am a bachelor, and only forty-one. It will be hard for you to believe that I, who am now but a shadow, was a hale, hearty man two short years ago—a man of iron, a very athlete!—yet such is the simple truth. But stranger still than this fact is the way in which I lost my health. I lost it through helping to take care of a box of guns on a two-hundred-mile railway journey one winter's night. It is the actual truth, and I will tell you about it.

I belong in Cleveland, Ohio. One winter's night, two years ago, I reached home just after dark, in a driving snowstorm, and the first thing I heard when I entered the house was that my dearest boyhood friend and schoolmate, John B. Hackett, had died the day before, and that his last utterance had been a desire that I would take his remains home to his poor old father and mother in Wisconsin. I was greatly shocked and grieved, but there was no time to waste in emotions; I must start at once. I took the card, marked "Deacon Levi Hackett, Bethlehem, Wisconsin," and hurried off through the whistling storm to the railway station. Arrived there I found the long white pine box which had been described to me; I fastened the card to it with some tacks, saw it put safely aboard the express car, and then ran into the eating-room to provide myself with a sandwich and some cigars. When I returned, presently, there was my coffin-box *back again,* apparently, and a young fellow examining around it, with a card in his hands, and some tacks and a hammer! I was astonished and puzzled. He began to nail on his card, and I rushed out to the express car, in a good deal of a state of mind, to ask for an explanation. But no—there was my box all right, in the express car; it hadn't been disturbed. (The fact is that without my suspecting it a prodigious mistake had been made. I was carrying off a box of *guns* which that young fellow had come to the station to ship to a rifle company in Peoria, Illinois, and *he* had got my corpse!) Just then the conductor sang out "All aboard," and I jumped into the express car and got a comfortable seat on a bale of buckets. The expressman was there, hard at work—a plain man of fifty, with a simple, honest, good-natured face, and a breezy, practical heartiness in his general style. As the train moved off a stranger skipped into the car and set a package of peculiarly mature and capable Limburger cheese on one end of my coffin box—I mean my box of guns. That is to say, I know *now* that it was Limburger cheese, but at that time I never had heard of the article in my life, and of course was wholly ignorant of its character. Well, we sped through the wild night, the bitter storm raged on, a cheerless misery stole over me, my heart went down, down, down! The old expressman made a brisk remark or two about the tempest and the arctic weather, slammed his sliding doors to, and bolted them, closed his window down tight, and then went bustling around, here and there and yonder, setting things to rights, and all the time contentedly humming "Sweet By and By," in a low tone, and flatting a good deal. Presently I began to detect a most evil and searching odor stealing about on the frozen air. This depressed my spirits still more, because of course I attributed it to my poor departed friend. There was something infinitely saddening about his calling himself to my remembrance in this dumb, pathetic way, so it was hard to keep the tears back. Moreover, it distressed me on account of the old expressman, who, I was afraid, might notice it. However, he went humming tranquilly on and gave no sign; and for this I was grateful. Grateful, yes, but still uneasy; and soon I began to feel more and more uneasy every minute, for every minute that went by that odor thickened up the more, and got to be more and more gamy and hard to stand. Presently, having got things arranged to his satisfaction, the expressman got some wood and made up a tremendous fire in his stove. This distressed me more than I can tell, for I could not but feel that it was a mistake. I was sure that the effect would be deleterious upon my poor departed friend. Thompson—the expressman's name was Thompson, as I found out in the course of the night—now went poking around his car, stopping up whatever stray cracks he could find, remarking that it didn't make any difference what kind of a night it was outside, he calculated to make *us* comfortable, anyway. I said nothing, but I believed he was not choosing the right way. Meantime he was humming to himself just as before; and meantime, too, the stove was getting hotter and hotter, and the place closer and closer. I felt myself growing pale. I noticed that the "Sweet By and By" was gradually fading out; next it ceased altogether, and there was an ominous stillness. After a few moments Thompson said—

"Pfew! I reckon it ain't no cinnamon 't I've loaded up thish-yer stove with!"

He gasped once or twice, then moved toward the cof—gun-box, stood over that Limburger cheese part of a moment, then came back and sat down near me, looking a good deal impressed. After a contemplative pause, he said, indicating the box with a gesture—

"Friend of yourn?"

"Yes," I said with a sigh.

"He's pretty ripe, *ain't* he!"

Nothing further was said for perhaps a couple of minutes,

each being busy with his own thoughts; then Thompson said, in a low, awed voice—

"Sometimes it's uncertain whether they're really gone or not—*seem* gone, you know—body warm, joints limber—and so, although you *think* they're gone, you don't really know. I've had cases in my car. It's perfectly awful, becuz *you* don't know what minute they'll rise up and look at you!" Then, after a pause, and slightly lifting his elbow toward the box,—"But *he* ain't in no trance! No, sir, I go bail for *him!*"

We sat some time, in meditative silence, listening to the wind and the roar of the train; then Thompson said, with a good deal of feeling:

"Well-a-well, we've all got to go, they ain't no getting around it. Man that is born of woman is of few days and far between, as Scriptur' says. Yes, you look at it any way you want to, it's awful solemn and cur'us: they ain't *nobody* can get around it; *all's* got to go—just *everybody*, as you may say. One day you're hearty and strong"—here he scrambled to his feet and broke a pane and stretched his nose out at it a moment or two, then sat down again while I struggled up and thrust my nose out at the same place, and this we kept on doing every now and then—"and next day he's cut down like the grass, and the places which knowed him then knows him no more forever, as Scriptur' says. Yes'ndeedy, it's awful solemn and cur'us; but we've all got to go, one time or another; they ain't no getting around it."

There was another long pause; then—

"What did he die of?"

I said I didn't know.

"How long has he been dead?"

It seemed judicious to enlarge the facts to fit the probabilities, so I said:

"Two or three days."

But it did no good; for Thompson received it with an injured look which plainly said, "Two or three *years*, you mean." Then he went right along, placidly ignoring my statement, and gave his views at considerable length upon the unwisdom of putting off burials too long. Then he lounged off toward the box, stood a moment, then came back on a sharp trot and visited the broken pane, observing:

"Twould 'a' ben a dum sight better, all around, if they'd started him along last summer."

Thompson sat down and buried his face in his red silk handkerchief, and began to slowly sway and rock his body like one who is doing his best to endure the almost endurable. By this time the fragrance—if you may call it fragrance —was just about suffocating, as near as you can come at it. Thompson's face was turning gray; I knew mine hadn't any color left in it. By and by Thompson rested his forehead in his left hand, with his elbow on his knee, and sort of waved his red handkerchief toward the box with his other hand, and said:

"I've carried a many a one of 'em—some of 'em considerable overdue, too—but, lordy, he just lays over 'em all!— and does it *easy*. Cap, they was heliotrope to *him!*"

This recognition of my poor friend gratified me, in spite of the sad circumstances, because it had so much the sound of a compliment.

Pretty soon it was plain that something had got to be done. I suggested cigars. Thompson thought it was a good idea. He said:

"Likely it'll modify him some."

We puffed gingerly along for a while, and tried hard to imagine that things were improved. But it wasn't any use. Before very long, and without any consultation, both cigars were quietly dropped from our nerveless fingers at the same moment. Thompson said, with a sigh:

"No, Cap, it don't modify him worth a cent. Fact is, it makes him worse, becuz it appears to stir up his ambition. What do you reckon we better do, now?"

I was not able to suggest anything; indeed, I had to be swallowing and swallowing all the time, and did not like to trust myself to speak. Thompson fell to maundering, in a desultory and low-spirited way, about the miserable experiences of this night; and he got to referring to my poor friend by various titles—sometimes military ones, sometimes civil ones; and I noticed that as fast as my poor friend's effectiveness grew, Thompson promoted him accordingly—gave him a bigger title. Finally he said:

"I've got an idea. Suppos'n' we buckle down to it and give the Colonel a bit of a shove toward t'other end of the car? —about ten foot, say. He wouldn't have so much influence, then, don't you reckon?"

I said it was a good scheme. So we took in a good fresh breath at the broken pane, calculating to hold it till we got through; then we went there and bent over that deadly cheese and took a grip on the box. Thompson nodded "All ready," and then we threw ourselves forward with all our might; but Thompson slipped, and slumped down with his nose on the cheese, and his breath got loose. He gagged and gasped, and floundered up and made a break for the door, pawing the air and saying hoarsely, "Don't hender me!—gimme the road! I'm a-dying; gimme the road!" Out on the cold platform I sat down and held his head awhile, and he revived. Presently he said:

"Do you reckon we started the Gen'rul any?"

I said no; we hadn't budged him.

"Well, then, *that* idea's up the flume. We got to think up something else. He's suited wher' he is, I reckon; and if that's the way he feels about it, and has made up his mind that he don't wish to be disturbed, you bet he's a-going to have his own way in the business. Yes, better leave him right wher' he is, long as he wants it so; becuz he holds all the trumps, don't you know, and so it stands to reason that the man that lays out to alter his plans for him is going to get left."

But we couldn't stay out there in that mad storm; we should have frozen to death. So we went in again and shut the door, and began to suffer once more and take turns at the break in the window. By and by, as we were starting away from a station where we had stopped a moment Thompson pranced in cheerily, and exclaimed:

"We're all right, now! I reckon we've got the Commodore this time. I judge I've got the stuff here that'll take the tuck out of him."

It was carbolic acid. He had a carboy[1] of it. He sprinkled it all around everywhere; in fact he drenched everything with it, rifle-box, cheese and all. Then we sat down, feeling pretty hopeful. But it wasn't for long. You see the two perfumes began to mix, and then—well, pretty soon we made a break for the door; and out there Thompson swabbed his face with his bandanna and said in a kind of disheartened way:

"It ain't no use. We can't buck agin *him*. He just utilizes everything we put up to modify him with, and gives it his own flavor and plays it back on us. Why, Cap, don't you know, it's as much as a hundred times worse in there now than it was when he first got a-going. I never *did* see one of 'em warm up to his work so, and take such a dumnation interest in it. No, sir, I never did, as long as I've been on the road; and I've carried a many a one of 'em, as I was telling you."

We went in again after we were frozen pretty stiff; but my, we couldn't *stay* in, now. So we just waltzed back and forth, freezing, and thawing, and stifling, by turns. In about

[1] *Carboy:* a large bottle enclosed in a box or in wicker; used for corrosives.

an hour we stopped at another station; and as we left it Thompson came in with a bag, and said—

"Cap, I'm a-going to chance him once more—just this once; and if we don't fetch him this time, the thing for us to do, is to just throw up the sponge and withdraw from the canvass. That's the way *I* put it up."

He had brought a lot of chicken feathers, and dried apples, and leaf tobacco, and rags, and old shoes, and sulphur, and asafetida,[1] and one thing or another; and he piled them on a breadth of sheet iron in the middle of the floor, and set fire to them.

When they got well started, I couldn't see, myself, how even the corpse could stand it. All that went before was just simply poetry to that smell—but mind you, the original smell stood up out of it just as sublime as ever—fact is, these other smells just seemed to give it a better hold; and my, how rich it was! I didn't make these reflections there—there wasn't time—made them on the platform. And breaking for the platform, Thompson got suffocated and fell; and before I got him dragged out, which I did by the collar, I was mighty near gone myself. When we revived, Thompson said dejectedly:

"We got to stay out here, Cap. We got to do it. They ain't no other way. The Governor wants to travel alone, and he's fixed so he can out-vote us."

And presently he added:

"And don't you know, we're *pisoned*. It's *our* last trip, you can make up your mind to it. Typhoid fever is what's going to come of this. I feel it a-coming right now. Yes, sir, we're elected, just as sure as you're born."

We were taken from the platform an hour later, frozen and insensible, at the next station, and I went straight off into a virulent fever, and never knew anything again for three weeks. I found out, then, that I had spent that awful night with a harmless box of rifles and a lot of innocent cheese; but the news was too late to save *me*; imagination had done its work, and my health was permanently shattered; neither Bermuda nor any other land can ever bring it back to me. This is my last trip; I am on my way home to die.

For Writing and Discussion

1. If Birdey Doggett had tried to set up the trick described in Twain's story, what roles do you think he might have assumed in order to

---

[1] *asafetida:* fetid gum resin from Oriental plants.

see that the two boxes were exchanged and that the offensive cheese was placed in the express car?

2. This story is a kind of "burlesque," or wildly improbable distortion of a commonplace situation done in a broad, crude manner. It is "low" comedy in several respects, one of them being that it deals with matters not usually discussed in polite society (the bad smells that we don't talk about in company, for example). What are some of the situations and the uses of language in this story and in general that would be considered "low" or in poor taste by such arbiters of manners as Emily Post or Amy Vanderbilt?

3. Another attribute of low comedy is its dependence upon coincidence to explain the absurd situations that arise in this type of humor. Enumerate all the coincidences in the plot of this tale. Do you expect that Twain, or any other practitioner of this form, tries to convince the reader of the realism of his plot?

4. Why do you think the reader is informed at the very beginning of the story that the boxes were switched? Where else in the story is he reminded of the mistake? Would the story have worked as well if the fact that a mistake was made had not been revealed until the end of the story? Explain.

5. In Twain's story of the senator and his secretary (page 14), the secretary was a kind of "deadpan" trickster. Is there a similar straight-faced comic and a stooge in this story? Explain.

6. How does the story employ contrast between types of language, between the subject matter of the story and the way in which the story is told, and between the narrator and the expressman in order to create the surprise at the unexpected that is the essence of humor, especially of low comedy?

7. Compare the reader's, the narrator's, and the expressman's knowledge of the true state of affairs in the freight car. Who never does become aware of the true nature of the difficulty? What may have happened to him as a result of the experience that turned the forty-one-year-old bachelor into an invalid? How would you have felt in his place?

8. Exaggeration is the hallmark of low comedy. Cite examples of exaggerated situation, language, and characterization in this story.

The Petrified Man

MARK TWAIN

Birdey Doggett is an example of a successful practitioner of low comedy, although occasionally even one of Birdey's jokes failed to come off. Twain's invalid was not so successful. In the sketch you are about to read, Mark Twain offers himself as an illustration of a joker whose trick backfires in a way that produces another type of success. Twain's intention, at least his stated intention, is to satirize a fad by making such an obvious joke of it that everyone will recognize the absurdity of his hoax as well as of the fad itself. But this is not how things turn out in "The Petrified Man." Anyone who knows what a joker Mark Twain was might think he intended to play a joke on the reader. What do you think?

The Petrified Man Now, to show how really hard it is to foist a moral or a truth upon an unsuspecting public through a burlesque without entirely and absurdly missing one's mark, I will here set down two experiences of my own in this thing. In the fall of 1862, in Nevada and California, the people got to running wild about extraordinary petrifications and other natural marvels. One could scarcely pick up a paper without finding in it one or two glorified discoveries of this kind. The mania was becoming a little ridiculous. I was a bran-new local editor in Virginia City, and I felt called upon to destroy this growing evil; we all have our benignant fatherly moods at one time or another, I suppose. I chose to kill the petrifaction mania with a delicate, a very delicate satire. But maybe it was altogether too delicate, for nobody ever perceived the satire part of it at all. I put my scheme in the shape of the discovery of a remarkably petrified man.

I had had a temporary falling out with Mr. ——, the new coroner and justice of the peace of Humboldt, and thought I might as well touch him up a little at the same time and make him ridiculous, and thus combine pleasure with business. So I told, in patient belief-compelling detail, all about the finding of a petrified man at Gravelly Ford (exactly a hundred and twenty miles, over a breakneck mountain trail from where —— lived); how all the savants of the immediate neighborhood had been to examine it (it was notorious that there was not a living creature within fifty miles of there, except a few starving Indians, some crippled grasshoppers,

The
Release
of
Laughter

82

and four or five buzzards out of meat and too feeble to get away); how those savants all pronounced the petrified man to have been in a state of complete petrifaction for over ten generations; and then, with a seriousness that I ought to have been ashamed to assume, I stated that as soon as Mr. —— heard the news he summoned a jury, mounted his mule, and posted off, with noble reverence for official duty, on that awful five days' journey, through alkali, sagebrush, peril of body, and imminent starvation, to *hold an inquest* on this man that had been dead and turned to everlasting stone for more than three hundred years! And then, my hand being "in," so to speak, I went on, with the same unflinching gravity, to state that the jury returned a verdict that deceased came to his death from *protracted exposure*. This only moved me to higher flights of imagination, and I said that the jury, with that charity so characteristic of pioneers, then dug a grave, and were about to give the petrified man Christian burial, when they found that for ages a limestone sediment had been trickling down the face of the stone against which he was sitting, and this stuff had run under him and cemented him fast to the "bed-rock"; that the jury (they were all silver miners) canvassed the difficulty a moment, and then got out their powder and fuse, and proceeded to drill a hole under him, in order to *blast him from his position,* when Mr. ——, "with that delicacy so characteristic of him, forbade them, observing that it would be little less than sacrilege to do such a thing."

From beginning to end the "Petrified Man" squib was a string of roaring absurdities, albeit they were told with an unfair pretense of truth that even imposed upon me to some extent, and I was in some danger of believing in my own fraud. But I really had no desire to deceive anybody, and no expectation of doing it. I depended on the way the petrified man was *sitting* to explain to the public that he was a swindle. Yet I purposely mixed that up with other things, hoping to make it obscure—and I did. I would describe the position of one foot, and then say his right thumb was against the side of his nose; then talk about his other foot, and presently come back and say the fingers of his right hand were spread apart; then talk about the back of his head a little, and return and say the left thumb was hooked into the right little finger; then ramble off about something else, and by and by drift back again and remark that the fingers of the left hand were spread like those of the right. But I was too ingenious. I mixed it up rather too much; and so all that description of

Jokes,
Jests,
and Tall Tales

the attitude, as a key to the humbuggery of the article, was entirely lost, for nobody but me ever discovered and comprehended the peculiar and suggestive position of the petrified man's hands.

As a *satire* on the petrifaction mania, or anything else, my Petrified Man was a disheartening failure; for everybody received him in innocent good faith, and I was stunned to see the creature I had begotten to pull down the wonder-business with, and bring derision upon it, calmly exalted to the grand chief place in the list of the genuine marvels our Nevada had produced. I was so disappointed at the curious miscarriage of my scheme, that at first I was angry, and did not like to think about it; but by and by, when the exchanges began to come in with the Petrified Man copied and guile-lessly glorified, I began to feel a soothing secret satisfaction; and as my gentleman's field of travels broadened, and by the exchanges I saw that he steadily and implacably penetrated territory after territory, State after State, and land after land, till he swept the great globe and culminated in sublime and unimpeached legitimacy in the august London *Lancet*, my cup was full, and I said I was glad I had done it. I think that for about eleven months, as nearly as I can remember, Mr. ———'s daily mail-bag continued to be swollen by the addition of half a bushel of newspapers hailing from many climes with the Petrified Man in them, marked around with a prominent belt of ink. I sent them to him. I did it for spite, not for fun. He used to shovel them into his back yard and curse. And every day during all those months the miners, his constituents (for miners never quit joking a person when they get started), would call on him and ask if he could tell them where they could get hold of a paper with the Petrified Man in it. He could have accommodated a continent with them. I hated ——— in those days, and these things pacified me and pleased me. I could not have gotten more real comfort out of him without killing him.

For Writing and Discussion

1. Thurber tells the story of Birdey from the point of view of an observer who disapproves (at least publicly) of Birdey and who wants to avoid being Birdey's victim. Twain tells the tale of "The Petrified Man" from a first-person point of view, from the trickster's point of view, as he also does in "My Late Senatorial Secretaryship." What difference would it have made if "The Petrified Man" had been told from the point of view of a miner observing the joke, but not

being quite in on it, or from the point of view of the justice of the peace? In either case, what would the reader have learned of Twain's mixed motives?

2. Most practical jokes have some physical effect—a bodily injury or an embarrassment that produces a blush or some other physical evidence of psychological stress. Twain's joke is purely verbal; that is, he did not intend that an expedition be undertaken or that physical hardship should result. There is some evidence, though, that the story verifies the idea of some critics that low comedy is an "acceptable" release of deep-seated hostility as well as momentary pleasure at getting the better of someone. What is this evidence? Does Mark Twain's admission of his own belligerence make his pleasure at his victim's discomfort less objectionable to the reader? Explain.

3. This story combines elements of the tall tale with the practical joke. A tall tale is a kind of verbal joke. Typical of the humor of the American West, it combines the techniques of low comedy— exaggeration and understatement contrasted and carried to extremes of absurdity in situation and language. It is usually told in the form of what might be called a "whopping lie." The narrator is a braggart who presents his tale in deadpan fashion, often in order to fool his audience. Sometimes he even seems to believe his own whoppers—especially if, over a period of time, he has continued to embroider them. According to this definition, what elements of the tall tale does "The Petrified Man" exemplify?

4. Although much frontier humor was directed at exposing frauds, much of this humor, like the tall tale and the practical joke, was itself a fraud. The critic Marcus Cunliffe has said that in the West "humor softened a swindle as moonlight beautified the shapeless streets of the Western town. If everyone was a showman, nobody ultimately was victimized." Does "The Petrified Man" bear out this statement? Explain.

5. In what way are Twain's inventions for the tall tale as complicated and exaggerated as Birdey's preparations for his jokes?

6. How does the tall tale take advantage of people's compulsive adherence to repeated routines or rumors?

7. Twain tells us that "From beginning to end the 'Petrified Man' squib was a string of roaring absurdities." Identify all the ridiculous or illogical elements in the original story. How does Twain's manner of telling the story convey a sense of truth?

8. What details did the narrator purposely include to gradually give away his little joke? What distractions did he add to embellish his

Jokes,
Jests,
and Tall Tales

story? What was the position of the petrified man's hands, and how was it suggestive of the very gesture Twain was symbolically and verbally engaging in himself? At whom was Twain directing this gesture?

The Horse in the Parlor

JAMES THURBER

The absurd situations of low comedy most often appear in tall tales, orally delivered or written in a style intended to imitate spontaneous, down-to-earth, even crude speech. Note, however, how James Thurber manages to convey a world of absurdity of situation in this cartoon.

Q. How would you feel if every time you looked up from your work or anything, there was a horse peering at you from behind something? He prowls about the house at all hours of the day and night. Doesn't seem worried about anything, merely wakeful. What should I do to discourage him?

Mrs. Grace Voynton

Now, the matter-of-fact answer would be to get the horse out of the house in a jiffy. In fact, you would like to know how he got there in the first place. (But that comes up in the next chapter.) Here's Thurber's answer. What elements of low comedy are present in it?

> A. The horse is probably sad. Changing the flowered decorations of your home to something less like open meadows might discourage him, but then I doubt whether it is a good idea to discourage a sad horse. In any case speak to him quietly when he turns up from behind things. Leaping at a horse in a house and crying "Roogie, roogie!" or "Whoosh!" would only result in breakage and bedlam. Of course you might finally get used to having him around, if the house is big enough for both of you.

5

Clowning
Around

Mark Twain and James Thurber have shown you some of the tricks used in writing low comedy. Now it's your turn to put yourself in their place and to try your hand at clowning around with words. And because being funny deliberately is much harder than laughing at or criticizing someone else's jokes, we'll begin with a version of the tall tale that we've all told, though some of us are more adept at it than others.

THE WAY-OUT WHOPPER

The Situation

The tall tale, as told by Mark Twain, exemplifies a brand of humor typical of the American West. Not many of us go around telling contrived stories like "The Petrified Man" or "The Invalid's Story." All of us, however, have been caught in a situation where we wanted to avoid telling the truth, either to save someone else's feelings or reputation, or to save ourselves from some sort of unpleasant penalty that telling the truth would incur. The first sort of lie, the "white lie," is, by definition, not an extravagance. Questions like "Did you see Mary with Helen's boyfriend last weekend?" or "What do you think of Henry's new hairpiece? Doesn't it make him look ridiculous?" may leave us squirming and floundering in a manner that is a dead giveaway. But often, we simply respond with "No" (when we actually mean "Yes"), or

"I didn't even notice his hairpiece, so it must be very natural." We can, of course, take off on flights of additional fabrications in answer to the question about Henry's crowning glory, flights calculated to take the questioner's mind off the suspicion that we may not be giving a completely honest answer, even though it is a considerate one. We could, for example, start talking about all the extraordinary hairpieces we've seen, including as we go along some we've never seen, and ending with an imaginary wig so ridiculous that no human head could bear it, quite literally.

The Purpose

The purpose, in this case, is accomplished when our questioner becomes so captivated or amused at our story that he forgets his original question and goes away chuckling to himself. If we are really successful in evading the truth, your questioner may be prompted to tell Henry how natural his hairpiece is—and it will be, in comparison with the wigments of your imagination.

Sources of Invention

To get in practice for a more artfully constructed tall tale, à la Mark Twain's examples, spend a few moments thinking of a succession of hairpieces for Henry's competitors in wiggery. Try, for instance, to visualize a tiny, middle-aged, dark-haired woman who has suddenly decided she wants to be a tall, glamorous blonde, or a teen-aged boy who wishes he had been born with straight instead of curly hair, or an old man who is trying to recapture his youth and whose only remnants of scalp-cover are a few wisps of white encircling the back of his skull. Keep at your mental hairdressing until you find yourself smiling inwardly at your creations. Before going on to the next stage in preparing to write a tall tale, fix this final picture in your mind. Jot down the details that you think are most amusing. Next, list enough details of some other possibilities that occurred to you as you worked your way toward your climactic version of outrageous "fake" hairstyles. Arrange your examples of wigs in a kind of ascending order, from the acceptable to the obviously ridiculous.

One way to fix in your mind the exact details of your extreme version is to try drawing it. If you are not a good sketcher, select a model from a newspaper or magazine advertisement, preferably an ad for hair tonic or restorative, or for wigs. Embellish the basic drawings with the details of your imaginary creation, in somewhat the same way you must have pencilled extravagant mustaches and blackened teeth over magazine illustrations when you were a child. (You did this as a joke—for fun, most often—though you also may have done it to make someone you disliked look ugly or foolish.)

If you want to show a progression of hairdos in increasingly "far-out" styles, you can draw your ideas onto a series of illustrations of bald models. But when you have completed your drawn visualization, see whether you are satisfied with the result. Does it convey the same impression your mental picture conveys to you? After you have tried drawing your idea, you will almost certainly discover that, even though you may be a talented and imaginative artist, utterly ridiculous images of a progressive kind may be better portrayed in words. Imagine, for example, what consecutive drawings of the hand gestures of Twain's petrified man might look like. If you saw the final drawing and immediately recognized the meaning of the hand gesture, the element of surprise and gradual realization that preceded your amusement on discovering the joke would have been diminished, at the very least.

To understand why this is so, we have to question our purpose in making a kind of tall tale or exaggerated joke out of an innocent lie.

Purpose and Method

Following that question, we must ask ourselves what method best achieves our purpose. We have already said that, in the case of Henry's hairpiece, the purpose was to distract our questioner's attention from our false response as well as from Henry himself. The method used was to lend credibility by *gradually* leading our listener from a fairly believable but slightly distorted picture of a hairpiece we may actually have seen, through a series of increasingly preposterous descriptions, to a final climax with an absolute absurdity or joke that produces amusement or some sort of surprise. We might, for example, end our hairpiece description with a personal version of Medusa's snaky locks, worded in such a way that our listener might not get the point until after we have left him. This is much the same way Mark Twain leads us on in "The Petrified Man." The main elements of our method, then, are *gradualness*, an increasing *incongruity* between accepted ideas of what hairpieces may reasonably look like and our own examples of unusual hairdos, and *a final exaggerated example*. This final example is so extreme that, when our listener considers it in the cold light of reason, it is clearly absurd, an obvious joke. By the time we arrive at the end of our little story, we have—if we skillfully arranged each example in a sequence from slightly to very ridiculous—given it just enough semblance of truth to dupe our listener, or at least amuse him so much that he forgets the question he originally put to us.

A pictorial representation is not always as successful as a verbal one because it might at once seem unbelievable (think of Medusa's serpentine locks, for instance) or so real that it might fail to be humorous. It could even be pathetic, insulting, or cruel in its ridicule. On the other hand, the verbal whopping lie, a version of the tall tale that is told for the purpose of getting a laugh, ends up being so amusing that our listener or reader is led into forgiving our dishonesty. The gradual verbal buildup has another advantage over the picture in that it develops an acceptance or readiness to be taken in at the end. It keeps its surprise to the very last moment, and then that surprise gets a spontaneous response. Words, as Marshall McLuhan has pointed out, are "linear." That is, they are spoken over a period of time, in a sequence we must hear or see in terms of a beginning, a middle, and a conclusion. With words, we don't know the end until we get there, and the timing of this ending depends completely upon the speaker or writer. A picture, on the contrary, we view as a whole, with all its details and surprises usually revealed at once.

Another, more obvious, reason that any picture you might draw cannot achieve the same humorous effect as a skillful verbal description of it is the very nature of the verbal form. A whopping lie or tall tale is a verbal joke, not a pictorial trick. It is, of necessity, compounded of words strung together. This leads us to a third and final insight into the sources of verbal humor. Words are symbols of reality, not direct representations of it, as are photographs or realistic drawings. Words carry connotations that differ from individual to individual. Although we all must see essentially the same picture, we don't all see the same mental picture that results from our listening to or reading verbal descriptions. The verbal description *suggests*. It allows the listening or reading audience to create their own versions of your picture. If you are a good whopping liar, you will lead your listener to see what you want him to see and, at the same time, give him freedom to do some creative visualizing of his own.

Techniques

A tall tale in the form of a whopping lie is meant to be *told*, not written. So before writing your versions of outlandish hairdos that ultimately will make Henry's folly less ridiculous (or whatever other kind of whopper you choose), you might rehearse your story or put it on tape to play back for your own and, possibly, a friend's evaluation. In preparation for this step, consider some of the techniques you will want to use. Let's assume you have listed several kinds of hairdos in ascending order of "far-outness." You have visualized them well enough to describe them as accurately as if you were describing in detail a picture or drawing of these same heads. Your problem now is to find the right words, the right style, and the right tone to use in presenting your whopper either to a listening or to a reading audience. The most obvious thing might be to state exactly how ridiculous each hairdo is. But let's look at the way Mark Twain does it in both "The Petrified Man" and "The Invalid's Story." He applies a fundamental principle of leading his readers to accept distortions of truth—namely, by presenting the most absurd "facts" as if they were literally true. A deadpan delivery, like that of the narrator in the story of the petrified man or of the narrator in the story of the odorous box, is one that presents tales in a straightforward, almost expository way, and in a matter-of-fact tone, if not exactly a completely serious one. Think now of Medusa's head and jot down a short statement or two in which you describe the horror of the writhing snakes, the crowning ugliness of their loathsome faces. When you have done this, rewrite your short statements in a matter-of-fact, understated way, as if you saw people like Medusa every day in the week and were simply trying to describe her. Write as if you were describing a hairdo that is commonplace. When comparing your two descriptions, you should be able to see that the deadpan version is the more humorous of the two. The invalid's olfactory experience is an extended example of this sort of prosaic description of loathsome or vulgar detail.

Models to Imitate

In Mark Twain's "Story of the Old Ram," there are two excellent short examples of this type of understated, deadpan description of unpleasant, even crudely physical details, in what could be considered a ghoulish context. They are humorous mainly because they are told in a style that is very matter-of-fact and obviously not intentionally unkind. Humor is also created by juxtaposing exaggeration of details and an occasional exaggerated expression with this understated tone and almost expository description. Before you read this excerpt, think quickly of how you might humorously describe a glass eye that doesn't fit properly in size or color.

You see, Sile Hawkins was—no, it warn't Sile Hawkins, after all—it was a galoot by the name of Filkins—I disremember his first name; but he *was* a stump—come into pra'r meeting drunk, one night, hooraying for Nixon, becuz he thought it was a primary; and old deacon Ferguson up and scooted him through the window and he lit on old Miss Jefferson's head, poor old filly. She was a good soul—had a glass eye and used to lend it to old Miss Wagner, that hadn't any, to receive company in; it warn't big enough, and when Miss Wagner warn't noticing, it would get twisted around in the socket, and look up, maybe, or out to one side, and every which way, while t' other one was looking as straight ahead as a spy-glass. Grown people didn't mind it, but it most always made the children cry, it was so sort of scary. She tried packing it in raw cotton, but it wouldn't work, somehow—the cotton would get loose and stick out and look so kind of awful that the children couldn't stand it no way. She was always dropping it out, and turning up her old deadlight on the company empty, and making them oncomfortable, becuz *she* never could tell when it hopped out, being blind on that side, you see. So somebody would have to hunch her and say, "Your game eye has fetched loose, Miss Wagner dear"—and then all of them would have to sit and wait till she jammed it in again—wrong side before, as a general thing, and green as a bird's egg, being a bashful cretur and easy sot back before company. But being wrong side before warn't much difference, anyway, becuz her own eye was sky-blue and the glass one was yaller on the front side, so whichever way she turned it it didn't match nohow. Old Miss Wagner was considerable on the borrow, she was. When she had a quilting, or Dorcas S'iety at her house she gen'ally borrowed Miss Higgins's wooden leg to stump around on; it was considerable shorter than her other pin, but much *she* minded that. She said she couldn't abide crutches when she had company, becuz they were so slow; said when she had company and things had to be done, she wanted to get up and hump herself.

She was as bald as a jug, and so she used to borrow Miss Jacops's wig—

Writing a First Draft

Keeping in mind Mark Twain's matter-of-fact style and his combination of exaggerated detail and mundane choice of words, take your list of hairdos, select two or three progressively outlandish ones, and visualize them carefully before you begin writing. Now, talk through the answer to the original question: "What do you think of Henry's new hairpiece? Doesn't it make him look ridiculous?" Write as you talk, as quickly as you can, and write in a way that imitates talk without actually copying down every word you're saying.

Some Other Ideas

In case you're tired of Henry's hairpiece by this time, as well you might be, here are some other questions and quick answers that can lead into equally humorous possibilities for whoppers:

a. "Mary's voice is getting louder by the minute, don't you think?" "Oh, I don't know . . . I've heard much louder voices in my time."

b. "Helen's going much too far with her diet, don't you agree?" "Helen's fat compared to some people I've known."

c. "That house being built down the street looks as if the walls would scarcely shut out the cold, let alone the noise. Don't you agree?" "Those walls are positively thick compared with some I've lived with."

Another idea could easily come from answering any of these four questions sent to a columnist, requesting advice on hairdos:

> Question—I am 5 feet tall, have a tiny face and figure but my eyes are huge. A year ago, my boyfriend talked me into letting my hair grow. Now it is shoulder length and just hangs there. If I set my hair, it seems to balloon out. If I leave it straight, I look like a waif. What would be a good hairstyle for me?

> *Regrets Cut*

> Question—I am 20 years old, almost 6 feet tall and have a square-shaped face. I had my hair cut short with wisps of hair coming down my neck. It looked great when I was sit-

Clowning Around

95

ting in the beauty shop, but when I looked at myself in a full-length mirror I cried. What can I do while it grows out?

Hanging Bangs

Q.—Fifteen years ago, my home economics teacher told me I should wear bangs to hide my low forehead. A few months ago I decided to let the bangs grow out. They now cover my eyes, which are close-set. The rest of my hair is a few inches below chin length. What can I do?

Severe Style

Q.—I have a small face and delicate features. I love to wear my hair parted in the center and pulled back tightly or covered with a turban or scarf. Sometimes, however, I think this plastered-to-my-head hairstyle is rather severe. How can I soften it?

Review of Procedure

Here's a list of reminders to help you prepare the final version of your way-out whopper.

1. Establish a hypothetical situation in which someone asks a question about the absurdity of someone's dress, health, or manner, or about a particularly questionable characteristic of an article or object.
2. Prepare an offhand answer in which you reject the questioner's position.
3. Think through a series of objects or kinds of persons having a quality similar to the one introduced in the question. Make your examples progressively more extreme.
4. Be sure your last example is so ridiculous as to be utterly unbelievable if introduced as the only or first example.
5. Visualize each example carefully, and select the two or three that seem to offer the most gradual and most effective progression for producing a humorous effect.
6. Select details that call attention to the departures from the commonplace in the items you are describing, but associate these details with words that are usually associated with quite ordinary things.
7. Be sure to use frequently some of the following devices: exaggeration, understatement, incongruity, repetition, puns, humorous names.

8. Recite your whopper to yourself in a matter-of-fact way.

9. When you are satisfied that you have as funny a version as you can get, tape it for your own or some friend's enjoyment and evaluation.

10. Write down your final version in a conversational style in preparation for presenting it orally before a group of listeners who will swap their whoppers with yours to see whose gets the most laughs.

THE PERIPATETIC PREVARICATION

The Situation

Another version of the tall tale is the whopper one uses to evade punishment or a penalty of some sort, often the penalty of being made to feel foolish. We've all been caught without a homework assignment or a term paper that's due; or after going on an errand, we've shown up without the very item we were asked to buy. When we were very small children, we all must have taken that piece of candy we were not supposed to have, picked on our smaller brother or sister, or washed around the edges instead of taking that complete bath or shower. When we are questioned by whoever gave us our original directions, we often give ourselves away with a delayed response or one that seems too weak an excuse or too common a response for acceptance. Who believes us when, in answer to the question, "Why were you so late?", we answer, "Because my alarm clock didn't go off."? Or, when to the inquiry, "Why didn't you bring home the coffee?", we answer, "Because I lost the money." Yet when we give some long, circuitous, highly improbable excuse, we are frequently believed—perhaps because our interrogator is so exhausted by our rambling discourse that he's glad when we stop. Or perhaps because the usual excuse, though true, seems so trite as to be unbelievable, while the contrived excuse seems so unique that our hearer thinks it must be true.

The Purpose

The whopper that is a response to a question about our own conduct, then, puts a premium on two abilities. The first of these is the ability to respond without hesitation. The second is the skill of imaginative contrivance. This skill encourages us to follow our mind wherever it takes us, as it proceeds through a series of rambling and often illogical incidents that lead us to our conclusion

Clowning Around

and achieve our desired purpose—which is to be exonerated, un-punished, and even admired instead of being considered a dunce.

As in the case of the whopper told to evade a question about someone else, the tall tale one uses to avoid penalties does not have to be believed to be effective. If the listener is amused, or even frustrated by our tale, then he may well forget the original question and never think of it again.

The Method

There is not too much method involved in making an immediate response. Try to cultivate the habit of plunging in quickly. The trick is simply to begin unhesitatingly. Open your mouth or push your pencil, and say something—anything. One caution, though. You'll want to say that feeble, trite, perhaps "true" or reasonable thing at first. Simply erase it from your mind in the flash of time it takes to think of it, and proceed with the open mouth or flying pencil. The "method" lies in the manner of pursuing your story. The key word to describe this method is *peripatetic*. Originally used to describe a group of Aristotle's followers who walked with him in the Lyceum in Athens as he taught, the word has become a synonym for anyone who wanders from place to place. So start your wandering as soon as you are presented with the need to justify your conduct in some way. Say anything that occurs to you. The most far-out, improbable thing will give you a good start. Once you've said it, your problem of inventing other incidents becomes a matter of working your way back to that farthest-out event in some sort of loosely connected way. You'll then have a goal for your invention.

If the first thing you say is not that kind of way-out explanation or incident, you can proceed from the reasonable to the wildly absurd, attempting to provide a seemingly rational chain of events —at least at the beginning of your story. This involves keeping some sort of cause-and-effect relationship, no matter how prepos-terous the chain of events is. You can and should get off the track. Don't forget, however, to keep coming back to the main narrative.

If you're looking for help and ideas, there's no greater master of the "peripatetic" than Mark Twain. Thurber is also a master. Consider, for instance, the coincidences by which Darke's visitors arrive at his island, as well as the startling coincidences on which Birdey depends for his jokes. Mark Twain describes this very method in perfect detail in a story called "The Old Ram," from which the excerpt about the borrowing Miss Wagner was taken. The story begins as an attempt to get the narrator to tell a story about an old ram, but the narrator rambles on and on, and never gets around to talking about the ram. He tells numerous other little stories along the way, all with some ostensible but contrived connections. As you recall, the same technique is illustrated in the letters of the senator's secretary. In one letter, he completely avoids all mention of his questioner's concern; and in another, he begins with that concern or request, and gets so involved that he confuses the reader as well as his correspondent. He was, you remember, following directions to be "noncommittal" and "dubious," but he was really playing a joke on the senator.

Practice in Invention

But no doubt your interrogator is far from being interested in the fact that you are avoiding a subject; *you* are the one who, in setting up this humorous situation, wants to avoid it. So you have to appear to be making an attempt to give an exact and very detailed account of an actual occurrence.

Suppose, for instance, that while walking with your St. Bernard, you have met a German shepherd, and have, by being inattentive and not quite as strong as your animal friend, lost your dog. You return home without him, only to find him there ahead of you. The relative or friend you greet as you are effusively welcomed by the dog, asks, "Did Fritz lose you on the walk? We thought you had run away from home." You *could* tell the truth, but that would make you seem more foolish; so . . . you start out. Right now. No practice. Turn to your nearest neighbor, whether he is sitting there in the flesh or projected in your imagination, and begin talking. If you get interested in what you're saying, write it down as soon as you're finished, no matter how rough the draft. You may want to use it for a written version of a humorous monologue sometime.

Try this one, now. You have gone hunting or horseback riding. You meet a bull in a field; your horse rears up, throws you, and you limp home ignominiously. The horse is never seen again. What do you say when someone jeers, "Some rider you are. And where's your horse?"

Models to Imitate

After you've tried your hand at this kind of story, you might want to hear how a master did it. In Mark Twain's *Roughing It*, some passengers from a broken-down stagecoach—or "mud wagon"— wait out the five–six-hour delay for repairs by going off on horses to hunt buffalo. Bemis returns without his horse, but explains his plight in this fashion:

"Well, it was not funny, and there was no sense in those gawks making themselves so facetious over it. I tell you I was angry in earnest for a while. I should have shot that long gangly lubber they called Hank, if I could have done it without crippling six or seven other people—but of course I couldn't, the old 'Allen's' so confounded comprehensive. I wish those loafers had been up in the tree; they wouldn't have wanted to laugh so. If I had had a horse worth a cent— but no, the minute he saw that buffalo bull wheel on him and give a bellow, he raised straight up in the air and stood on his heels. The saddle began to slip, and I took him round the neck and laid close to him, and began to pray. Then he came down and stood up on the other end awhile, and the bull actually stopped pawing sand and bellowing to contemplate the inhuman spectacle. Then the bull made a pass at him and uttered a bellow that sounded perfectly frightful, it was so close to me, and that seemed to literally prostrate my horse's reason, and make a raving distracted maniac of him, and I wish I may die if he didn't stand on his head for a quarter of a minute and shed tears. He was absolutely out of his mind—he was, as sure as truth itself, and he really didn't know what he was doing. Then the bull came charging at us, and my horse dropped down on all fours and took a fresh start—and then for the next ten minutes he would actually throw one handspring after another so fast that the bull began to get unsettled, too, and didn't know where to start in—and so he stood there sneezing, and shoveling dust over his back, and bellowing every now and then, and thinking he had got a fifteen-hundred-dollar circus horse for breakfast, certain. Well, I was first out on his neck—the horse's, not the bull's—and then underneath, and next on his rump, and sometimes head up, and sometimes heels— but I tell you it seemed solemn and awful to be ripping and tearing and carrying on so in the presence of death, as you might say. Pretty soon the bull made a snatch for us and brought away some of my horse's tail (I suppose, but do not know, being pretty busy at the time), but *something* made him hungry for solitude and suggested to him to get up and hunt for it. And then you ought to have seen that spider-legged old skeleton go! And you ought to have seen the bull cut out after him, too—head down, tongue out, tail up, bellowing like everything, and actually mowing down the weeds, and tearing up the earth, and boosting up the sand like a whirlwind! By George, it was a hot race! I and the saddle were back on the rump, and I had the bridle in my teeth and holding onto the pommel with both hands. First we left the dogs behind; then we passed a jackass rabbit; then we overtook a coyote, and were gaining on an antelope when the rotten girth let go and threw me about thirty yards off to the left, and as the saddle went down over the horse's rump he gave it a lift with his heels that sent it more than four hundred yards up in the air, I wish I may die in a minute if he didn't. I fell at the foot of the only solitary tree there was in nine counties adjacent (as any creature could see with the naked eye), and the next second I had hold of the bark with four sets of nails and my teeth, and the next second after that I was astraddle of the main limb and blaspheming my luck in a way that made my breath smell of brimstone. I *had* the bull now, if he did not think of *one* thing. But that one thing I dreaded. I dreaded it very seriously. There was a possibility that the bull might not think of it, but there were greater chances that he would. I made up my mind what I would do in case he did. It was a little over forty feet to the ground from where I sat. I cautiously unwound the lariat from the pommel of my saddle—"

"Your *saddle?* Did you take your saddle up in the tree with you?"

"Take it up in the tree with me? Why, how you talk. Of course I didn't. No man could do that. It *fell* in the tree when it came down."

"Oh—exactly."

"Certainly. I unwound the lariat, and fastened one end of it to the limb. It was the best green rawhide, and capable of sustaining tons. I made a slip noose in the other end, and then hung it down to see the length. It reached down twenty-two feet—halfway to the ground. I then loaded every barrel of the Allen with a double charge. I felt satisfied. I said to myself, if he never thinks of that one thing that I dread, all right—but if he does, all right anyhow—I am fixed for him. But don't you know that the very thing a man dreads is the thing that always happens? Indeed it is so. I watched the bull, now, with anxiety—anxiety which no one can conceive of who has not been in such a situation and felt that at any moment death might come. Presently a thought came into the bull's eyes. I knew it! said I—if my nerve fails now, I am lost. Sure enough, it was just as I had dreaded, he started in to climb the tree—"

"What, the bull?"

"Of course—who else?"

"But a bull can't climb a tree."

"He can't, can't he? Since you know so much about it, did you ever see a bull try?"

"No! I never dreamt of such a thing."

"Well, then, what is the use of your talking that way, then? Because you never saw a thing done, is that any reason why it can't be done?"

"Well, all right—go on. What did you do?"

"The bull started up, and got along well for about ten feet, then slipped and slid back. I breathed easier. He tried it again—got up a little higher—slipped again. But he came at it once more, and this time he was careful. He got gradually higher and higher, and my spirits went down more and more. Up he came—an inch at a time—with his eyes hot, and his tongue hanging out. Higher and higher—hitched his foot over the stump of a limb, and looked up, as much as to say, 'You are my meat, friend.' Up again—higher and higher, and getting more excited the closer he got. He was within ten feet of me! I took a long breath—and then said I, 'It is now or never.' I had the coil of the lariat all ready; I paid it out slowly, till it hung right over his head; all of a sudden I let go of the slack, and the slip noose fell fairly round his neck! Quicker than lightning I out with the Allen and let him have it in the face. It was an awful roar, and must have scared the bull out of his senses. When the smoke cleared away, there he was, dangling in the air, twenty foot from the ground, and going out of one convulsion into another faster than you could count! I didn't stop to count, any-how—I shinned down the tree and shot for home."

"Bemis, is all that true, just as you have stated it?"

"I wish I may rot in my tracks and die the death of a dog if it isn't."

"Well, we can't refuse to believe it, and we don't. But if there were some proofs—"

"Proofs! Did I bring back my lariat?"

"No."

"Did I bring back my horse?"

"No."

"Did you ever see the bull again?"

"No."

"Well, then, what more do you want? I never saw anybody as particular as you are about a little thing like that."

I made up my mind that if this man was not a liar he only missed it by the skin of his teeth.

Composing a Prevarication

Using this model from Twain, but in miniature, imagine Mr. Preble's response to his wife if he should return to the cellar with a toy pistol instead of with a heavy murder weapon. She asks scathingly, "And couldn't you find a *real* one?" Or, if that idea doesn't get you started, try thinking of an explanation for the appearance of a horse in the living room as shown in Thurber's cartoon (page 86). Best of all, think of some time you've been caught red-handed and red-faced in a comparable situation not too long ago. Try to put yourself back in that place again, and now—with your greater know-how—concoct a peripatetic prevarication that you wish you had thought of at the time. Here is a list of reminders to help you.

1. Practice beginning to say or write something immediately, in response to whatever question you pose yourself. Questions like "Why didn't you bring the eggs?", "What did you do with all the money you earned last year?", "Why can't you visit your Aunt Emma in Blitzville?", "What happened to your eye?" are the kind to start with.
2. As you begin, think ahead to a circumstance that has nothing to do with the actual reason for your action or fault. Then, while you wander a bit to kill time, think of another circumstance, then still another even more improbable one that is tied to the others in some sort of wildly coincidental way.
3. The more unlikely coincidences you can include the better.
4. Establish a progression of circumstances that begins far out and explains itself in a kind of flashback technique; or begin at the beginning, with a fairly reasonable event and work up to more and more exaggerated material.
5. When you need time for more invention along the way, ramble a while.
6. Tell or write your explanation in a matter-of-fact way until you get to the circumstances that will not be accepted as truth. Then go all out to impress your questioner with your *own* sense of disbelief, your own fear, your own amazement

at these unheard-of circumstances. Use colorful language and exaggerated description.

7. Retalk or rewrite your little prevarication until you can say it in less than five minutes, or write it out in less than two typed pages (about 500 words).

8. Check to see that you have included examples of exaggeration, dead pan, narration, coincidence, or incongruously linked chains of events.

9. Practice telling your prevarication to someone, and don't forget *not* to keep the straight-faced delivery all the way, as you did for the "whopper." Act out your imagined feelings as they would normally occur if you really had lived through the events you are narrating.

GOING ONE BETTER

The Situation

A more classic form of the tall tale, and another variation of the "whopper," is the boasting speech that in a sequence of more and more exaggerated detail and language recounts seemingly impossible exploits of strength, ability, and feeling. With no intention of creating humor, the form is used in myths that catalogue the trials and conquests of gods and demigods; it is also used in legends that recount feats requiring almost superhuman ability. With its hardy, courageous, rough-and-ready pioneers—who climbed the highest, ruggedest mountains; crossed the widest, hottest deserts; suffered the greatest hardships; roped the wildest horses; herded the most cattle; fed the hugest appetites; and fought the fiercest Indians— it was inevitable that the American West developed legends of prowess and converted them, in the end, into the swaggering, bragging tall tale that was meant primarily for amusement. Two or three miners, cowboys, or cardsharps would sit around a fire or a table in a saloon. One of them would begin describing something that had happened, an event in which he was the "hero," and in which he exaggerated every detail toward a wildly improbable climax of wildly improbable coincidences. When he was finished— or even as he was talking—the next miner, or cowboy, or cardsharp would interrupt and try to go him one better. And so on and on.

The Purposes and the Method

The speaker's purposes were varied—to portray himself as a

superior person, to get the better of a verbal antagonist, and, more often, to entertain the available audience.

The method combines one feature at least of the "whopper"—the piling on of more and more absurd details, and one of the "peripatetic prevarication"—the joining together of a series of wildly improbable coincidences in some kind of connected chain of events. The differences in method are mainly in the language used and in the manner of oral delivery. The key device in choice of language is known as *hyperbole*. The manner of delivery is hyperbolic as well.

The Technique of Hyperbole

A collegiate dictionary defines hyperbole as "exaggeration for effect, not meant to be taken literally." The literary definition of hyperbole calls it an "extravagant exaggeration of fact, used either for serious or comic effect." As a figure of speech, hyperbole is used as one of the main devices in low comedy, which is the most "exaggerated" form of humor. You already have read, and probably spoken or written, a number of examples of hyperbole. Recall some from "The Invalid's Story," "Shake Hands with Birdey Doggett," and "The Petrified Man." Twain's story of the buffalo hunt is full of hyperbole. It is, in fact, a kind of boasting lie; it is aimed, though, at the avoidance of looking foolish rather than at outdoing someone else at describing an exploit. It is certainly a "tall tale," and a model one, to be sure.

For a little preliminary practice in composing some hyperboles as a warmup for writing a short, boastful anecdote, think of one or two sentences that would provide the most exaggerated description you can think of for a climate that vacillates between heat and cold, even in the summer. After satisfying yourself that you have done your best, compare your example with this one from Mark Twain. Twain says of a region called Lake Mono: "So uncertain is the climate in summer that a lady who goes out visiting cannot hope to be prepared for all emergencies unless she takes her fan under one arm and her snowshoes under the other. When they have a Fourth of July procession it generally snows on them, and they do say that as a general thing when a man calls for a brandy toddy there, the barkeeper chops it off with a hatchet and wraps it up in a paper, like maple sugar. And it is further reported that the old soakers haven't any teeth—wore them out eating gin cocktails and brandy punches."

For further practice, try describing the following in hyperbolic fashion: (1) a windy day in the city; (2) a shaggy dog; (3) a hungry person—you, perhaps; (4) a person on a diet; (5) a cookout on a camping trip or picnic.

Here's an example of the bragging tall tale in its purest form. It is a passage from *Life on the Mississippi*, in which Twain imitates the kind of talk heard on the Mississippi keelboats. Evidently, a test of strength (verbal, of course) is going on:

> "Whoo-oop! I'm the old original iron-jawed, brass-mounted, copper-bellied corpse-maker from the wilds of Arkansaw! Look at me! I'm the man they call Sudden Death and General Desolation! Sired by a hurricane, dam'd by an earthquake, half-brother to the cholera, nearly related to the small-pox on the mother's side! Look at me! I take nineteen alligators and a bar'l of whiskey for breakfast when I'm in robust health, and a bushel of rattle-snakes and a dead body when I'm ailing! I split the everlasting rocks with my glance, and I squench the thunder when I speak! Whoo-oop! Stand back and give me room according to my strength! Blood's my natural drink, and the wails of the dying is music to my ear! Cast your eye on me, gentlemen! and lay low and hold your breath, for I'm 'bout to turn myself loose!"
>
> All the time he was getting this off, he was shaking his head and looking fierce, and kind of swelling around in a little circle, tucking up his wrist-bands, and now and then straightening up and beating his breast with his fist, saying, "Look at me, gentlemen!" When he got through, he jumped up and cracked his heels together three times, and let off a roaring "Whoo-oop! I'm the bloodiest son of a wildcat that lives!"
>
> Then the man that had started the row tilted his old slouch hat down over his right eye; then he bent stooping forward, with his back sagged and his south end sticking out far, and his fists a-shoving out and drawing in in front of him, and so went around in a little circle about three times, swelling himself up and breathing hard. Then he straightened, and jumped up and cracked his heels together three times before he lit again (that made them cheer), and he began to shout like this:
>
> "Whoo-oop! bow your neck and spread, for the kingdom of sorrow's a-coming! Hold me down to the earth, for I feel my powers a-working! whoo-oop! I'm a child of sin, *don't* let me get a start! Smoked glass, here, for all! Don't attempt

to look at me with the naked eye, gentlemen! When I'm playful I use the meridians of longitude and parallels of latitude for a seine, and drag the Atlantic Ocean for whales! I scratch my head with the lightning and purr myself to sleep with the thunder! When I'm cold, I bile the Gulf of Mexico and bathe in it; when I'm hot I fan myself with an equinoctial storm; when I'm thirsty I reach up and suck a cloud dry like a sponge; when I range the earth hungry, famine follows in my tracks! Whoo-oop! bow your neck and spread! I put my hand on the sun's face and make it night in the earth; I bite a piece out of the moon and hurry the seasons; I shake myself and crumble the mountains! Contemplate me through leather—*don't* use the naked eye! The massacre of isolated communities is the pastime of my idle moments, the destruction of nationalities the serious business of my life! The boundless vastness of the great American desert is my enclosed property, and I bury my dead on my own premises!" He jumped up and cracked his heels together three times before he lit (they cheered him again), and as he come down he shouted out: "Whoo-oop! bow your neck and spread, for the Pet Child of Calamity's a-coming!"

What exaggerated details have been selected by each speaker? What words are used to describe them? If you were going to give a reading of this "tall talk," how would you interpret it? How would you differentiate between the two speakers? If you are good at speaking or interested in acting, try practicing this reading; then put it on tape and play it for any interested audience you can find.

You don't hear anyone going around talking like that nowadays; it just isn't done, even for entertainment. What you do hear, though, is a kind of perversion of the boasting tall tale—that is, the exaggerated underrating of oneself that often passes, mistakenly, for modesty. It seems perfectly all right, in our time, to diminish one's skill to the point of nullity. This is done in a kind of hyperbolic understatement. Denigrating oneself often terminates in a kind of boasting about one's incapacities or weaknesses. The sinner who confesses in public meeting at every opportunity is a kind of inverted braggart, as is the clinging vine who makes a virtue of her inability to do anything for herself, the lazy person whose accounts of his idleness make you positively envy him, or the sloppy dresser who runs down his own habits until you'd almost think he was setting a new style. There is also the professional comedian, like Jack Benny, who makes a display of his cheapness, and the professional singer whose comic musical errors make up for talent. And there are countless other examples.

Practice in Invention

Here is a newspaper article concerning the age-old problem of cheating—hardly an admirable act, and one that is frowned on in most societies. After reading the article, imagine that you have mastered all the ways to cheat that are mentioned in the article. Exaggerate the ones that seem most absurd or impossible to achieve, and then try to go even those one better.

New Delhi.

Examination time at many Indian universities and colleges instills fear among the students and causes disruptions and campus demonstrations.

The examination "season" this year has set off a wave of violence reminiscent of the language riots in Northern India during the early sixties. Many campuses resembled armed police camps and teachers in Uttar Pradesh and West Bengal would not be exam proctors unless they had police protection.

These instructors have good cause for their concern since proctors in at least three northern states have been killed or maimed in recent years. School officials fear that the violence may become an annual ritual at examination time.

Students at many colleges will use any device to postpone their exams. When all other methods fail they often see to it that the tests themselves are disrupted.

Among some of the grievances, students have complained that courses have not been fully completed in class, or that the examination papers were too "stiff," or that some of the questions were not included in the course of study. Some students have even walked out on a test, claiming that the particular questions were not expected to be asked until the next term.

Since a college degree is essential if the student is to get a salaried job or enter a profession, many students cheat by whatever means possible.

A generation ago copying or cheating in examinations was considered reprehensible—parents were shocked and friends and colleagues disapproved. But today, successful cheating often merits praise from a parent and the help of other students.

Both men and women students carry concealed notes into the examination room to be consulted when the appropriate questions arise. Some students simply peek at their neighbors' answers.

In Bihar, parents installed loudspeakers to provide answers for their sons and daughters taking an examination. Some parents with influential connections try to get test questions in advance or attempt to get the test score changed in their child's favor.

At Kanpur University, examinations for all 4,000 students were canceled because students engaged in mass copying. Lucknow University had to postpone exams until a student caught cheating was punished. The student culprit later beat up the proctor who caught him.

The problem has reached such proportions that the issue has been debated in India's Parliament. Suggestions have been made for reform in the examination system, but little has been done to combat the violence.

One member of Parliament thought he had the answer: Let students take books, notes and ready-made answers into the examination room. Presumably the cure for cheating is to allow everyone to cheat.

Clinching the Process

1. Agree with a partner to go each other one better on your incompetency in any skill or field in which you both feel inadequate.
2. List a series of progressively more unflattering adjectives to describe your lack of ability. Make your adjectives as hyperbolic as possible.
3. Devise for each adjective an example, frequently in the form of a comparison, to illustrate an experience that proved you to be disastrously inept. ("I am so clumsy at throwing a softball that when I pitched to the batter, the ball flew into the stands behind home plate."
4. Arrange your examples in order of exaggerated ineptitude.
5. Challenge your partner to a "going one better" contest before an audience that will select the most hyperbolically competent incompetent.

THE PRACTICAL JOKE

The Tale and The Joke

All of the three low comic forms that we have tried up to this point are forms of *verbal* humor. All are intended primarily for a listening rather than for a reading audience. If these forms are practiced in writing, either a narrator reports them in the form of a monologue delivered by someone he is listening to or recording, or—more often—he tells them in the first person, in a colloquial style appropriate to the speaker's social and vocational identity and to the kind of audience he is addressing. The essential devices are gross exaggeration and wild coincidence, either heightened by hyperbole or counterpointed by understatement. Played straight to contribute to the incongruity, they constitute a kind of "verbal slapstick."

The Method

The practical joke, on the other hand, has very little verbal accompaniment. It is acted out with some physical energy and often with physical rather than verbal outcomes. Birdey Doggett's victims—and his mother's, in some cases—flail their flaming umbrellas about, take off unexpectedly on a single skate, or find themselves clasping a hand without an accompanying forearm. The practical joke shares with the tall tale its complex chain of surprising coincidences, except that usually there is only one main surprise—the one that comes at the end of the chain of coincidences. To write about practical jokes, or make them the subjects of humorous anecdotes, as Thurber did so well, one must put oneself in the joker's place rather than in the victim's place. After working through the details of the joke as if one were to play it, visualize how it would look if acted out on the stage by a slapstick comedian, or if carried out in an actual situation. Here an exact mental image is really worth a thousand words, whereas a thousand words make a better "whopper" than one picture does, as we already have seen. Unless you can make your listener or reader, in this case, see what you have seen, he won't laugh.

Setting Up a Situation

To get an idea for your joke, ask yourself how the practical joker knows what kind of situation to set up for particular kinds of people, or for a special person he has in mind. If you think about it, you'll come to the conclusion that the practical joker succeeds if he takes advantage of his victim's slavish adherence to routines or unexamined conventions of social behavior. He counts on our reacting in the "usual" way when we are in situations in which a particular behavior seems expected or routine. Recall some of the ordinary situations that Birdey Doggett took advantage of, such as the custom of shaking hands in greeting, rising from a sitting position and expecting to be able to walk naturally, sitting down without examining what one is sitting on, putting one's hands in one's pockets, addressing people by name, carrying an unfurled umbrella between showers. The joker, in order to take advantage of the routine reactions of his victims, often has to make elaborate preparations. Remember some of Birdey's most complex operations, for example.

Sources of Invention

If you are going to write an anecdote using a practical joke as the central situation, you can get an idea for the plot by basing your joke on a routine that is common to everyone, such as shaking hands. Or, you can base your joke on a habit that is peculiar to your particular victim, perhaps the gesture of blowing one's nose even when there is no symptom of a cold, or washing one's hands after the slightest exertion, or parking a car in precisely the same spot every day. After you have decided on the routine you want to use, decide on the way in which it is to be disrupted. For example, suppose you decide to take advantage of the habit we all have of saying "Hello" and "How are you?" as we pass people on the street or in a hallway, usually in such a routine way that we continue walking without expecting an answer. Think of the possible ways this kind of routine meeting of an acquaintance could be interrupted in such a way as to shock the person who is greeting you. You could, of course, stop dead in your tracks when asked how you are and proceed to tell a long, involved story about your troubles; or you might pretend you are not the person he takes you for; or you might—if you were like Birdey—have set up the situation well in advance. You could, for instance, have inserted the end of a blunt-tipped knife into a suction cup; placed the cup over your heart; cut a hole in your shirt so that the knife handle would look as if it were protruding from you; covered it with your jacket; then, as soon as you were greeted with "How are you?", say something like "Okay, considering . . ."; then quickly open your coat, give a brief but meaningful shrug, and be off down the hall.

Point of View

The outcome of your joke would depend upon the length of your story, and whether or not you were the narrator, an observer like

Thurber, or the victim himself. Take off from here, and assume the role of each in turn. Which role and which ending produce the most amusement? Did you disclose the joke, keep it hidden, or reveal it at the very end to the audience you expect to write for? What variations of effect can be produced by changes of this sort?

The Problem of Visualizing

Your problem in writing your joke down, aside from the choice of a point of view, is to transmit to the reader the same picture of the action of the joke that you have in your mind, or—if you have actually seen or planned a joke that came off—of one that you remember. Because speed is the essence of both a practical joke and of humor, don't slow down your short narrative by stopping to describe objects, people, and settings in detail. You want to catch your victim quickly, before he realizes that the routine situation has been disturbed; you want to catch your reader in a quick gasp of surprise or chuckle of amusement. Insert your descriptive notes as you move along, and learn to use the briefest possible ways of getting exact pictures across. These are short phrases or single words, first of all—words that make the finest rather than the most general distinctions, words that carry an element of unexpectedness or originality. Consider some of the words used by James Thurber in "Shake Hands with Birdey Doggett": "waggishness," "wears his years with a smirk," "a brief, desperate semicircle," "attacked by her muzzled Scotty," "a citizen with a floppy umbrella," "a tapioca brain." Close your eyes and think back over each expression. Try to see a picture of the movement, the situation, the expression, the kind of person described. Think of the different effect if, instead of "brief, desperate semicircle," which presents an exact picture of someone who unexpectedly finds himself skating, Thurber had used the phrase, "going around in circular movements, quickly, with a desperate look on his face."

Practice for your more extended narration of a joke by describing in no more than four words each of these actions: (a) the movements of someone who unexpectedly walks onto a newly waxed floor; (b) the motions of a car, seen from behind, that skids on a wet pavement; (c) the movement of a baby who knows how to crawl, but is trying to walk.

Now, develop into a short anecdote your idea for interrupting a routine situation in order to play a practical trick on someone.

If you still don't have an idea that appeals to you, try one of these routines for a starter:

1. Eating what is considered a well-balanced meal of meat, potatoes, green vegetable, salad, dessert, and beverage in the evening at about six or seven o'clock.
2. Eating juice, toast, eggs and coffee in the morning.
3. Taking a shower every morning or evening.
4. Expecting to get light when we flip a switch.
5. Taking flowers to a sick friend at the hospital.

Perhaps you know of someone who is almost Birdey's equal. You could describe some of his tricks, trying to equal Thurber in letting your reader visualize the joke. Or maybe you have been a victim of a really clever April Fool's prank.

Summary of Procedure

Here now is a summary of the procedure for writing about practical jokes.

1. Think of a routine involving some action that has become a habit.
2. Imagine ways the routine could be interrupted by substituting some unexpected outcome.
3. Put yourself in the joker's place and think of a way your prank could be accomplished.
4. Visualize the execution of your prank as if you were watching it on the stage or on film.
5. Write down what you visualized, using as few words as possible, and making every word count. When you have finished the first draft, read it over and underline the expressions you think convey a picture. See if you can improve on them.
6. Read your joke to someone else, or better yet, have them read a typed or clearly handwritten copy of your anecdote. Listen for a laugh or watch for a quiet smile. If you don't get it, try it on someone else. If you don't get a laugh after two or three tries, begin again.

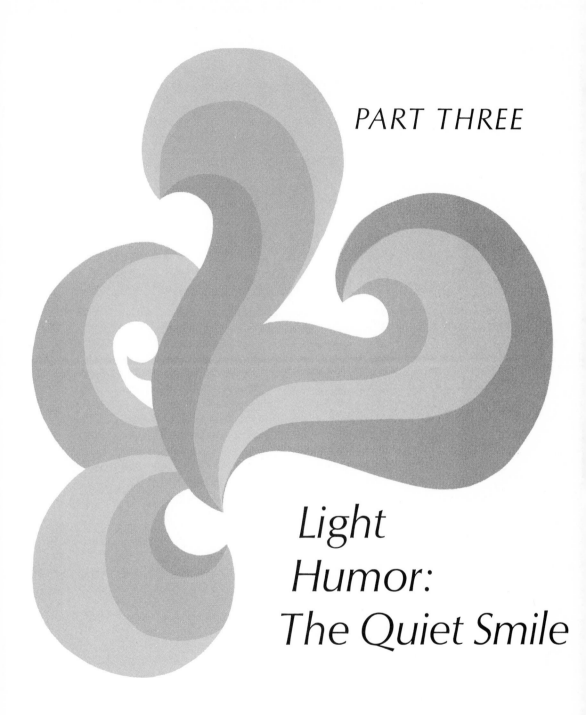

PART THREE

Light
Humor:
The Quiet Smile

6

Geniuses
for Minor
Difficulties

The forms of low comedy—whether designed to be seen, read, or listened to—aim for the loud laugh, the one frequently called a "belly laugh." "Belly laugh" is a colorful and accurate way of describing the response to low comedy. This kind of response is spontaneous and instinctive, a "gut" reaction that scarcely has time to pass through the censors of the mind. The actor-clown or the author-clown rely on age-old tricks of surprise, wild exaggeration, and patent nonsense pawned off in a deadpan manner that occasionally becomes as extravagant as its subject matter.

The subject matter of low comedy is earthy, obeying the dictates of the belly rather than the etiquette of the linen-clad table. It deals in physical accident and situation, getting its physical response from the trickster's victim as well as from his audience. But the audience for low comedy is, unlike the joker's victim, "in" on the joke. Its laughter is frequently an expression of delight in knowing that some sort of unexpected joke is in store, a joke that will prove as harmless as the tricks most children play. Low comedy, though, can descend to a more sadistic level, like the games children play in good spirits until the competition becomes too keen and the desire to trick someone too overpowering. Whatever the motives or the response, however, the guffaw is immediate, loud, and quickly over, forgotten until the next situation arises to trigger the expectancy that ends in the release of laughter.

We all like to laugh, but we tire very quickly of the indefatigable Birdeys and of the clowns who never let up. These buffoons evidently have not learned that the only restraint they *must* exercise is one against the temptation to go themselves one better one too many times in succession. For the essence of all humor, including low comedy, lies in its transience, its impermanence, its surprise. And a surprise is *not* a surprise unless it is infrequent and shocking. We can stand only a few shocks, even pleasant ones, before becoming "shock-proof." Mark Twain, the prince of pranksters and of the tall tale, knew this, for most of his burlesques are interwoven in his longer, more serious (at least more realistically told) works. Admittedly, even he could not resist the temptation to go too far once in a while. James Thurber, however, rarely goes too far into the realms of low comedy. A self-styled writer "of light pieces running from a thousand to two thousand words," usually for publication in periodicals like *The New Yorker*, Thurber was the master of the more subtle humorous sketch, the genius for "getting into minor difficulties."

You will recall that in the first chapter of this book we discussed the difficulty of classifying the varieties of comedy. It is easier, and perhaps less arbitrary, to differentiate among them by contrasting them with each other—classifying by exclusion, saying what "X" type of humor is *not* rather than what it is. In a way, "low comedy" might seem a better name for the humorous essay or story than it is for the comic forms to which the word "low" is usually applied: forms characterized by the antonyms of "lowness" —namely, loudness, wildness, extravagance.

The humorous pieces at which Thurber excels are low-keyed, "quiet" humor—"high-styled" rather than high-voiced. They deal with the ordinary rather than the extraordinary, the lack of surprise rather than the expectancy of delight, the minor rather than the major. Instead of blowing us up, like the supermen of the tall tale, they deflate us. Humorists, says Thurber, view human dignity as "not only silly but a little sad. So are dreams and conventions and illusions. The fine brave fragile stuff that men live by. They look so well, and go to pieces so easily." Instead of shouting with glee at the victim's dilemma, we smile sardonically, and much more slowly, when we learn that *we* are the victims of life's little jokes.

Low comedy springs from situation; humor, from character, or more accurately, personality. Humor results from identifying with a particular person who finds himself in a mildly distressing situation that we have all experienced at some time or other. The purpose of this quieter kind of humor is relief rather than release— relief, perhaps, that we are no longer the victims of the painful past, or that we are able to view a distressing situation with balance, perspective, and detachment. Humor of the kind Thurber writes looks back on a given situation from the objective, reasonable viewpoint of a narrator who remembers rather than reports. It deals with the "then" rather than the "now," filtering out the unpleasantness and transforming the momentarily embarrassing into the amusingly absurd. This kind of humor is mental rather than visceral, for the intelligence recognizes the absurdity of the situation and rationalizes the pain that the body forgets as soon as the physical manifestations of pain have disappeared.

Mark Twain also knew that present humor springs from its opposite in the past. In "Pudd'nhead Wilson's New Calendar" he remarked that "Everything human is pathetic. The secret source of humor itself is not joy but sorrow." And, in *My Life and Hard Times*, Thurber elaborates: "This type of writing is not a joyous form of self-expression but the manifestation of twitchiness at once cosmic and mundane. Authors of such pieces have, nobody knows why, a genius for getting into minor difficulties: they walk into the wrong apartments; they drink furniture polish for stomach bitters; they drive their cars into the prize tulip beds of haughty neighbors; they playfully slap gangsters, mistaking them for old school friends. To call such persons 'humorists,' a loose-fitting and ugly word, is to miss the nature of their dilemma and the dilemma of their nature. The little wheels of their invention are set in motion by the damp hand of melancholy. Such a writer . . . talks largely about small matters and smally about great affairs. . . . Your short piece writer's time is not Walter Lippmann's time, or Stuart Chase's time, or Professor Einstein's time. It is his own personal time, circumscribed by the short boundaries of his pain and embarrassment, in which what happens to his digestion, the rear axle of his car, and the confused flow of his relationships with six or eight persons and two or three buildings, is of greater importance than what goes on in the nation."

Whatever is used as the subject matter of humorous pieces, as Thurber has said, is frightfully crucial at the time it happens, sometimes so important that it becomes an obsession—which you will see in at least two of the selections in this book. But the stance of the humorist is the backward glance over his shoulder. He sees himself or the character he describes from a distance. And his audience sees with his eyes. "The things we laugh at are awful while they are going on, but get funny when we look back. And other people laugh because they've been through it too. . . . Humor is a kind of emotional chaos told about calmly and quietly in retrospect. There is always a laugh in the utterly familiar. . . . People can laugh out of a kind of mellowed self-pity as well as out of superiority."

Humor of this sort is a kind of therapy, a recovery of a sense of balance in life. It's the alternative to a tearful and fearful response to unpleasant events and feelings or to the dehumanizing effect of mechanical routines. Usually it is this kind of comic response that is referred to in the expression "sense of humor." A sense of proportion about life comes through the intelligent appraisal of things such as the discrepancies between ideals and realities, between the aspirations of human beings and their limitations, between the emotional reactions of the moment and the cooler evaluations that follow in time. A sense of humor comes from awareness of contrasts like these, and it comes with the humbling discovery that *we* are more often the victims of life and of our own foolishness or frailty than we are the slickers who put one over on the other fellow. Instead of satisfying our competitive, aggressive instincts, this sort of smiling amusement brings us closer to our neighbors because we recognize the Everyman in life's absurdities and inevitable minor difficulties. Unfortunately, however, we are not born with a sense of humor. A sense of humor is not instinctive in the same way that playing games and laughing at tricks and jokes are. Happily, though, it can be acquired and sharpened. Humor is rational rather than instinctive, retrospective rather than immediate, cultivated rather than natural.

And now let Twain and Thurber have a chance to help you refine and sharpen your sense of humor.

The Dog That Bit People

The main reservoir of ideas for light humor lies in one's own experience. One of Thurber's most famous collections of stories is based on his experiences in Columbus, Ohio, where he grew up. In *My Life and Hard Times* he deals with such commonplace events as going to school and dealing with relatives—and dogs. Most of us would groan with boredom at an assignment to write a theme on "My Pet," but look what Thurber came up with when he gave himself this assignment.

The Dog That Bit People Probably no one man should have as many dogs in his life as I have had, but there was more pleasure than distress in them for me except in the case of an Airedale named Muggs. He gave me more trouble than all the other fifty-four or -five put together, although my moment of keenest embarrassment was the time a Scotch terrier named Jeannie, who had just had six puppies in the clothes closet of a fourth floor apartment in New York, had the unexpected seventh and last at the corner of Eleventh Street and Fifth Avenue during a walk she had insisted on taking. Then, too, there was the prizewinning French poodle, a great big black poodle—none of your little, untroublesome white miniatures—who got sick riding in the rumble seat of a car with me on her way to the Greenwich Dog Show. She had a red rubber bib tucked around her throat and, since a rainstorm came up when we were halfway through the Bronx, I had to hold over her a small green umbrella, really more of a parasol. The rain beat down fearfully and suddenly the driver of the car drove into a big garage, filled with mechanics. It happened so quickly that I forgot to put the umbrella down and I will always remember, with sickening distress, the look of incredulity mixed with hatred that came over the face of the particular hardened garage man that came over to see what we wanted, when he took a look at me and the poodle. All garage men, and people of that intolerant stripe, hate poodles with their curious haircut, especially the pom-poms that you got to leave on their hips if you expect the dogs to win a prize.

But the Airedale, as I have said, was the worst of all my

Geniuses for Minor Difficulties

dogs. He really wasn't my dog, as a matter of fact: I came home from a vacation one summer to find that my brother Roy had bought him while I was away. A big, burly, choleric dog, he always acted as if he thought I wasn't one of the family. There was a slight advantage in being one of the family, for he didn't bite the family as often as he bit strangers. Still, in the years that we had him he bit everybody but mother, and he made a pass at her once but missed. That was during the month when we suddenly had mice, and Muggs refused to do anything about them. Nobody ever had mice exactly like the mice we had that month. They acted like pet mice, almost like mice somebody had trained. They were so friendly that one night when mother entertained at dinner the Friraliras, a club she and my father had belonged to for twenty years, she put down a lot of little dishes with food in them on the pantry floor so that the mice would be satisfied with that and wouldn't come into the dining room. Muggs stayed out in the pantry with the mice, lying on the floor, growling to himself—not at the mice, but about all the people in the next room that he would have liked to get at. Mother slipped out into the pantry once to see how everything was going. Everything was going fine. It made her so mad to see Muggs lying there, oblivious of the mice—they came running up to her—that she slapped him and he slashed at her, but didn't make it. He was sorry immediately, mother said. He was always sorry, she said, after he bit someone, but we could not understand how she figured this out. He didn't act sorry.

Mother used to send a box of candy every Christmas to the people the Airedale bit. The list finally contained forty or more names. Nobody could understand why we didn't get rid of the dog. I didn't understand it very well myself, but we didn't get rid of him. I think that one or two people tried to poison Muggs—he acted poisoned once in a while—and old Major Moberly fired at him once with his service revolver near the Seneca Hotel in East Broad Street—but Muggs lived to be almost eleven years old and even when he could hardly get around he bit a Congressman who had called to see my father on business. My mother had never liked the Congressman—she said the signs of his horoscope showed he couldn't be trusted (he was Saturn with the moon in Virgo)—but she sent him a box of candy that Christmas. He sent it right back, probably because he suspected it was trick candy. Mother persuaded herself it was all for the best that the dog had bitten him, even though father lost an im-

Nobody knew exactly what was the matter with him.

portant business association because of it. "I wouldn't be associated with such a man," mother said. "Muggs could read him like a book."

We used to take turns feeding Muggs to be on his good side, but that didn't always work. He was never in a very good humor, even after a meal. Nobody knew exactly what was the matter with him, but whatever it was it made him irascible, especially in the mornings. Roy never felt very well in the morning, either, especially before breakfast, and once when he came downstairs and found that Muggs had moodily chewed up the morning paper he hit him in the face with a grapefruit and then jumped up on the dining room table, scattering dishes and silverware and spilling the coffee. Muggs' first free leap carried him all the way across the table and into a brass firescreen in front of the gas grate, but he was back on his feet in a moment and in the end he got Roy and gave him a pretty vicious bite in the leg. Then he was all over it; he never bit anyone more than once at a time. Mother always mentioned that as an argument in his favor; she said he had a quick temper but that he didn't hold a grudge. She was forever defending him. I think she liked him because he wasn't well. "He's not strong," she would say,

Geniuses for Minor Difficulties

pityingly, but that was inaccurate; he may not have been well but he was terribly strong.

One time my mother went to the Chittenden Hotel to call on a woman mental healer who was lecturing in Columbus on the subject of "Harmonious Vibrations." She wanted to find out if it was possible to get harmonious vibrations into a dog. "He's a large tan-colored Airedale," mother explained. The woman said that she had never treated a dog but she advised my mother to hold the thought that he did not bite and would not bite. Mother was holding the thought the very next morning when Muggs got the iceman but she blamed that slip-up on the iceman. "If you didn't think he would bite you, he wouldn't," mother told him. He stomped out of the house in a terrible jangle of vibrations.

One morning when Muggs bit me slightly, more or less in passing, I reached down and grabbed his short stumpy tail and hoisted him into the air. It was a foolhardy thing to do and the last time I saw my mother, about six months ago, she said she didn't know what possessed me. I don't either, except that I was pretty mad. As long as I held the dog off the floor by his tail he couldn't get at me, but he twisted and jerked so, snarling all the time, that I realized I couldn't hold him that way very long. I carried him to the kitchen and flung him onto the floor and shut the door on him just as he crashed against it. But I forgot about the backstairs. Muggs went up the backstairs and down the frontstairs and had me cornered in the living room. I managed to get up onto the mantelpiece above the fireplace, but it gave way and came down with a tremendous crash throwing a large marble clock, several vases, and myself heavily to the floor. Muggs was so alarmed by the racket that when I picked myself up he had disappeared. We couldn't find him anywhere, although we whistled and shouted, until old Mrs. Detweiler called after dinner that night. Muggs had bitten her once, in the leg, and she came into the living room only after we assured her that Muggs had run away. She had just seated herself when, with a great growling and scratching of claws, Muggs emerged from under a davenport where he had been quietly hiding all the time, and bit her again. Mother examined the bite and put arnica on it and told Mrs. Detweiler that it was only a bruise. "He just bumped you," she said. But Mrs. Detweiler left the house in a nasty state of mind.

Lots of people reported our Airedale to the police but my father held a municipal office at the time and was on friendly terms with the police. Even so, the cops had been

Lots of people reported our dog to the police.

out a couple times—once when Muggs bit Mrs. Rufus Sturtevant and again when he bit Lieutenant-Governor Malloy—but mother told them that it hadn't been Muggs' fault but the fault of the people who were bitten. "When he starts for them, they scream," she explained, "and that excites him." The cops suggested that it might be a good idea to tie the dog up, but mother said that it mortified him to be tied up and that he wouldn't eat when he was tied up.

Muggs at his meals was an unusual sight. Because of the fact that if you reached toward the floor he would bite you, we usually put his food plate on top of an old kitchen table with a bench alongside the table. Muggs would stand on the bench and eat. I remember that my mother's Uncle Horatio, who boasted that he was the third man up Missionary Ridge, was splutteringly indignant when he found out that we fed the dog on a table because we were afraid to put his plate on the floor. He said he wasn't afraid of any dog

Geniuses for Minor Difficulties

Muggs at his meals was an unusual sight.

that ever lived and that he would put the dog's plate on the floor if we would give it to him. Roy said that if Uncle Horatio had fed Muggs on the ground just before the battle he would have been the first man up Missionary Ridge. Uncle Horatio was furious. "Bring him in! Bring him in now!" he shouted. "I'll feed the —— on the floor!" Roy was all for giving him a chance, but my father wouldn't hear of it. He said that Muggs had already been fed. "I'll feed him again!" bawled Uncle Horatio. We had quite a time quieting him.

In his last year Muggs used to spend practically all of his time outdoors. He didn't like to stay in the house for some reason or other—perhaps it held too many unpleasant memories for him. Anyway, it was hard to get him to come in and as a result the garbage man, the iceman, and the laundryman wouldn't come near the house. We had to haul the garbage down to the corner, take the laundry out and bring it back, and meet the iceman a block from home. After this had gone on for some time, we hit on an ingenious arrangement for getting the dog in the house so that we could lock him up while the gas meter was read, and so on. Muggs was afraid of only one thing, an electrical storm. Thunder and lightning frightened him out of his senses (I think he thought a storm had broken the day the mantel-piece fell). He would rush into the house and hide under a bed or in a clothes closet. So we fixed up a thunder ma-chine out of a long narrow piece of sheet iron with a wooden handle on one end. Mother would shake this vigorously when she wanted to get Muggs into the house. It made an excellent imitation of thunder, but I suppose it was the most roundabout system for running a household that was ever devised. It took a lot out of mother.

A few months before Muggs died, he got to "seeing things." He would rise slowly from the floor, growling low, and stalk stiff-legged and menacing toward nothing at all. Sometimes the Thing would be just a little to the right or left of a visitor. Once a Fuller Brush salesman got hysterics. Muggs came wandering into the room like Hamlet following his father's ghost. His eyes were fixed on a spot just to the left of the Fuller Brush man, who stood it until Muggs was about three slow, creeping paces from him. Then he shouted. Muggs wavered on past him into the hallway grumbling to himself but the Fuller man went on shouting. I think mother had to throw a pan of cold water on him before he stopped. That was the way she used to stop us boys when we got into fights.

Muggs died quite suddenly one night. Mother wanted to bury him in the family lot under a marble stone with some such inscription as "Flights of angels sing thee to thy rest," but we persuaded her it was against the law. In the end we just put up a smooth board above his grave along a lonely road. On the board I wrote with an indelible pencil "Cave Canem." Mother was quite pleased with the simple classic dignity of the old Latin epitaph.

For Writing and Discussion

1. "The Dog That Bit People" contains almost all the elements of the sketch based on personal experiences that are embarrassing at the time they occur but funny in retrospect. How does Thurber use in this story all the elements and techniques listed below?

   a. plot based on loose succession of commonplace situations

b. situation arising from characters' personalities rather than from coincidence. (Don't forget to include the dog as a character!)

c. understatement used to describe unusual situations

d. repetitive actions and expressions

e. variations on one's expectancies of behavior in ordinary circumstances.

2. One of the pitfalls of writing about dogs and mothers is the danger of allowing some sympathetic emotional response, verging on sentimentality, to cancel out the objectivity and detachment that this kind of humor requires. How does Thurber avoid this danger? When, if ever, do you feel he comes close to becoming too involved with what he describes?

3. Repetitive actions that become conditioned responses to any situation, regardless of their appropriateness, are compulsive. They form the stock in trade of the humorist. What is the dog's compulsion? What is Thurber's mother's? How are they complementary? What variations in reactions to the dog keep the compulsive acts from becoming truly conditioned responses?

4. Another major device for creating humor is to portray characters who try to impose their own illogical logic on the practical problems of the world. What are some examples of Thurber's mother's solutions to the problem of a biting dog that illustrate this technique? How do the kinds of people from whom she seeks advice reinforce her dream-world reasoning?

5. Explain how the "topsy-turvy" or reversal-of-expectancy technique is also illustrated in Thurber's mother's logic.

6. Why is the epitaph the family chooses for the dog appropriate? Why does it seem unlikely that Thurber's mother will ever investigate the true meaning of the Latin inscription?

Curing a Cold

MARK TWAIN

Thurber said that writers of humorous pieces "talk largely about small matters." Nothing seems smaller, in retrospect, than a head cold. The adjective "common," which is usually associated with a cold, attests to the ordinariness of the ailment. We've all had not one, but several; and we scarcely remember them once they've gone. But while we're wheezing and sniffling it's a different matter:

pure misery . . . acute embarrassment at having to blow that dripping red trumpet of a nose at the most inopportune moments! The British poet and literary critic Samuel Taylor Coleridge (the author of "The Rime of the Ancient Mariner," which is anything but funny) also commented on the humorist's "bringing forward into distinct consciousness those minutiae of thought and feeling which appear to be trifles, yet have an importance for the moment, and which almost every man feels in one way or another. Thus is produced the novelty of an individual peculiarity together with the interest of a something that belongs to our common nature. . . . The propensity to notice these things does itself constitute the humorist, and the superadded power of so presenting them to men in general gives us the man of humor." In this passage Coleridge was speaking of the English humorist, Laurence Sterne. What he said applies equally well to Twain's treatment of the common cold.

Curing a Cold It is a good thing, perhaps, to write for the amusement of the public, but it is a far higher and nobler thing to write for their instruction, their profit, their actual and tangible benefit. The latter is the sole object of this article. If it prove the means of restoring to health one solitary sufferer among my race, of lighting up once more the fire of hope and joy in his faded eyes, or bringing back to his dead heart again the quick, generous impulses of other days, I shall be amply rewarded for my labor; my soul will be permeated with the sacred delight a Christian feels when he has done a good, unselfish deed.

Having led a pure and blameless life, I am justified in believing that no man who knows me will reject the suggestions I am about to make, out of fear that I am trying to deceive him. Let the public do itself the honor to read my experience in doctoring a cold, as herein set forth, and then follow in my footsteps.

When the White House was burned in Virginia City, I lost my home, my happiness, my constitution, and my trunk. The loss of the two first-named articles was a matter of no great consequence, since a home without a mother, or a sister, or a distant young female relative in it, to remind you, by putting your soiled linen out of sight and taking your boots down off the mantelpiece, that there are those who think about you and care for you, is easily obtained. And I cared nothing for the loss of my happiness, because, not being a poet, it could not be possible that melancholy would abide

Geniuses for Minor Difficulties

with me long. But to lose a good constitution and a better trunk were serious misfortunes. On the day of the fire, my constitution succumbed to a severe cold, caused by undue exertion in getting ready to do something. I suffered to no purpose, too, because the plan I was figuring at for the extinguishing of the fire was so elaborate that I never got it completed until the middle of the following week.

The first time I began to sneeze, a friend told me to go and bathe my feet in hot water and go to bed. I did so. Shortly afterwards, another friend advised me to get up and take a cold shower-bath. I did that also. Within the hour, another friend assured me that it was policy to "feed a cold and starve a fever." I had both. So I thought it best to fill myself up for the cold, and then keep dark and let the fever starve a while.

In a case of this kind, I seldom do things by halves; I ate pretty heartily; I conferred my custom upon a stranger who had just opened his restaurant that morning; he waited near me in respectful silence until I had finished feeding my cold, when he inquired if the people about Virginia City were much afflicted with colds. I told him I thought they were. He then went out and took in his sign.

I started down toward the office, and on the way encountered another bosom friend, who told me that a quart of salt water, taken warm, would come as near curing a cold as anything in the world. I hardly thought I had room for it, but I tried it anyhow. The result was surprising. I believed I had thrown up my immortal soul.

Now, as I am giving my experience only for the benefit of those who are troubled with the distemper I am writing about, I feel that they will see the propriety of my cautioning them against following such portions of it as proved inefficient with me, and acting upon this conviction, I warn them against warm salt water. It may be a good enough remedy, but I think it is too severe. If I had another cold in the head, and there were no course left me but to take either an earthquake or a quart of warm salt water, I would take my chances on the earthquake.

After the storm which had been raging in my stomach had subsided, and no more good Samaritans happening along, I went on borrowing handkerchiefs again and blowing them to atoms, as had been my custom in the early stages of my cold, until I came across a lady who had just arrived from over the plains, and who said she had lived in a part of the country where doctors were scarce, and had from necessity acquired considerable skill in the treatment of simple "family complaints." I knew she must have had much experience, for she appeared to be a hundred and fifty years old.

She mixed a decoction composed of molasses, aquafortis, turpentine, and various other drugs, and instructed me to take a wine glass full of it every fifteen minutes. I never took but one dose; that was enough; it robbed me of all moral principle, and awoke every unworthy impulse of my nature. Under its malign influence my brain conceived miracles of meanness, but my hands were too feeble to execute them; at that time, had it not been that my strength had surrendered to a succession of assaults from infallible remedies for my cold, I am satisfied that I would have tried to rob the graveyard. Like most other people, I often feel mean, and act accordingly; but until I took that medicine I had never revelled in such supernatural depravity and felt proud of it. At the end of two days I was ready to go doctoring again. I took a few more unfailing remedies, and finally drove my cold from my head to my lungs.

I got to coughing incessantly, and my voice fell below zero; I conversed in a thundering bass, two octaves below my natural tone; I could only compass my regular nightly repose by coughing myself down to a state of utter exhaustion, and then the moment I began to talk in my sleep, my discordant voice woke me up again.

My case grew more and more serious every day. Plain gin was recommended; I took it. Then gin and molasses; I took that also. Then gin and onions; I added the onions, and took all three. I detected no particular result, however, except that I had acquired a breath like a buzzard's.

I found I had to travel for my health. I went to Lake Bigler with my reportorial comrade, Wilson. It is gratifying to me to reflect that we traveled in considerable style; we went in the Pioneer coach, and my friend took all his baggage with him, consisting of two excellent silk handkerchiefs, and a daguerreotype of his grandmother. We sailed and hunted and fished and danced all day, and I doctored my cough all night. By managing in this way, I made out to improve every hour in the twenty-four. But my disease continued to grow worse.

A sheet-bath was recommended. I had never refused a remedy yet, and it seemed poor policy to commence then; therefore I determined to take a sheet-bath, notwithstanding I had no idea what sort of arrangement it was. It was administered at midnight, and the weather was very frosty. My

*Geniuses
for Minor
Difficulties*

131

breast and back were bared, and a sheet (there appeared to be a thousand yards of it) soaked in ice-water, was wound around me until I resembled a swab for a Columbiad.[1]

It is a cruel expedient. When the chilly rag touches one's warm flesh, it makes him start with sudden violence, and gasp for breath just as men do in the death agony. It froze the marrow in my bones, and stopped the beating of my heart. I thought my time had come. . . .

Never take a sheet-bath—never. Next to meeting a lady acquaintance, who, for reasons best known to herself, don't see you when she looks at you, and don't know you when she does see you, it is the most uncomfortable thing in the world.

But, as I was saying, when the sheet-bath failed to cure my cough, a lady friend recommended the application of a mustard plaster to my breast. I believe that would have cured me effectually, if it had not been for young Wilson. When I went to bed, I put my mustard plaster—which was a very gorgeous one, eighteen inches square—where I could reach it when I was ready for it. But young Wilson got hungry in the night, and—here is food for the imagination.

After sojourning a week at Lake Bigler, I went to Steamboat Springs, and, beside the steam baths, I took a lot of the vilest medicines that were ever concocted. They would have cured me, but I had to go back to Virginia City, where, notwithstanding the variety of new remedies I absorbed every day, I managed to aggravate my disease by carelessness and undue exposure.

I finally concluded to visit San Francisco, and the first day I got there, a lady at the hotel told me to drink a quart of whisky every twenty-four hours, and a friend uptown recommended precisely the same course. Each advised me to take a quart; that made half a gallon. I did it, and still live.

Now, with the kindest motives in the world, I offer for the consideration of consumptive patients the variegated course of treatment I have lately gone through. Let them try it; if it don't cure, it can't more than kill them.

[1] Columbiad: An obsolete, heavy, long-chambered gun.

For Writing and Discussion

1. In these two stories, both Twain and Thurber are dealing with personal experiences viewed in retrospect. Which of the two stories seems more detached from the experience, more inclined to keep an objective, understated tone and point of view? How does this

difference reflect the personalities of the authors as they are revealed in the selections you have read?

2. As in "The Petrified Man," Mark Twain states his purpose for writing this "lighter" piece. How do the stated purposes contrast with each other and with the actual purposes the reader infers rather than accepts literally? What humorous techniques do both statements of purpose employ?

3. How does Twain use repetition as the organizational principle of his sketch in much the same way Thurber uses it in "The Dog That Bit People"? Where also does he use it as a humorous device? What variations on the repetitive theme of cold symptoms and cures does Twain make use of to avoid unadulterated obsessiveness?

4. Coleridge, also in speaking of Laurence Sterne, said that "Humorous writers . . . delight, after much preparation, to end in nothing, or in direct contradiction." How does Twain use directly contradictory remedies to create a humorous effect?

5. How much of the humor depends on your ability to identify with the sufferer? Explain.

6. Do you think Twain was able to keep the "light touch," or do you think he occasionally gets carried away? If so, where?

7. What keeps Twain's exaggeration from merging into the impossible extravagances of the tall tale? Where is exaggerated language used to describe mundane, factual details? Compare this with Thurber's uses of understated language to describe Muggs.

8. How do expressions like "breath like a buzzard's" and "a swab for a Columbiad" inject elements of low comedy? Why are they suitable for the subject?

A Genuine Turkish Bath

MARK TWAIN

Both "The Dog That Bit People" and "Curing a Cold" use the raw material of ordinary life in unique presentations of the general. The narrators view their own unpleasant or embarrassing experiences from a distance. They were the victims; the joke was on them. Looking back, they both understand that the hope of substituting wishful thinking for hard logic in problems of everyday life is an illogical expectation, and therefore a fit subject for humor. It is too much to expect that an irascible dog can be sweetened by

Geniuses for Minor Difficulties

harmonious vibrations and that a cold can be cured before its ordained course has been run. But the stamp of the narrator's personality, his reaction to the experience, makes the event humorous.

Another frequently used subject for humorous sketches is the stereotyped character in a stereotyped situation reacting in a stereotyped way. Think of the variations that have been made on stock humorous characters such as henpecked husbands, innocent country girls, city slickers, muscle-bound athletes, and egghead intellectuals. Humor is also created when the stereotyped character is reacting to an actual situation that is different from the ideal one he envisages—that is, when the fulfillment fails to meet the high standards of the expectation. And because we have all had hopes that either were not realized or, when realized, failed to turn out as we had anticipated, we can all identify with the recurrent theme of the discrepancy between the ideal and the real.

In his book, *Traveling with the Innocents Abroad*, Mark Twain includes several humorous sketches of the stereotype of the American tourist, sketches in which the American tourist comes off better in Twain's slightly jaundiced view than his foreign hosts. In the following sketch from *Innocents Abroad*, Twain pokes fun at his own typically tourist notions about exotic customs that turn out to be more attractive in anticipation than in reality. Observe how he uses the contrast between the ideal and the real, between a dreamlike picture of the world and the actual world, as devices for achieving the deflation of human aspirations. This is one of the main features of the quieter kinds of humor.

A Genuine Turkish Bath

Constantinople, Aug. 31, 1867.

When I think how I have been swindled by books of Oriental travel, I want a tourist for breakfast. For years and years I have dreamed of the wonders of the Turkish bath; for years and years I have promised myself that I would yet enjoy one. Many and many a time, in fancy, I have lain in the marble bath, and breathed the slumbrous fragrance of Eastern spices that filled the air; then passed through a weird and complicated system of pulling and hauling, and drenching and scrubbing, by a gang of naked savages who loomed vast and vaguely through the steaming mists, like demons; then rested for a while on a divan fit for a King; then passed through another complex ordeal, and one more fearful than the first;

and finally, swathed in soft fabrics, was conveyed to a princely saloon and laid upon a bed of eiderdown, where eunuchs, gorgeous of costume, fanned me while I drowsed and dreamed, or contentedly gazed at the rich hangings of the apartment, the soft carpets, the sumptuous furniture, the pictures; and drank delicious coffee, smoked the soothing narghili [narghile], and dropped, at the last, into tranquil repose, lulled by sensuous odors from unseen censors [censers], by the gentle influence of the narghili's Persian tobacco, and by the music of fountains that counterfeited the pattering of summer rain.

That was the picture, just as I got it from incendiary books of travel. It was a poor, miserable fraud. The reality is no more like it than the Five Points are like the Garden of Eden. They received me in a great court, paved with marble slabs; around it were broad galleries, one above another, carpeted with seedy matting, railed with unpainted balustrades, and furnished with huge, rickety chairs, cushioned with rusty old mattresses indented with impressions left by the forms of nine successive generations of men who had reposed upon them. The place was vast, naked, dreary—its court a barn, its galleries stalls for human horses. The cadaverous, half-nude varlets that served in the establishment had nothing of poetry in their appearance, nothing of romance, nothing of Oriental splendor. They shed no entrancing odors —just the contrary. Their hungry eyes and their lank forms continually suggested one glaring, unsentimental fact—they wanted a "square meal."

I went up into one of the racks and undressed. An unclean starveling wrapped a gaudy tablecloth about my loins, and hung a white rag over my shoulders. If I had had a tub then, it would have come natural to me to take in washing. I was then conducted downstairs into the wet, slippery court, and the first things that attracted my attention were my heels. My fall excited no comment. They expected it, no doubt. It belonged in the list of softening, sensuous influences peculiar to this home of Eastern luxury. It was softening enough, certainly, but its application was not happy. They now gave me a pair of wooden clogs—benches in miniature, with leather straps over them to confine my feet (which they would have done, only I do not wear No. 13s). These things dangled uncomfortably by the straps when I lifted up my feet, and came down in awkward and unexpected places when I put them on the floor again, and sometimes turned sideways and wrenched my ankles out of joint.

However, it was all Oriental luxury, and I did what I could to enjoy it.

They put me in another part of the barn and laid me on a stuffy sort of pallet, which was not made of cloth of gold or Persian shawls, but was merely the unpretending sort of thing I have seen in the slave quarters of Arkansas. There was nothing whatever in this dim marble prison but five more of these biers. It was a very solemn place. I expected that the spiced odors of Araby were going to steal over my senses now, but they didn't. A copper-colored skeleton, with a rag around him, brought me a glass decanter of water, with a lighted tobacco pipe in the top of it, and a pliant stem a yard long, with a brass mouthpiece to it. It was the famous "narghili" of the East—the thing the Grand Turk smokes in the pictures. This began to look like luxury. I took one blast at it, and it was sufficient. The smoke all went down my throat. It came back in convulsive snorts through my nose. It had a vile taste, and the taste of a thousand infidel tongues that remained on that brass mouthpiece was viler still. I was getting discouraged. Whenever hereafter I see the cross-legged Grand Turk smoking his narghili, in pretended bliss, on the outside of a paper of Connecticut tobacco, I shall know him for the shameless humbug he is.

This prison was filled with hot air. When I had got warmed up sufficiently to prepare me for a still warmer temperature, they took me where it was—into a marble room, wet, slippery, and steamy, and laid me out on a raised platform in the center. It was very warm. Presently my man sat me down by a tank of hot water, drenched me well, gloved his hand with a coarse mitten, and began to polish me all over with it. I began to smell disagreeably. The more he polished, the worse I smelt. It was alarming. I said to him: "I perceive that I am pretty far gone. It is plain that I ought to be buried without any unnecessary delay. Perhaps you had better go after my friends at once, because the weather is warm, and I cannot 'keep' long." He went on scrubbing, and paid no attention. I soon saw that he was reducing my size. He bore hard on his mitten, and from under it rolled little cylinders, like macaroni. It could not be dirt, for it was too white. He pared me down in this way for a long time. Finally I said: "It is a tedious process; it will take hours to trim me to the size you want me. I will wait; go and borrow a jack-plane." He paid no attention at all.

After a while he brought a basin, some soap, and something that seemed to be the tail of a horse. He made up a prodigious quantity of soapsuds, deluged me with them from head to foot without warning me to shut my eyes, and then swabbed me viciously with the horse tail. Then he left me there, a statue of snowy lather, and went away. When I got tired of waiting, I went and hunted him up. He was propped against the wall, in another room, asleep. I woke him. He was not disconcerted. He took me back and flooded me with exhausting hot water, then turbaned my head, swathed me with dry tablecloths, and conducted me to a latticed chicken-coop in one of the galleries, and pointed to one of those Arkansas beds. I mounted it, and vaguely expected the odors of Araby again. They did not come. The blank, unornamented coop had nothing about it of that Oriental voluptuousness one reads of so much. It was more suggestive of the county hospital than anything else. The skinny servitor brought a narghili, and I got him to take it out again without wasting any time about it. Then he brought the world-renowned Turkish coffee that poets have sung so rapturously for many generations, and I seized upon it as the last hope that was left of my old dreams of Eastern luxury. It was another swindle. Of all the unchristian beverages that ever passed my lips, Turkish coffee is the worst. The cup is small, it is smeared with grounds; the coffee is black, thick, unsavory of smell, and execrable in taste. The bottom of the cup has a muddy sediment in it half an inch deep. This goes down your throat, and portions of it lodge by the way and produce a tickling aggravation that keeps you barking and coughing for an hour.

Here endeth my experience of the celebrated Turkish bath, and here also endeth my dream of the bliss the mortal revels in who passes through it. It is a malignant swindle. The man who enjoys it is qualified to enjoy anything that is repulsive to sight or sense, and he that can invest it with the charm of poetry is able to do the same with anything else in the world that is tedious, and wretched, and dismal, and nasty.

For Writing and Discussion

1. Comment on "A Genuine Turkish Bath" as an illustration of this remark by James Thurber: "Human dignity, the humorist believes, is not only silly but a little sad. So are dreams and conventions and illusions."

2. Explain the role of contrast, repetition, and "topsy-turvy" reversal of either expectation or reality in the creation of humor.

Geniuses for Minor Difficulties

3. Twain's tendency to overstatement is held in stricter check than usual in this anecdote. Where does it begin to get out of hand?

4. How does Twain use exaggeration and hyperbole to diminish human nature rather than to make it godlike or superhuman, as in the tall tale?

5. This sketch is a model of tight organization. Trace Twain's development of thought on the Turkish bath from the ideal to the real, from the sublime to the ridiculous. How are both contrast and chronological sequence combined in the organizational pattern?

6. Select the three expressions or sentences that contribute most to the verbal humor of this piece. What language choices are involved? what particular devices or figures of speech?

The Private Life of Mr. Bidwell

JAMES THURBER

The unusual situation gets the belly laugh in low comedy. It is a character's response to an ordinary experience that prompts the smile of light humor. You have just met one of the favorite types of characters for the humorous sketch—the stereotype whose stock expectations are not realized because they are based on a topsy-turvy picture of the real world, a world in which his own mind imposes the "rules" as he would like to see them applied. Also a favorite—one that appeals more to Thurber than to Twain—is the obsessive character, the person whose daily life is so monotonous that he creates out of repetition itself a kind of reason for being, a way of life. The obsessive person's compulsive behavior and fixed ideas, especially as they relate to creating humor, can also be considered as a means of not being human, a way of escaping from the indignities, the unforeseeable and uncontrollable vagaries of real life into the more ordered and mechanical but predictable and "safe" existence of the machine. The computerized man is the opposite of the quixotic man, though both exhibit repetitive behavior. The quixotic man's behavior is a kind of theme with variations, while the computerized man's responses are as conditioned as those of Pavlov's dogs. The humor of the quixotic man is in his attempt to impose a dream-logic on the real world; the humor of the automaton is in his acting like a machine instead of like a human being. Mr. Bidwell, the compulsive character you are about to meet, is so frustrated and trapped in unpleasant situations in real life that he is willing to sell his birthright as a quixotic human being to become permanently less than human.

The Private Life of Mr. Bidwell

From where she was sitting, Mrs. Bidwell could not see her husband, but she had a curious feeling of tension: she knew he was up to something.

"What are you doing, George?" she demanded, her eyes still on her book.

"Mm?"

"What's the matter with you?"

"Pahhhhh-h-h," said Mr. Bidwell, in a long, pleasurable exhale. "I was holding my breath."

Mrs. Bidwell twisted creakingly in her chair and looked at him; he was sitting behind her in his favorite place under the parchment lamp with the street scene of old New York on it. "I was just holding my breath," he said again.

"Well, please don't do it," said Mrs. Bidwell, and went back to her book. There was silence for five minutes.

"George!" said Mrs. Bidwell.

"Bwaaaaaa," said Mr. Bidwell. "What?"

"Will you please *stop* that?" she said. "It makes me nervous."

"I don't see how that bothers you," he said. "Can't I breathe?"

"You can breathe without holding your breath like a goop," said Mrs. Bidwell. "Goop" was a word that she was fond of using; she rather lazily applied it to everything. It annoyed Mr. Bidwell.

"Deep breathing," said Mr. Bidwell, in the impatient tone he used when explaining anything to his wife, "is good exercise. You ought to take more exercise."

"Well, please don't do it around me," said Mrs. Bidwell, turning again to the pages of Mr. Galsworthy.

At the Cowans' party, a week later, the room was full of chattering people when Mrs. Bidwell, who was talking to Lida Carroll, suddenly turned around as if she had been summoned. In a chair in a far corner of the room, Mr. Bidwell was holding his breath. His chest was expanded, his chin drawn in; there was a strange stare in his eyes, and his face was slightly empurpled. Mrs. Bidwell moved into the line of

his vision and gave him a sharp, penetrating look. He deflated slowly and looked away.

Later, in the car, after they had driven in silence a mile or more on the way home, Mrs. Bidwell said, "It seems to me you might at least have the kindness not to hold your breath in other people's houses."

"I wasn't hurting anybody," said Mr. Bidwell.

"You looked silly!" said his wife. "You looked perfectly crazy!" She was driving and she began to speed up, as she always did when excited or angry. "What do you suppose people thought—you sitting there all swelled up, with your eyes popping out?"

"I wasn't all swelled up," he said, angrily.

"You looked like a goop," she said. The car slowed down, sighed, and came to a complete, despondent stop.

"We're out of gas," said Mrs. Bidwell. It was bitterly cold and nastily sleeting. Mr. Bidwell took a long, deep breath.

The breathing situation in the Bidwell family reached a critical point when Mr. Bidwell began to inhale in his sleep, slowly, and exhale with a protracted, growling "wooooo-ooo." Mrs. Bidwell, ordinarily a sound sleeper (except on nights when she was sure burglars were getting in), would wake up and reach over and shake her husband. "George!"

she would say.

"Hawwwwww," Mr. Bidwell would say, thickly. "Wahs maa nah, hm?"

After he had turned over and gone back to sleep, Mrs. Bidwell would lie awake, thinking.

One morning at breakfast she said, "George, I'm not going to put up with this another day. If you can't stop blowing up like a grampus, I'm going to leave you." There was a slight, quick lift in Mr. Bidwell's heart, but he tried to look surprised and hurt.

"All right," he said. "Let's not talk about it."

Mrs. Bidwell buttered another piece of toast. She described to him the way he sounded in his sleep. He read the paper.

With considerable effort, Mr. Bidwell kept from inflating his chest for about a week, but one night at the McNallys' he hit on the idea of seeing how many seconds he could hold his breath. He was rather bored by the McNallys' party, anyway. He began timing himself with his wristwatch in a remote corner of the livingroom. Mrs. Bidwell, who was in the kitchen talking children and clothes with Bea McNally, left her abruptly and slipped back into the livingroom. She stood quietly behind her husband's chair. He knew she was there, and tried to let out his breath imperceptibly.

"I see you," she said, in a low, cold tone. Mr. Bidwell jumped up.

"Why don't you let me alone?" he demanded.

"Will you please lower your voice?" she said, smiling so that if anyone were looking he wouldn't think the Bidwells were arguing.

"I'm getting pretty damned tired of this," said Bidwell in a low voice.

"You've ruined my evening!" she whispered.

"You've ruined mine, too!" he whispered back. They knifed each other, from head to stomach, with their eyes.

"Sitting here like a goop, holding your breath," said Mrs. Bidwell. "People will think you are an idiot." She laughed, turning to greet a lady who was approaching them.

Mr. Bidwell sat in his office the next afternoon, a black, moist afternoon, tapping a pencil on his desk, and scowling, "All right, then, get out, get out!" he muttered. "What do I care?" He was visualizing the scene when Mrs. Bidwell would walk out on him. After going through it several times, he returned to his work, feeling vaguely contented. He made up his mind to breathe any way he wanted to, no matter what she did. And, having come to this decision, he oddly enough, and quite without effort, lost interest in holding his breath.

Everything went rather smoothly at the Bidwells' for a month or so. Mr. Bidwell didn't do anything to annoy his wife beyond leaving his razor on her dressing table and forgetting to turn out the hall light when he went to bed. Then there came the night of the Bentons' party.

Mr. Bidwell, bored as usual, was sitting in a far corner of the room, breathing normally. His wife was talking animatedly with Beth Williamson about negligees. Suddenly her voice slowed and an uneasy look came into her eyes: George was up to something. She turned around and sought him out. To anyone but Mrs. Bidwell he must have seemed like any husband sitting in a chair. But his wife's lips set tightly. She walked casually over to him.

"What are you doing?" she demanded.

"Hm?" he said, looking at her vacantly.

"What are you *doing*?" she demanded, again. He gave her a harsh, venomous look, which she returned.

"I'm multiplying numbers in my head," he said, slowly and evenly, "if you must know." In the prolonged, probing examination that they silently, without moving any muscles save those of their eyes, gave each other, it became solidly, frozenly apparent to both of them that the end of their endurance had arrived. The curious bond that held them together snapped—rather more easily than either had supposed was possible. That night, while undressing for bed, Mr. Bidwell calmly multiplied numbers in his head. Mrs. Bidwell stared coldly at him for a few moments, holding a stocking in her hand; she didn't bother to berate him. He paid no attention to her. The thing was simply over.

George Bidwell lives alone now (his wife remarried). He never goes to parties any more, and his old circle of friends rarely sees him. The last time that any of them did see him, he was walking along a country road with the halting, uncertain gait of a blind man: he was trying to see how many steps he could take without opening his eyes.

For Writing and Discussion

1. How does Mr. Bidwell's obsessive behavior represent an attempt to escape from life's indignities? How is his frustration both similar to and different from Mr. Preble's?

2. What is ironic about the acquisition of an obsessive habit that was acquired initially as a way to free oneself of something unpleasant?

3. How many examples of repetition (words and phrases, actions, situations) do you find in this story? How does Thurber vary each of these, both to avoid boring the reader and to create humor through repetition?

4. Like so much slang that is in vogue, is overused, and then disappears, the word *goop* is no longer heard very often. If you were Mr. Bidwell's mate, what word would you use instead? Locate any other examples of dated slang in this story. Would you update these terms, or do you think they still contribute effectively to the humor of this story?

5. In spite of Mr. Bidwell's strange behavior, it should not be difficult to laugh *with* him as well as *at* him. What irrational habits have you ever indulged in to the point that you found you could not stop even when you tried? Why did you cultivate the habits in the first place?

6. If you had to live with either Mr. or Mrs. Bidwell, whom would you choose? Why?

Geniuses
for Minor
Difficulties

Men, Women, and Dogs

JAMES THURBER

Here are three cartoons from Thurber's collection called *Men, Women, and Dogs*—all subjects that obsessed Thurber as a writer. Each of these cartoons deals with obsessions of different types. How does the first cartoon relate to the causes of the frustrations of Mr. Preble and Mr. Bidwell? In the second cartoon, what psychological pattern of response does Mrs. Sprague have in common with Mr. Bidwell? In what sense is the third cartoon an illustration of the *reverse* side of the coin for Mr. Preble and Mr. Bidwell?

Home

"Have you seen my pistol, Honey-Bun?"

"You said a moment ago that everybody you look at seems to be a rabbit. Now just what do you mean by that, Mrs. Sprague?"

Geniuses
for Minor
Difficulties

7

Making Trouble Pay

The Situation

Most of us, at some time or other, have pulled some practical jokes, told a few whoppers, made boastful remarks or wagers, or exaggerated adventures. Not many of us, though, would be proud to be called perennial tricksters, expert liars, and the best of the big-mouthed braggarts—unless we were professional humorists or clowns. In the course of daily conversation, however, we all tell stories about ourselves and interesting people we've met. Occasionally we'll get such an engrossed response that we'll be asked to repeat the same anecdote on another occasion. Someone may, for example, be talking about a fire reported in the paper or on a television newscast, and suddenly we'll find ourselves being asked about that fire we were actually involved in. Or, more naturally, we'll be one of a group of people who've begun a round of snake stories, or stories about automobiles, pets, or parties. Or we might be trading stories about the brightest or the stupidest or the clumsiest person we've ever known.

Not all the stories are humorous. Many are serious, some pathetic, some tragic. Usually they represent some high point in life, something out of the ordinary. But they can also be stories of anticlimax, of great expectations followed by flat realizations. They can be moments of quiet, smiling recollection as we look back on life's experiences that seemed, at the time, so monotonously trivial that they went unnoticed, or so exaggeratedly important or intense that only time and distance can put them in proper perspective. It is this backward glance at life's little absurdities that provides the subject matter for another kind of humor—for the humor of heretofore unnoticed idiosyncrasies, or for the humor found in the detection of routines that have become so repetitive that they are comic in their obsessiveness.

LIFE'S LITTLE ABSURDITIES

Sources of Invention

If you're looking for material for a light humorous sketch in the manner of Twain or Thurber, or if you are thinking of brushing up an anecdote in order to build your reputation as an entertaining raconteur, take Thurber's advice: "I think that humor is the best that lies closest to the familiar, to that part of the familiar which is humiliating, distressing, even tragic. . . . There is always a laugh in the utterly familiar." Humorists, as E. B. White observed, have "always made trouble pay." Look for the experiences that seemed at the time to diminish life, to lower your dignity; and look at the familiar habits we all indulge in even when they are no longer useful or necessary. Think of yourself, if you can, as a character that you are observing from a distance in time. Get outside yourself. And if you notice someone else's habits and obsessions, think about the ways they are similar to, rather than different from, some of your own. You'll end up laughing at yourself as well as at him; or, more likely, laughing with him instead of at him. Like Twain, we've all had colds, and we've had favorite remedies that seemed to us as unsatisfactory though not as strenuous as his. Our dogs may not have bitten quite as many people as Thurber's dogs, but we've all known pets whose habits haven't endeared them to the neighborhood and who yet were loved beyond sense by their owners. Mr. Bidwell *does* seem ridiculous, but who hasn't walked down the pavement and carefully avoided stepping on lines, and who hasn't stumbled into a curb while avoiding a ladder? And though we may never have visited Turkey, which of us hasn't had a soap-bubble dream of a faraway, luxurious place or of something else that turned into a lead cloud?

Start thinking of the most ordinary events of life—eating, sleeping, going to work or school, getting up in the morning, wearing clothes, buying things, watching television, getting sick, going to the dentist, using the telephone, asking for a date, falling in love or out of love, getting into arguments and fights.

Problems

Do you get very far before you begin to bore yourself? That's because the hardest thing to write or talk about is the familiar. If the experience or emotion we select is so ordinary that everyone has gone through it, we of course run the risk of being dull. We all know people who consider themselves amusing conversationalists, but who put us to sleep with their elaborate accounts of trivia or of unusual events made trivial by the piling on of endless, mundane details. The humor of the quiet smile isn't as spontaneous as the humor of the belly laugh, and it doesn't come as easily.

The Unusual Approach to the Usual

How, we ask, does Twain make a common cold funny? And how does Thurber create an unforgettable and amusing portrait of humans and dogs and a man who simply holds his breath—something we all do at times. Both Twain and Thurber agree that the humor of retrospect arises from unpleasant, humiliating, undignified, or even painful experiences rather than from pleasant or simply uneventful ones, or ones that are funny at the time they happen in the same way that the situations of low comedy are funny in a kind of everlastingly spontaneous "now." Your familiar experiences with getting dressed, for example, are not subjects for humor unless you've had the habit of putting things on backwards, or of mistakenly and sleepily struggling into your smaller or larger brother's or sister's clothes. Your visits to the dentist might produce discomfort that seems excruciating, fatal at the time, but is actually minor when viewed from a distance. Dropping things gets to be an irritating and often embarrassing situation for most of us, but there are nevertheless humorous possibilities for telling about our butterfinger days, depending upon what we drop, where we drop it, and what the penalties or results are. Think of the difference, for instance, between dropping a sweater on a rug and spilling a package of pins or a carton of small tacks on a freshly waxed floor, or on a newly cemented or hot tarred pavement.

The You in Humor

The main thing we learn from Twain and Thurber is that their humor arises from the stamp of their personalities on the situation. We would expect Twain's cold to be the worst ever, the remedies the most outlandish. It was; they were. We would expect Thurber to present an upside-down world where dogs instead of humans rule the household, and where intuitive guesses replace rational decisions. Twain's descriptions of his troubles are extravagant, colorful, flamboyant, overstated; Thurber's recollections of his troubles are more subtle, more dependent on the oblique view, the understatement, the awareness of the innate absurdity of people and life. Your cold and your dog are different simply because your reactions to them are different. Unlike the humor of low comedy, the humor of the quiet smile and the "buried" laugh depends upon the person in the situation as much as upon the situation itself. Humor arises from character more often than from event—either as a result of a unique character in an ordinary situation or a mundane character in an extraordinary situation. It may arise from the actions of a dull, computerized, frustrated person in a repetitively ordinary or unusual situation (Preble caught in the routine of a bad marriage and suddenly becoming obsessed with a most unusual solution, or Bidwell caught in a similar situation and taking an even more mundane escape). Dropping that package of pins or carton of tacks on a hopelessly slippery or sticky surface is dealt with differently by a methodical, middle-aged man, by a flittery female, or by a gawky teen-age boy.

Details That Sharpen Contrasts

Another cue we get from considering the selections in the preceding chapter is that humor, like all good writing, depends upon selecting the specific instances, the uniquely revealing details that help you to see, hear, feel, and touch with the observer and the protagonist. We see visitors retreating before Muggs's staring eyes; we cough with Twain; we feel a tightness in the chest as we hold our breath with Bidwell. These sensory details underscore the major elements of humor—our illogical actions, our absurdly disproportionate reactions to what eventually turns out to be minor or at least temporary, our feelings and responses that we find practical and rational ways of coping with only after they have passed. Remember Thurber's statement that humorists talk "largely about small matters and smally about great affairs." This implies the possibility of also finding humor in an important event that is originally underrated rather than overrated. In order to dramatize the "topsy-turvy" responses we make at the time things happen as compared with our evaluation of the happenings much later, we want to emphasize the detail that best demonstrates the contrast between the irrational immediate response and the rational response in retrospect. For example, the rational response to Muggs's habit would be to get rid of *him* instead of one's friends and the services of the laundryman, iceman, and trash collector. The rational response to a cold is to seek a doctor's advice rather than to follow the folklore medicine of friends. The irrational response, however, is humorous, and it strikes other people funny because it is such a human kind of illogic, one with which all of us can identify. It makes us feel pleasantly amused to know that we are not alone in our idiosyncrasies.

Writing Your Anecdote

Now let's start to select material and details for a humorous anecdote based on a humiliating or embarrassing personal experience. Let us say you have just dropped a package of pins or a carton of tacks on a sticky surface. Stop whatever you're thinking about at this moment and picture the situation you're in. Exactly what did you drop? How many? In what kind of container? Onto what surface? Where? Are there other people around, or are you alone? What do you immediately do, without thinking, to retrieve your pins or tacks? What happens? What other actions *might* you undertake if your first unthinking response fails?

Jot down all of the actions you imagine until you hit on a solution. Then, very quickly, write a rough draft of a paragraph or two describing these actions in succession, as exactly as possible. Make no comment on their absurdity. Write as if whatever you did was perfectly sensible. You might be interested in comparing the sort of thing you imagined, and the language you used to describe your actions, with Thurber's account in "Nine Needles" of a man who finds himself in a similar situation. After spending the weekend with a couple who have just left for work, he cuts himself while shaving:

> More angry than hurt, I jerked open the door of the medicine cabinet to see if I could find a styptic pencil and out fell, from the top shelf, a little black paper packet containing nine needles. It seems that this wife kept a little paper packet containing nine needles on the top shelf of the medicine

cabinet. The packet fell into the soapy water of the washbowl, where the paper rapidly disintegrated, leaving nine needles at large in the bowl. I was, naturally enough, not in the best condition, either physical or mental, to recover nine needles from a washbowl. No gentleman who has lather on his face and whose ear is bleeding is in the best condition for anything, even something involving the handling of nine large blunt objects.

It did not seem wise to me to pull the plug out of the washbowl and let the needles go down the drain. I had visions of clogging up the plumbing system of the house, and also a vague fear of causing short circuits somehow or other (I know very little about electricity and I don't want to have it explained to me). Finally, I groped very gently around the bowl and eventually had four of the needles in the palm of one hand and three in the palm of the other—two I couldn't find. If I had thought quickly and clearly, I wouldn't have done that. A lathered man whose ear is bleeding and who has four wet needles in one hand and three in the other may be said to have reached the lowest known point of human efficiency. There is nothing he can do but stand there. I tried transferring the needles in my left hand to the palm of my right hand, but I couldn't get them off my left hand. Wet needles cling to you. In the end, I wiped the needles off onto a bathtowel which was hanging on a rod above the bathtub. It was the only towel that I could find. I had to dry my hands afterward on the bathmat. Then I tried to find the needles in the towel. Hunting for seven needles in a bathtowel is the most tedious occupation I have ever engaged in. I could find only five of them. With the two that had been left in the bowl, that meant there were four needles in all missing—two in the washbowl and two others lurking in the towel or lying in the bathtub under the towel. Frightful thoughts came to me of what might happen to anyone who used that towel or washed his face in the bowl or got into the tub, if I didn't find the missing needles. Well, I didn't find them. I sat down on the edge of the tub to think, and I decided finally that the only thing to do was wrap up the towel in a newspaper and take it away with me. I also decided to leave a note for my friends explaining as clearly as I could that I was afraid there were two needles in the bathtub and two needles in the washbowl, and that they better be careful.

I looked everywhere in the apartment, but I could not find a pencil, or a pen, or a typewriter. I could find pieces of paper, but nothing with which to write on them. I don't know what gave me the idea—a movie I had seen, perhaps, or a story I had read—but I suddenly thought of writing a message with a lipstick. The wife might have an extra lipstick lying around and, if so, I concluded it would be in the medicine cabinet. I went back to the medicine cabinet and began poking around in it for a lipstick. I saw what I thought looked like the metal tip of one, and I got two fingers around it and began to pull gently—it was under a lot of things. Every object in the medicine cabinet began to slide. Bottles broke in the washbowl and on the floor; red, brown, and white liquids spurted; nail files, scissors, razor blades, and miscellaneous objects sang and clattered and tinkled. I was covered with perfume, peroxide, and cold cream.

It took me half an hour to get the debris all together in the middle of the bathroom floor. I made no attempt to put anything back in the medicine cabinet. I knew it would take a steadier hand than mine and a less shattered spirit. Before I went away (only partly shaved) and abandoned the shambles, I left a note saying that I was afraid there were needles in the bathtub and the washbowl and that I had taken their towel and that I would call up and tell them everything—I wrote it in iodine with the end of a toothbrush. I have not yet called up, I am sorry to say. I have neither found the courage nor thought up the words to explain what happened. I suppose my friends believe that I deliberately smashed up their bathroom and stole their towel. I don't know for sure, because they have not yet called me up, either.

Notice these elements in Thurber's story: (1) the actions that were illogical; (2) the sequence of actions that permitted the author to develop a "thin situation" into a more extended series of cause-and-effect events; (3) objectivity, and exactness of details and description. Can you see the guest? Have you ever been in a similar bind? What would have been a logical way to handle the situation?

Language and Point of View

Selecting exactly the right details to create humor is the crucial step. But the tone must be right, too. Language and point of view create the tone. Usually the point of view in the quiet, retrospective kind of humor we've been discussing is third person, objective. The narrator, usually the protagonist or subject of his story, is looking back on an experience in a cool, rational frame of mind. He is struck by the contrast between his present feelings and appraisal of the experience and his irrational feelings and erratic responses at the time the incident took place. If he writes in the first person, which is the usual way to speak of one's own experiences, he is the "I" narrator viewing himself as a character in the same detached way he would view another person. If he does *not* adopt a detached point of view, regardless of whether he is speaking from the viewpoint of a third or a first person, he runs the danger of sympathizing with himself and becoming emotionally involved with his own past problems. The result may be pathetic instead of humorous. Humor requires coolness and distance. Without these, the essential contrast between intense reactions to minor problems or inadequate responses to major events is lost.

Notice how Thurber helps us identify with his butterfingered needledropper without feeling sorry for him. He does get dangerously near the sentimental in "The Dog That Bit People," in which he skirts between humorous acceptance of and sentimental attachment to both mother and dog. But we don't really feel sorry for either of them, and we can't if we wish to maintain a humorous, detached tone. Even Twain's tourist, in describing the disappointing Turkish bath, is viewed as a ludicrous rather than as a pathetic or exploited object. This tourist's experience provides an example of another commonly used subject for humorous personal reminiscence—the longed-for, dreamed-about desire that, when granted, is disappointing. Here the contrast is between ideal and real, expectation and fulfillment, goal and accomplishment. Humorous experiences of this kind are often comments on the saying that "All that glitters is not gold."

Your choice of language also helps to convey the proper tone of detachment. Language provides another kind of contrast to the topsy-turvy logic of action and emotion, the reversal of hope and fulfillment, when viewed immediately and from a distance. Language is the most effective way to make the "great small" or the "small great," as you observed in Twain's "My Late Senatorial Secretaryship" and Thurber's "Casuals of the Keys." In the Twain story, the secretary's literal language, exaggeratedly applied to quite practical requests, creates a contrast with both the request and the employer's euphemisms and circumlocutions. In the Thurber tale, understated language contrasts with bizarre situations. For a little preliminary practice in understatement and overstatement, write a short phrase or sentence in which the language you use to describe your reactions to a series of similar, increasingly unpleasant experiences is the opposite in tone and intensity from the experience itself. Understate the most unpleasant experience; exaggerate the least distasteful experience.

   a. a mosquito bite; a bee sting; a deep cut
   b. a sniffle; a sneeze; a persistent, hacking cough
   c. a slight draught; a cool breeze; a bone-chilling wind
   d. the hum of traffic; the screech of a fire siren; the blare of hundreds of horns

Now select a personal experience that was intensely unpleasant or embarrassing at the time, or an experience that represented the disappointing fulfillment of a wish, and prepare a short anecdote to tell your friends. Or write a brief sketch to submit to a school newspaper or magazine. The suggestions that follow should help recall the steps you may want to follow in preparing your story.

Summary of Procedure
   1. Try to recall an experience which, at the time it occurred, seemed either much more distasteful and humiliating than it does in retrospect or which was far more important than it seemed at the time.
   2. Try to imagine yourself back in that experience. Analyze your original feelings. How did your emotions result in actions that now seem inappropriate for the situation you were in? (Remember that you are trying to describe not only your emotions, but also the behavior caused by these emotions.)
   3. Select for your anecdote the responses that now seem most illogical. Exaggerate some, or invent others, if you think your story will seem more ludicrous by their addition. List these in order of increasing illogicality.
   4. Establish the context or setting in which your over- or understated behavior occurred. Describe it in a matter-of-fact way.
   5. If your story is one of underreaction to an important event, adopt a tone and method that are understated. If it is a tale of overreaction to a comparatively trivial or temporary event, stick to overstatement and exaggeration. Be sure,

Making Trouble Pay

however, that your tone and method contrast with the events you are describing.

6. In order to achieve proper detachment from your personal involvement, you might try telling your story in the third person. If you like, rewrite it in the first person, keeping the same cool distance between yourself and your "I" narrator.

THE HUMOR OF HABIT: COMPULSIVE CHARACTERS

The familiar experience of disproportionate distress viewed in balanced perspective is a chief source of the quieter types of humor. Its appeal lies in our recognition of ourselves, the Everyman concealed in the highly individualized character who responds to an ordinary but typically human situation in a very human way. To be human, in this sense, implies weakness as well as strength, error as well as infallibility, discrepancy between desire and fulfillment, conflict between reason and impulse and between the feeling that nothing in life ever stands still and the wish that it would.

Since humor is built on contrast, it should not be surprising to learn that the opposite of the human and individualized can also be funny. In fact, one of the most astute analysts of the comic, the French philosopher Henri Bergson, believed that comedy arises whenever a person ceases to behave in an unpredictable way, attempting to solve new problems by trial and error, and acts instead like an automaton, a mechanized toy, a "piece of clockwork wound up once and for all." Bergson would have enjoyed Mr. Bidwell, whose breath-holding habit became so automatic a response to certain situations that it was replaceable only by habits of exactly the same mechanical nature. He would have considered humorous Harrison Cammery, who couldn't resist grabbing any goldfish in sight. Bergson might have thought Muggs and his mistress funny because of the dog's clockwork regularity of biting and his mistress's equally clockwork habit of excusing him. We smile, then, at the familar experience that seemed distressing at the time, and we smile, too, at the person whose habits are more like the behavior of machines than of human beings. (Sometimes, of course, that "person" is oneself.) Unlike the tall tale and other low comic forms, which tend to exaggerate our abilities, both the distressing experience and the mechanized behavior reduce the stature of us humans. The distressing experience reminds us of our vulnerability and weakness; the clockwork response shows us how easy it is for human creativity to become dehumanized into machinelike reactions.

Habits and Compulsions

Two kinds of people who behave in mechanized ways are the compulsive character and the human machine. We all know or have met a few of each. We all, perhaps, are similarly "de-humans" ourselves at one time or another in our lives, though one of the differences between the humor of the familiar indignity and the humor of mechanical toys is that we readily recognize ourselves in the one and almost never in the other. In your role as storyteller or party raconteur, before you can begin to look around for compulsive subjects, you have to know what a compulsive character is and how to recognize him when you see him.

Compulsive people are not merely creatures of habit; nor are they, like the human machine, "computerized" to react in a sort of automatic progression of behavior patterns when their habit-machine is triggered by some special stimulus. Most habits are not compulsive, though they are mechanical. The ordinary habits of daily life are often reasonable and efficient responses to the need to establish routines in matters that occur over and over, where *thinking about* the appropriate behavior would waste time and be just as absurd as compulsive behavior. Think, for example, of the difficulty young children have in learning to tie shoelaces, button clothes, or brush teeth. If you had to think consciously about all the routines you have set up just to get going in the morning, you'd be late every day. It would be absurd to give up these useful habits. Compulsive habits, on the other hand, are inappropriate responses to the situations in which they are practiced. And further, they are irrational in origin; that is, they are developed not in response to an originally reasonable purpose, but as reactions that are illogical from the start. The dictionary defines a compulsion as "the irresistible impulse to perform an irrational act." Compulsions become habits in time—habits like Mr. Bidwell's breath-holding, Thurber's mother's defense of Muggs's machinelike lunges, or Birdey Doggett's compulsive and invariable response to the opportunity (real or imagined) for a joke.

Origins of Compulsions

The origins of Mr. Preble's and Mr. Bidwell's compulsions are irrational because they are both completely illogical solutions to their real problems—which may, in both cases, have been underlying dissatisfactions with their wives, logically to be dealt with through marriage counseling or rational compromise. But their compulsive insistence on solving their problems in one way and one way only is not only compulsive, but obsessive. *Obsession* is a very interesting word. It is derived from a Latin root meaning "to sit on" or "besiege." Gradually the word came to signify the act of an evil spirit or devil that possessed a person, literally "sitting" on his reason and rendering him impotent to act sensibly. He is possessed by demons, preoccupied by a fixed idea, which he acts out in mechanical, repetitive patterns of irrational behavior, or compulsions. The obsessive person dwells on an idea and thinks about his compulsive needs, in addition to acting them out in his habits. Mr. Preble, once he has decided to murder his wife, seems taken over by an irrational spirit and from then on, his actions are compulsive. The absurdity in this story is compounded by Mrs. Preble's seeming acquiescence in the topsy-turvy logic that pervades the whole piece. Mr. Bidwell, too, seems unable to control his own machinelike acts. He is like a toy wound up to hold its breath a certain number of seconds. Both men are dehumanized, though one is inhuman and the other merely a self-made robot.

Topsy-Turvy Technique

Ordinary habits are automatic, unthinking responses to situations; compulsive, obsessive habits are those that are irrational in origin and in continued practice. People who have compulsive and obsessive habits are characteristically consciously preoccupied with them. They are examples of the "topsy-turvy" or "upside-down" in humor in that they are uses of one's mind for "un-sane" or unreasonable purposes. Ironically, the obsessive-compulsive character often begins his march toward mechanization in an attempt to be free, to rid himself of restrictions that seem intolerable to him. Thus Mr. Preble wants to be rid of his marriage and Mr. Bidwell of wifely monologues and forced attendance at boring parties. The termination of this quest for freedom by self-imprisonment in one's own habits is another example of the topsy-turvy technique that is humorous at the same time as it pictures the dehumanizing of a person.

Sources of Invention

We don't meet compulsive types like Mr. Preble every day, but we *do* know people like the goldfish-holder or like Mr. Bidwell, people who have an obsession which consumes them and which they practice in the most unexpected places and at the most inappropriate times. Do you, for instance, know any health faddists who have a cure for all ills—just one habit or a cluster of habits that they engage in and, in addition, try to "sell" to their friends? Dieters are often obsessed with a particular diet and compulsive in their eating habits. Some, for example, are so convinced that grapefruit, if eaten before each and every meal, will reduce their weight that they carry a grapefruit with them to restaurants and dinners with friends. Others prefer carrot juice; still others eat nothing but meat, or skim milk and bananas. Consider the possibilities for humor when one of these dieters, captivated with a remedy for overweight, attends a reception for a visiting dignitary, goes on a picnic, or invites guests to his home for a meal. Think of your dieter in a number of similar situations, and mentally arrange three of the scenes you have imagined in ascending order of ridiculousness—perhaps the dieter no longer needs to diet, is, in fact, thin as a reed, or eats everything greedily (including his remedy) and is actually becoming more and more overweight. You are on your way to a sketch of a compulsive character.

Other excellent sources of invention come from observing or recalling people who collect things—pieces of string, rubber bands, stones, paper bags, box tops, pieces of glass, bottles. Other sources might be suggested by television programs—the character who breaks things, or the one who saves or spends money compulsively. Newspapers and magazines are also good places to look for ideas. Most newspapers carry a horoscope for those who let the stars guide their destinies. Think of the person who takes literally every single piece of advice from the stars, changing plans if they do not seem provided for in the daily horoscope. For example, look ahead for a period of a week or two at the horoscope for your own birthdate, and imagine what kinds of behavior you might exhibit if you tried to apply each admonition.

Columns of advice—medical, marital, and social—are also good places to look. Judging from a popular column of medical advice, Mr. Bidwell's opposite number is not an unusual compulsive type: evidently some people breathe too deeply and fre-

Making Trouble Pay

159

quently instead of not frequently enough. In his widely read syndicated medical column, Dr. Peter Steincrohn reports as follows:

Dear Dr. Steincrohn—I would like to say something about your column relating to the 14-year-old with fainting spells. My symptoms were exactly the same, and they were due to hyperventilation.

Six years ago, when I was in junior high school, it was an almost-unnoticed fad for kids to make themselves "blackout" by hyperventilating and then holding their breath and tensing their abdominal muscles. (Now it's drugs that produce a similar effect.)

I never did this with other kids, but later I began it as an escape from difficult or unpleasant situations. I did well in school, had friends and all the other good marks of "adjustment," but I was always looking for escape from—well, anything, or just diversion or maybe attention.

First it was pretty mild, but then it started to scare me. But I could not make myself stop breathing fast and deep. I'd get hysterical, numb in my hands and feet, and cry out with horrible headaches. When someone found me, my pulse was really scrambled and I couldn't talk.

My folks sent me to a neurologist who took a brain wave tracing (EEG). He concluded I had hyperventilation, which can be a totally unconscious reaction. My doctor prescribed tranquilizers.

At times I'd have to rebreathe for a few minutes into a paper bag to stop the extreme spells. Now I'm okay since I am able to control my rapid and deep breathing.—Miss O.

Dr. Steincrohn's reply implies that hyperventilation is not uncommon, though usually it is not compulsive or obsessive—at least not consciously so.

Hyperventilation is becoming a more recognizable term. A few years ago patients had no idea that it means overbreathing.

Often patients do not know they overbreathe. Unconsciously they breathe either too rapidly, too often or too deeply. Many sigh a lot or yawn often, losing greater amounts of carbon dioxide than normal.

This upsets the normal oxygen-carbon dioxide balance in the blood and causes such symptoms as nervousness, dizziness, apprehension, rapid pulse, palpitation, numbness, faintness and acute anxiety.

Often, just being aware that one overbreathes is the first step to cure.

Just skimming the headlines in your daily paper will soon put you on the trail of a compulsive person. The compulsive character in the following story is English, female, and obsessed by the demons of love:

GIRL, 20, JAILED FOR CHASING BEAU

Noisy Pursuit Of Boyfriend Basis For Court's Action

Reading, England, July 25 (AP)—A lovesick girl was jailed today for refusing to stop chasing the boy she wants to marry.

Irene Avery, 20, was led off to prison shouting: "I have to see him again and I will. Wait and see."

Miss Avery, a maid at the Royal Berkshire Hospital, was jailed for 28 days by local magistrates because she refused to agree to stop "continually pestering" Paul Taylor, 18.

The court was told that Miss Avery repeatedly visited Mr. Taylor's home, calling "I want Paul," after he broke off their four-month romance.

"She kept calling at the front gate and stood on the front lawn of the house," a police officer testified. "She refused to leave and finally the police was called and she was taken away by policemen.

"She was allowed to go but she persisted in pestering Mr. Taylor and followed him to work at a construction site where he is a dumper driver. This was embarrassing for him."

Technique

Develop a story using this article as a base. Or find another article and develop an idea in which you've become interested through the preceding discussion of compulsive characters. Remember to include in your sketch the situation that set off the obsession and the ways in which the obsession became computerized into an irrational series of responses to the same stimulus. Establish, if you wish, the point that your character's irrational act is a "topsy-turvy" result of a wish to be free instead of more restricted. When you have settled on your character, his compulsive habit, the obsessive nature of its origin and practice, and its humorous effect when applied to all sorts of inappropriate situations and settings, tell your anecdote in the matter-of-fact style of an objective news report or of Dr. Steincrohn's factual, "scientific," and serious explanation.

THE COMPULSIVE CHARACTER IN YOU

Sources of Invention

We usually tend to look outside ourselves for compulsive characters. *We* don't have obsessions. *We* don't do ridiculous things like carrying grapefruit or carrots to parties, or pursuing our romantic desires so outrageously and persistently, or . . . or do we? When did you last catch yourself avoiding that seam in the sidewalk, that ladder over the pavement, that black cat in your path? When did you last throw spilled salt over your shoulder? Superstitions are good sources for ideas about our own compulsions— and there are others. James Thurber tells a story about a man who could be any one of us, a man who receives this message from the Lost and Found Department of a hotel:

> An article was found after your departure in the room which you occupied. Kindly let us know if you have missed an article, and if so, send us a description and instructions as to what disposition you wish made of same. For lack of space, all Lost and Found articles must be disposed of within two months.

Suppose you receive such a letter, and after reviewing the contents of your luggage, cannot even remember the category of an object you might have left behind. Would you, like Thurber's forgetful guest, begin with the first letter of the alphabet and work through to Z? Or, have you ever run through the alphabet for the title of a song or for a name you've forgotten? After working out what you would do in a similar situation, see how Thurber takes a common obsession and makes it humorous.

Guessing Game

JAMES THURBER

An article was found after your departure in the room which you occupied. Kindly let us know if you have missed such an article, and if so, send us a description and instructions as to what disposition you wish made of same. For lack of

*Light
Humor:
The Quiet Smile*

space, all Lost and Found articles must be disposed of within two months.

Lost and Found Department
Hotel Lexington
Lexington Ave. & 48th St., New York
Per R. E. Daley.

Dear Mr. Daley:

This whole thing is going to be much more complicated than you think. I have waited almost two weeks before answering your postcard notification because I have been unable to figure out what article I left behind. I'm sorry now I didn't just forget the whole business. As a matter of fact, I did try to forget it, but it keeps bobbing up in my mind. I have got into an alphabetical rut about it; at night I lie awake naming articles to myself: bathrobe, bay rum, book, bicycle, belt, baby, etc. Dr. Prill, my analyst, has advised me to come right out and meet you on the subject.

So far, I have been able to eliminate, for certain, only two articles. I never remember to take pajamas or a hairbrush with me, so it couldn't be pajamas or a hairbrush you found. This does not get us very far. I have, however, ransacked the house and I find that a number of things are missing, but I don't remember which of them, if any, I had with me at the Lexington that night: the vest to my blue suit, my life-insurance policy, my Scotch terrier Jeannie, the jack out of the automobile tool case, the bottle-opener that is supposed to be kept in the kitchen drawer, the glass top to the percolator, a box of aspirin, a letter from my father giving my brother William's new address in Seattle, a roll of films (exposed) for a 2A Kodak, my briefcase (missing since 1927), etc. The article you have on hand might be any of these (with the exception of the briefcase). It would have been entirely possible for me, in the state of mind I was in that Friday, to have gone about all day with the automobile jack in my hand.

The thing that worries me most is the possibility that what I left in my room was something the absence of which I have not yet discovered and may never discover, unless you give me some hint. Is it animal, vegetable, or mineral? Is it as big as I am? Twice as big? Smaller than a man's hand? Does it have a screw-on top? Does it make any kind of regular ticking noise when in operation? Is it worth, new, as much as a hundred dollars? A thousand dollars? Fifty cents? It isn't a

Making
Trouble
Pay

bottle of toothache drops, is it? Or a used razor blade? Because I left them behind on purpose. These questions, it
seems to me, are eminently fair. I'm not asking you some
others I could think of, such as: Does it go with pants and
coat of a blue suit? Can it bark? Can it lift the wheel of an
automobile off the ground? Can it open a bottle? Does it re-
lieve pain? Is it a letter from somebody? Does anybody get
any money out of it when I am dead, providing I keep the
payments up?

I think you should let me know whether you are willing to
answer yes or no to my first set of questions, as in all games
of this sort. Because if you are going to stand there with a
silly look on your face and shake your head and keep repeating "Can't guess what it i-yis, can't guess what it i-yis!" to hell
with it. I don't care if it's a diamond ring.

I take it for granted, of course, that I really did leave an
article in the room I occupied. If I didn't, and this thing
turns out to be merely a guessing game in which the answer
is Robert E. Lee's horse, or something, you'll never be able to
answer your phone for a whole year without running the
chance of its being me, reserving dozens of rooms in a dis-
guised voice and under various assumed names, reporting a
fire on the twenty-third floor, notifying you that your bank
balance is overdrawn, pretending, in a husky guttural, that
you are the next man the gang is going to put on the spot
for the shooting of Joe the Boss over in Brooklyn.

Of course, I'm a little sore about the thing the way it is. If
you had been a guest at my house and had gone away leaving your watch or your keyring behind, would I send you a
penny postcard asking you to guess what you had left behind? I would now, yes; but I mean before this all happened.
Supposing everybody did business that way. Supposing your
rich and doting uncle wired you: "I'm arriving Grand Central
some time next month. Meet me." Or, worse yet, supposing
that instead of issuing a summons naming a definite crime or
misdemeanor, the courts sent out a postcard reading: "I
know what's going to happen to you-oo!" We'd all be
nervous wrecks.

The only thing I see to do right now is comply with your
request for a description of the article I left in that room. It is
a large and cumbersome iron object, usually kept in a kitchen
drawer, entitling my wife, upon my death, to a certain payment of money; it barks when in operation and, unless used
when the coffee reaches the boiling point, will allow the

liquid to spill out on the stove; it is signed by my father's name, is sensitive to light, relieves neuralgic pains, and is dark blue in color.

I have, of course, the same suspicion that you seem to have; namely, that maybe the object wasn't left behind by me but but by somebody else who occupied the room before I did or who occupied it at the same time I did, without either one of us knowing the other was there. And I'll tell you why. The night that I was at your hotel, the room clerk took a message out of my box when he reached for my key. The message was for a Mr. Donovan. I looked at it and said it didn't belong to me. "You haven't a Mr. Donovan with you?" he asked. I said no, but he didn't seem to be convinced. Perhaps whatever was left behind in my room was left behind by Mr. Donovan. I have an idea that, after all, Mr. Donovan and I may have occupied the same room, since his mail was in my box; perhaps he always arrived just after I had left the room and got out each time just before I came back. It's that kind of city.

I'm glad, anyway, that I have two months before the article

is returned to the insurance company or sent to the pound, or whatever. It gives me time to think.

Additional Devices

The overview section of this book presents a number of devices that recur in humorous writing of all kinds. "Guessing Game" is an excellent model with which to refresh your stock of such devices, little tricks that you can use in your own story of obsession. The most notable is the device of the *non sequitur*, the remark that seems to have no apparent connection with the one preceding it, or with a logical train of thought. One collegiate dictionary defines a *non sequitur* as "a conclusion or inference which does not follow from the premises or evidence upon which it is based." Since the obsession is illogical to begin with, the *non sequitur* is especially useful in writing about compulsive behavior, behavior in which the character, in a disordered way, is thinking constantly around a fixed idea. Thurber begins in a logical way, with the first letters of the alphabet, but notice the insertion of articles that could in no logical way be transported in suitcases: "bathrobe, bay rum, book, bicycle, belt, baby . . ." The only common denominator is the letter *b*. Under no logical inference could the bicycle or the baby be associated with the premise that hand luggage carries articles needed by the ordinary hotel guest, or that bicycles or babies are easy-to-forget articles. To get the feel of this sort of device, begin thinking of articles for which you were sent to the store, but which you forgot. Like Thurber, let's start with the letter *a*: apples, artichokes, acrobats, adding machines . . ." It's very easy once you get the idea.

And when Thurber gets out of the alphabet and begins to ransack the house for missing articles, notice how he uses the same general device. "The vest to my blue suit" could logically have been lost at the hotel, but what about the "life insurance policy, my Scotch terrier Jeannie, the jack out of the automobile tool case." Not only is the inference illogical and a *non sequitur*, but the picture of the articles conjured up in the reader's mind—the picture of these particular articles sitting together in a suitcase—adds to the humor because of the absurdity and the incongruity of the idea. Get back to that list of items from the grocery. Add to your problem the fact that you don't have a car or a bicycle to transport them. You are walking. Now think of some of the things you might have forgotten that would have been impossible to carry: "apples, artichokes, adding machines, one alligator, an antique suit of armor, two automobile tires, . . ."

A "Trial-Run" Assignment

As an assignment, try working out a short interior monologue, to be presented later orally or in writing, that is based on a "fixed idea" that you have had or can imagine. Demonstrate both the *non sequitur* technique and the technique of juxtaposing ordinarily unrelated items. If you haven't done any obsessive thinking lately, complete the hypothetical store list you have forgotten, or try to remember the name of a tune you liked three years ago, a tune beginning, say, with *P* or *R*. And, incidentally, what's the name of that movie you saw three times when you were twelve? (Don't ask anyone; start racking your brains for the answer.)

THE HUMOR OF HABIT: HUMAN MACHINES

As we have seen, the compulsive habit is often indulged in by the person obsessed with a fixed or irrational idea, or the person whose habit was originally a response to a necessary routine but who perpetuates the habit beyond its actual need or exaggerates its importance out of proportion to its value. We all act like machines at times, and indeed, one wonders occasionally if modern man in the electronic age isn't idealized as a kind of biological machine (which he is) with appropriately desirable programmed habits, all individuality carefully weeded out and transformed into computer-like responses that minimize his humanness as well as his capacity for "mistakes." Mechanized Everyman, however, is a fitter subject for satire (the humor of man in groups and institutions) than it is for a character sketch of a particular person with a compulsive habit.

The kind of person needed for this type of sketch is the average sort of human being—not someone who has irrational impulses to murder his wife or uncontrollable desires to hold goldfish, but someone who has cultivated a habit that fills a sensible need, a habit that is an end in itself instead of a means to an end. Often habits of this kind are developed in line with one's vocations or avocations. They are the routines and skills associated with certain recurring activities like playing musical instruments, fishing, carpentering, examining patients, trying legal cases, baby-sitting,

Making Trouble Pay

167

playing baseball, repairing electrical equipment, installing motors or zippers, making models, baking cakes, or map-making.

Sources of Invention

You probably have habits of this kind yourself, but because they have become such a mechanized part of you, you probably find it difficult to recognize them. If so, look around for a person, preferably someone you like, who has a compulsive habit that is annoying or irritating to you, and develop a sketch of that person as an automaton with a habit he can't—and doesn't want to—shake.

Techniques

This type of sketch is somewhat like the anecdote based on a distressing personal experience in that it is a story told with tolerance or amused detachment from a personal point of view. Our focus here, however, is on a distressing person rather than a distressing experience, or it can center on a distressing experience *caused* by a compulsive person. Frequently, this sketch is narrated from a distance in time and place. Sometimes, too, the narrator betrays his suspicion that the habits he is describing in someone else might indeed be similar to some of his own automatic, unthinking responses. What creates the humor, outside of the repetitive, clockworklike habit, is the human machine's own unawareness of his compulsion. He is, in fact, convinced that it is this very routine that makes him a superior fisherman, lawyer, cook, or . . .

Probably everyone can think of a teacher with an irritating habit that never varies, a habit that is important to him out of all proportion to its value and on which the teacher prides himself, thinking that it makes him a superior instructor. Think for a while about teachers you have had. Remember the one who insisted that all notes be kept in outline form, the one who required that all writing be in ink, or the one who wouldn't let anyone leave the room without a written excuse from the principal? Take it from there. But before you develop your tale of a teacher with a machine-like response to certain situations, or a student whose compulsive habits drove teachers wild, you might like to see what Thurber does with a similar subject. In this case, it's a teacher of English, Miss Groby, who has a thing about dissecting literature and hunting down figures of speech.

Light Humor: The Quiet Smile

Here Lies Miss Groby

JAMES THURBER

Miss Groby taught me English composition thirty years ago. It wasn't what prose said that interested Miss Groby; it was the way prose said it. The shape of a sentence crucified on a blackboard (parsed, she called it) brought a light to her eye. She hunted for Topic Sentences and Transitional Sentences the way little girls hunt for white violets in springtime. What she loved most of all were Figures of Speech. You remember her. You must have had her, too. Her influence will never die out of the land. A small schoolgirl asked me the other day if I could give her an example of metonymy. (There are several kinds of metonymies, you may recall, but the one that will come to mind most easily, I think, is Container for the Thing Contained.) The vision of Miss Groby came clearly before me when the little girl mentioned the old, familiar word. I saw her sitting at her desk, taking the rubber band off the roll-call cards, running it back upon the fingers of her right hand, and surveying us all separately with quick little henlike turns of her head.

Here lies Miss Groby, not dead, I think, but put away on a shelf with the other T squares and rulers whose edges had lost their certainty. The fierce light that Miss Groby brought to English literature was the light of Identification. Perhaps, at the end, she could no longer retain the dates of the birth and death of one of the Lake poets. That would have sent her to the principal of the school with her resignation. Or perhaps she could not remember, finally, exactly how many Cornishmen there were who had sworn that Trelawny should not die, or precisely how many springs were left to Housman's lad in which to go about the woodlands to see the cherry hung with snow.

Verse was one of Miss Groby's delights because there was so much in both its form and content that could be counted. I believe she would have got an enormous thrill out of Wordsworth's famous lines about Lucy if they had been written this way:

> A violet by a mossy stone
> Half hidden from the eye,
> Fair as a star when ninety-eight
> Are shining in the sky.

It is hard for me to believe that Miss Groby ever saw any famous work of literature from far enough away to know what it meant. She was forever climbing up the margins of books and crawling between their lines, hunting for the little gold of phrase, making marks with a pencil. As Palamides hunted the Questing Beast, she hunted the Figure of Speech. She hunted it through the clangorous halls of Shakespeare and through the green forests of Scott.

Night after night, for homework, Miss Groby set us to searching in *Ivanhoe* and *Julius Caesar* for metaphors, similes, metonymies, apostrophes, personifications, and all the rest. It got so that figures of speech jumped out of the pages at you, obscuring the sense and pattern of the novel or play you were trying to read. "Friends, Romans, countrymen, lend me your ears." Take that, for instance. There is an unusual but perfect example of Container for the Thing Contained. If you read the funeral oration unwarily—that is to say, for its meaning—you might easily miss the C.F.T.T.C. Antony is, of course, not asking for their ears in the sense that he wants them cut off and handed over; he is asking for the function of those ears, for their power to hear, for, in a word, the thing they contain.

At first I began to fear that all the characters in Shakespeare and Scott were crazy. They confused cause with effect, the sign for the thing signified, the thing held for the thing holding it. But after a while I began to suspect that it was I myself who was crazy. I would find myself lying awake at night saying over and over, "The thinger for the thing contained." In a great but probably misguided attempt to keep my mind on its hinges, I would stare at the ceiling and try to think of an example of the Thing Contained for the Container. It struck me as odd that Miss Groby had never thought of that inversion. I finally hit on one, which I still remember. If a woman were to grab up a bottle of Grade A and say to her husband, "Get away from me or I'll hit you with the milk," that would be a Thing Contained for the Container. The next day in class I raised my hand and brought my curious discovery straight out before Miss Groby and my astonished schoolmates. I was eager and serious about it and it never occurred to me that the other children would laugh. They laughed loudly and long. When Miss Groby had quieted them she said to me rather coldly, "That was not really amusing, James." That's the mixed-up kind of thing that happened to me in my teens.

In later years I came across another excellent example of

this figure of speech in a joke long since familiar to people who know vaudeville or burlesque (or radio, for that matter). It goes something like this:

> A: What's your head all bandaged up for?
> B: I got hit with some tomatoes.
> A: How could that bruise you up so bad?
> B: These tomatoes were in a can.

I wonder what Miss Groby would have thought of that one.

Devices and Techniques

Non sequitur, irrelevant or absurd juxtapositions, and irrational dreamlike logic characterize the sketch of the compulsive-obsessive person. Repetition-with-variations is the major technique of the "human machine" sketch. The habit in action is the content; its various manifestations as they are observed or experienced by the narrator are the variations on the theme. The situation changes, the people in the situation change, but the same stimulus produces the same response. A page of prose—regardless of time, place, purpose, or interest of readers—prompts in all Miss Grobys the relentless search for "containers-for-things-contained." The Miss Grobys of this world are unaware that their tactics are actually "search and destroy" methods, with negative—if not murderous—results. Miss Groby's pupils may never recover sufficiently from her onslaughts on figures of speech to be able to enjoy literature. We assume that Miss Groby's habit is more important to her than her former ability to love the art she dissects.

Suggestions for Writing

Try your hand at writing a sketch modelled on "Here Lies Miss Groby." Use as your principal character a teacher you have had, a classmate, a friend, or a neighborhood character, perhaps with a trash-burning obsession or something similar. Remember to adopt a tolerant, amused attitude in your writing—even if you don't feel so tolerant, even if you are the victim of the obsessions. Humor, as you now know, demands objectivity and detachment. Some humor is explicitly hostile—but *that's* the humor of the scornful, mournful laugh, which follows in Part Five of this book.

Or, if you prefer, develop, with help from another student, a comic strip narration or an informal dramatization which shows your obsessive character in action.

The Humor of Habit: Summary of Procedures for Composing

1. Look around for or try to recall a person of your acquaintance who engages frequently in an unusual habit of some sort or who has cultivated a habit, perhaps connected with some interest or job, that seems obsessively or unnecessarily practiced.

2. Imagine the kinds of situations in which the person's habit might seem inappropriate, insane, or overvalued to a practical, down-to-earth observer.

3. Try to picture in your mind (or, on paper, if you're an artist) the "acting out" of each repetition of the compulsive behavior pattern as it occurs in different circumstances and settings. Think of each recurrence as a small scene in a play or a succession of shots in a film sequence. Or picture a series of frames in a comic strip.

4. For the sake of diversity, vary the situation or the reactions of the people affected by the habit, but do not vary the nature and mechanical iteration of the compulsive act itself. (Recall that Thurber changes the location of Mr. Bidwell's breath-stopping scenes and varies the descriptions of the sound he makes when he exhales, but he never varies the act of holding breath until the very end, when he substitutes a similar habit for the original one.)

5. Arrange in ascending order of inappropriateness to the situation or of demoralizing effect on others the "scenes" you consider most humorous.

6. If you are one of the people affected by the character's compulsive behavior, as Thurber was affected by his mother's and Muggs's actions, try adopting a first-person detached point of view. Be sure your language reflects the objective, impersonal, and tolerant tone you want to maintain.

7. If you have decided to describe one of your own obsessions or fixed ideas, as Thurber does in "Guessing Game," your own thought processes, in their progressive and often illogical relationships to each other and to reality, are the substitute for the "scenes" in the sketch of a compulsive character in action.

8. In addition to using the techniques of all possible repetitions with variations (words, phrases, actions, gestures), include devices that emphasize these types of contrast: contrast between practical and impractical responses to a situation; between problem-solving thought processes aimed at sensible solutions or increased efficiency, and circular thinking or concentration on an irrational or fixed idea; between the character's unawareness of his own insane and machinelike routines and the observer's conviction that the behavior is absurd and unnecessary.

9. Indicate illogical relationships by inserting *non sequiturs,* inappropriate juxtapositions, incongruities between action and situation or objects and between dream-logic and rational thinking.

10. Write your sketch and read it to some interested friends for their reactions. Or wait for the next opportunity to inject it as an amusing anecdote into an informal conversation or bull session.

PART FOUR

Satire

8

Humor
as Criticism

Offhand, one might wonder whether the light comedy illustrated in the previous chapters has anything in common with satire. On close examination, however, it is clear that humor is used in both, although satire paradoxically lacks humor even as it uses it. Both light humor and satire tend to reduce man, to deflate him; satire goes beyond light humor, of course, in leaving man virtually invisible. However, if we go back to check the characteristics of light humor, we discover that satire is in many respects its antithesis.

Satire does not induce the slow smile; the purpose of satire sees to that. The satirist wants to change the reader, or at least force him to face his follies. Satiric medicine is strong; and the smile that should come, since satire uses humor, will not be slow and quiet. Most likely it will be a grimace rather than a smile. Satire, unlike quiet humor, does not spring from mildly depressing situations that individuals happen to find themselves in. True, satire observes the individual, but it looks at his follies and crimes. It also concerns itself with the follies of man in the group—with the whole of mankind if necessary. It sees pride, vanity, foolishness, lust, envy everywhere, and it attacks. As one can see, satirists do not "talk largely about small matters." Moreover, satire does not find it necessary to look back. It fixes its eye on the immediate. It is not interested in filtering out old unpleasantnesses; it turns a 200-power glass on the present, magnifying every detail, every bit of stinginess, vice, and cunning. The incidents depicted in quiet humor, however painful as they occur, become bearable in retrospect. Satire allows no retrospect. If quiet humor is mental and low humor is visceral, satire is both—a one-two punch to the mind and the heart. Only metaphors of strength and violence can truly describe the satirist at work. In providing relief from tension, quiet humor may act as therapy. Satire, on the other hand, can be a shock treatment. If that is therapy, it is therapy that engages one in action, not in "mellowed self-pity." The satirist, unlike the humorist, is not known for his sense of humor or for his sense of proportion about life. He offers no competition to the humorist or even to the lowest of the low comics, who at least is grudgingly acknowledged as having a sense of humor. If the satirist is outraged, a sense of proportion will not serve; only outrageous techniques will. The writer of quiet humor may help the reader to refine and sharpen his sense of humor, but if that is all a satirist does, he is a failure.

Are James Thurber and Mark Twain satirists? Not in the sense that the bulk of their work is clearly satiric. But each man's work includes examples of satire. If a major purpose of satire is to expose the follies and crimes of society, then Twain and Thurber are satirists. If a major purpose of satire is to react against the follies and crimes of society, surely these writers have had some measurable success. If a satirist can arouse in the reader a degree of contempt for what is being satirized while at the same time enabling him to smile a little, then Twain and Thurber are satirists.

As to the subject matter of satire, it can be almost anything. In our first sample, James Thurber uses a sharp knife on a marriage relationship. In a nonfiction monologue, Mark Twain takes a bludgeon to racial injustice. Whether it is politics, religion, or any other area in which people have scope for stupidity, greed, baseness, satirists put their tools to work. Metaphorically, some of the tools are the knife (very sharp), the bludgeon, the whip, and the emetic. In literary terminology, the major tool is wit. The minor devices range through the alphabet from abuse, caricature, inversion, and irony, to paradox and vituperation, and include two dozen or so other devices that fall between *a* and *v*.

The speaker in a satire can be an optimist, like Horace, who likes people and thinks they quite possibly can be cured of their stupidity if he tells them the truth with a smile. He can also be a pessimist like Juvenal, who dislikes people and thinks that since they are not likely to be cured, they assuredly should be punished. Although it is not quite accurate to make the analogy, at the superficial level at least Thurber more resembles Horace and Twain Juvenal. Yet why must a satirist be consistent, let alone resemble Horace or Juvenal, estimable Roman satirists that they are? *Satura*, the root word for *satire*, is variously translated as "composed of many different things," "hash," "medley," and "coarse mix." There is no need for the satirist to be consistent in tone. Indeed, one of his purposes is to keep his reader off balance, and by what better way does one achieve this than by shifting tone from time to time? Whatever stance he takes, the satirist addresses his audience in a number of ways. In the selections that follow, Twain addresses the reader in monologue and in story form, Thurber in narrative only. Some satirists tend to dominate their works; others keep themselves more in the background. One would expect that the satirist who writes a monologue in which the author seems to speak for himself would be more likely to dominate the scene than the satirist who puts his message in the form of a story. Yet even in narrative, at least in the episode presented here, the figure of Mark Twain is seen—eyebrow cocked and mouth aslant—behind the clear, innocent face of Huck Finn. James Thurber is much less in evidence in his narratives.

The genre used for the writing of satire is hinted at above. When the satirist speaks directly to an audience, he uses such varied forms as the nonfiction essay, the letter, and the dramatic monologue to a hopefully aroused listener. The satirist may speak directly to a large audience, as Twain does in his newspaper essay, or he may appear to speak to an identifiable individual as Thurber does in his cartoon. The narrative satires represented in this chapter include fables, a short story, and an episode from a long work. The satire can range in length from a short verbal tag of a cartoon to a full-length work, such as a novel or a play. All of Thurber's works are relatively short. Many of Twain's, which were written as novels and long monologues, are long. Long satiric narratives are difficult to sustain: the writer generally manages by keeping his work episodic or by mixing satire and nonsatire, obviously a dangerous practice.

The settings of satire are as varied as their lengths. Of the representative settings that appear in this chapter, some are set in the everyday world, seen, though, through the satirist's cracked binoculars. Others, such as the fables, are set in a never-never world that resembles our own. Huck, Tom, and Jim take off in a traditional satiric setting, the fantastic voyage. Short or long, in this world or out of it, the satiric method is always the same. The satirist focuses on a situation that he feels requires attention— such as the process of running for office; the mutual baiting of those who once promised each other to love, honor, and cherish; or a particular individual that needs cutting down to size. Then he uses all the techniques at his disposal to induce the reader to change either himself or someone else. In the satire itself little happens, nothing changes; the plot and characterization are as restricted as the settings and lengths are varied. In narrative satire the reader does not find the growth or deterioration of character he comes to expect in much nonsatiric narrative. Why should he? He might not be challenged to act if the situation appeared too hopeful, or if the characters showed possibilities for change.

A Couple of Hamburgers

JAMES THURBER

It would be nice if authors would label their satiric work SATIRE. Is the following story satire? It must be. On the one hand, it is not pure invective or bitter irony. On the other, it is not light humor or pure comedy. It may not be funny, but it contains humor. It looks with scorn, and it challenges to action.

One of James Thurber's favorite subjects is the battle of the sexes. In "A Couple of Hamburgers" he portrays probably as unloving a pair as have managed to stay together without killing each other. The story is a masterpiece showing the nastiness that couples too long in harness can display. Each has long known what most infuriates the other. Each relishes opportunities to irritate. Satire exaggerates, and this vignette demonstrates the lack of attention satire gives to the complexity of, in this case, marriage. Before he can exaggerate, however, the satirist must observe people at their worst. Juvenal stood on the streets of Rome with his notebook. So careful an observer is Thurber that one might accuse him of traveling through his Connecticut neighborhood with tape recorder and camera. Thurber's caricatures of husband and wife make the reader regard such waste of life with scorn. The author thus challenges his readers to generosity in their own lives.

Satire aside, "A Couple of Hamburgers" is typical of Thurber's narrative technique, his use of sharp descriptive touches, his considerable use of painfully accurate dialogue. This sketch, like many other Thurber sketches, is highly dramatic and could be easily turned into a short play.

A Couple of Hamburgers It had been raining for a long time, a slow, cold rain falling out of iron-colored clouds. They had been driving since morning and they still had a hundred and thirty miles to go. It was about three o'clock in the afternoon. "I'm getting hungry," she said. He took his eyes off the wet, winding road for a fraction of a second and said, "We'll stop at a dog-wagon." She shifted her position irritably. "I wish you wouldn't call them *dog*-wagons," she said. He pressed the klaxon button and went around a slow car. "That's what they are," he said. "Dog-wagons." She waited a few seconds. "*Decent* people call them *diners*," she told him, and added, "Even if you call them diners, I don't like them." He speeded up a hill. "They have better stuff than most restaurants," he said. "Anyway, I want to get home before dark and it takes too long in a restaurant. We can stay our stomachs with a couple hamburgers." She lighted a cigarette and he asked her to light one for him. She lighted one deliberately and handed it to him. "I wish you wouldn't say 'stay our stomachs,'" she said. "You know I hate that. It's like 'sticking to your ribs.' You say that all the time." He grinned. "Good old American expressions, both of them," he said. "Like sow belly. Old pioneer term, sow belly." She sniffed. "My ancestors were pioneers, too. You don't have to be vulgar just because you were a pioneer." "Your ancestors never got as far west as mine did," he said. "The real pioneers travelled on their sow belly and got somewhere." He laughed loudly at that. She looked out at the wet trees and signs and telephone poles going by. They drove on for several miles without a word; he kept chortling every now and then.

"What's that funny sound?" she asked, suddenly. It invariably made him angry when she heard a funny sound. "What funny sound?" he demanded. "You're always hearing funny sounds." She laughed briefly. "That's what you said when the bearing burned out," she reminded him. "You'd never have noticed it if it hadn't been for me." "I noticed it, all right," he said. "Yes," she said. "When it was too late." She enjoyed bringing up the subject of the burned-out bear-

ing whenever he got to chortling. "It was too late when *you* noticed it, as far as that goes," he said. Then, after a pause, "Well, what does it sound like *this* time? All engines make a noise running, you know." "I know all about that," she answered. "It sounds like—it sounds like a lot of safety pins being jiggled around in a tumbler." He snorted. "That's your imagination. Nothing gets the matter with a car that sounds like a lot of safety pins. I happen to know that." She tossed away her cigarette. "Oh, sure," she said. "You always happen to know everything." They drove on in silence.

"I want to stop somewhere and get something to *eat!*" she said loudly. "All right, all right!" he said. "I been watching for a dog-wagon, haven't I? There hasn't been any. I can't make you a dog-wagon." The wind blew rain in on her and she put up the window on her side all the way. "I won't stop at just any old diner," she said. "I won't stop unless it's a cute one." He looked around at her. "Unless it's a *what* one?" he shouted. "You know what I mean," she said. "I mean a decent, clean one where they don't slosh things at you. I hate to have a lot of milky coffee sloshed at me." "All right," he said. "We'll find a cute one, then. You pick it out. I wouldn't know. I might find one that was cunning but not cute." That struck him as funny and he began to chortle again. "Oh, shut up," she said.

Five miles farther along they came to a place called Sam's Diner. "Here's one," he said, slowing down. She looked it over. "I don't want to stop there," she said. "I don't like the ones that have nicknames." He brought the car to a stop at one side of the road. "Just what's the matter with the ones that have nicknames?" he asked with edgy, mock interest. "They're always Greek ones," she told him. "They're always Greek ones," he repeated after her. He set his teeth firmly together and started up again. After a time, "Good old Sam, the Greek," he said, in a singsong. "Good old Connecticut Sam Beardsley, the Greek." "You didn't see his name," she snapped. "Winthrop, then," he said. "Old Samuel Cabot Winthrop, the Greek dog-wagon man." He was getting hungry.

On the outskirts of the next town she said, as he slowed down, "It looks like a factory kind of town." He knew that she meant she wouldn't stop there. He drove on through the place. She lighted a cigarette as they pulled out into the open again. He slowed down and lighted a cigarette for himself. "Factory kind of town than *I* am!" he snarled. It was ten miles before they came to another town. "Torrington," he growled. "Happen to know there's a dog-wagon here because I stopped in it once with Bob Combs. Damn cute place, too, if you ask me." "I'm not asking you anything," she said, coldly. "You think you're *so* funny. I think I know the one you mean," she said, after a moment. "It's right in the town and it sits at an angle from the road. They're never so good, for some reason." He glared at her and almost ran up against the curb. "What the hell do you mean 'sits at an angle from the road'?" he cried. He was very hungry now. "Well, it isn't silly," she said, calmly. "I've noticed the ones that sit at an angle. They're cheaper, because they fitted them into funny little pieces of ground. The big ones parallel to the road are the best." He drove right through Torrington, his lips compressed. "Angle from the *road*, for God's sake!" he snarled, finally. She was looking out her window.

On the outskirts of the next town there was a diner called The Elite Diner. "This looks—" she began. "I see it, I see it!" he said. "It doesn't happen to look any cuter to me than any goddam—" she cut him off. "Don't be such a sorehead, for Lord's sake," she said. He pulled up and stopped beside the diner, and turned on her. "Listen," he said, grittingly, "I'm going to put down a couple of hamburgers in this place even if there isn't one single inch of chintz or cretonne in the whole—" "Oh, be still," she said. "You're just hungry and mean like a child. Eat your old hamburgers, what do I care?"

*Humor
as Criticism*

Inside the place they sat down on stools and the counterman walked over to them, wiping up the counter top with a cloth as he did so. "What'll it be, folks?" he said. "Bad day, ain't it? Except for ducks." "I'll have a couple of—" began the husband, but his wife cut in. "I just want a pack of cigarettes," she said. He turned around slowly on his stool and stared at her as she put a dime and a nickel in the cigarette machine and ejected a package of Lucky Strikes. He turned to the counterman again. "I want a couple of hamburgers," he said. "With mustard and lots of onion. *Lots* of onion!" She hated onions. "I'll wait for you in the car," she said. He didn't answer and she went out.

He finished his hamburgers and his coffee slowly. It was terrible coffee. Then he went out to the car and got in and drove off, slowly humming "Who's Afraid of the Big Bad Wolf?" After a mile or so, "Well," he said, "what was the matter with the Elite Diner, milady?" "Didn't you *see* that cloth the man was wiping the counter with?" she demanded. "Ugh!" She shuddered. "I didn't happen to want to eat any of the counter," he said. He laughed at that comeback. "You didn't even notice it," she said. "You never notice anything. It was filthy." "I noticed they had some damn fine coffee in there," he said. "It was swell." He knew she loved good coffee. He began to hum his tune again; then he whistled it; then he began to sing it. She did not show her annoyance, but she knew that he knew she was annoyed. "Will you be kind enough to tell me what time it is?" she asked. "Big *bad* wolf, big *bad* wolf—five minutes o' five—tum-dee-*doo*-dee-dum-m-m." She settled back in her seat and took a cigarette from her case and tapped it on the case. "I'll wait till we get home," she said. "If you'll be kind enough to speed up a little." He drove on at the same speed. After a time he gave up the "Big Bad Wolf" and there was deep silence for two miles. Then suddenly he began to sing, very loudly, *H-A-double-R-I-G-A-N spells Harr-i-gan—*" She gritted her teeth. She hated that worse than any of his songs except "Barney Google." He would go on to "Barney Google" pretty soon, she knew. Suddenly she leaned slightly forward. The straight line of her lips began to curve up ever so slightly. She heard the safety pins in the tumbler again. Only now they were louder, more insistent, ominous. He was singing too loud to hear them. "Is a *name* that *shame* has never been con-nec-ted with—*Harri-i-gan, that's me!*" She relaxed against the back of the seat, content to wait.

For Writing and Discussion

1. One of the characteristics of the short story is that during the unfolding of the plot the character changes, albeit slightly, either growing or deteriorating somewhat. A satire in the form of a short story generally is characterized by a plot movement that brings no measurable change in the character. Discuss "A Couple of Hamburgers" in terms of the above statements.

2. Who is the narrator of the story? How detached or involved is he? What evidence do you have for your opinion?

3. Why do you think Thurber has not assigned names to the characters?

4. One of Mae West's most famous sayings is, "Marriage is a great institution, but I'm not ready for an institution." What appears to be Thurber's view of the institution of marriage? Is there any hint in the story that the relationship between these two people is ever different from what we see of it? What do you think is the purpose of this satirical story?

5. What weapons are employed in this battle of the sexes? How much is calculated, how much is unplanned in their skirmishes?

6. Which of the following devices is more effective: the sarcasm the characters use on each other, or the exaggeration the author employs? Explain.

Picturing the Battle of the Sexes

JAMES THURBER

"Where did you get those big brown eyes and that tiny mind?"

Thurber here takes another look at the continuing battle of the sexes, just at the moment when the man has won a major engagement. What woman could soon recover from a thrust such as this? Note the condescending tone. Are you properly dazzled by the use of a question begun with a perfect interrogative? and by the simplicity of the verbal tag, a masterpiece of incongruity with its sharp contrast in size and with the whole point held in suspense until that last unexpected word is uttered? The question could scarcely be posed with safety to the marvelously alert but aloof dog. Notice also the incongruity of the male figure, the perfect bend of the body coupled with the boldness of the look, and contrasted with the absence of legs for flight. Incongruous? Perhaps not. Perhaps this is further assurance of the invincibility of the male in this instance. Notice the relaxed yet wary posture of the woman.

The satiric metaphor in this cartoon is surely that of the long pin thrust into the wax image.

For Writing and Discussion

1. What major cause for combat in the battle of the sexes does James Thurber illustrate in this cartoon?

2. Pit yourself against Thurber by trying to write one or two captions of your own for this cartoon. Use Thurber's device of placing incongruous phrases in grammatical parallels. Try to achieve the same two contrasts that are built into his caption.

3. Write a statement that you think the woman might have made to elicit Thurber's great answer.

Running for Governor

MARK TWAIN

Appearing to wear the mantle of Horace rather than that of Juvenal, Mark Twain writes of the perils of running for political office. Taking the role of the victim, he speaks in a satiric monologue. The reader will never be able to hold his smile down to a sneer in reading this account. In fact, he may laugh out loud and doubt that he is reading satire. Let's look again at the definition of *satura:* "coarse mix," "composed of many different things," "hash," "medley." The narrator is certainly besieged with a coarse mix of public and private opprobrium, some set down in print, some inflicted on him personally. Metaphorically, you could say the narrator took a barrage of garbage, from decayed cabbage leaves to rock-hard turnips. The account is a structural mixture, a stylistic hash. The satirist appears to the reader to be suffering from the right degree of obsession. The reader feels amused contempt for those attacking the narrator. He could be moved, as some people are, to write letters to the editor. He could be moved, as others are, to vote the straight ticket in protest. Before you quite finish this funny satire, take a hard look behind the narrator's pose of being an honest, common-sense contender who can hardly conceive of being the object of such a malicious attack. Look behind the pretense of "the whole truth and nothing but the truth." Perhaps you can see a grim smile on the writer's face.

Humor as Criticism

Running
for Governor

A few months ago I was nominated for Governor of the great state of New York, to run against Mr. John T. Smith and Mr. Blank J. Blank on an independent ticket. I somehow felt that I had one prominent advantage over these gentlemen, and that was—good character. It was easy to see by the newspapers that if ever they had known what it was to bear a good name, that time had gone by. It was plain that in these latter years they had become familiar with all manner of shameful crimes. But at the very moment that I was exalting my advantage and joying in it in secret, there was a muddy undercurrent of discomfort "riling" the deeps of my happiness, and that was—the having to hear my name bandied about in familiar connection with those of such people. I grew more and more disturbed. Finally I wrote my grandmother about it. Her answer came quick and sharp. She said:

You have never done one single thing in all your life to be ashamed of—not one. Look at the newspapers—look at them and comprehend what sort of characters Messrs. Smith and Blank are, and then see if you are willing to lower yourself to their level and enter a public canvass with them.

It was my very thought! I did not sleep a single moment that night. But, after all, I could not recede. I was fully committed, and must go on with the fight. As I was looking listlessly over the papers at breakfast I came across this paragraph, and I may truly say I never was so confounded before.

Perjury.—Perhaps, now that Mr. Mark Twain is before the people as a candidate for Governor, he will condescend to explain how he came to be convicted of perjury by thirty-four witnesses in Wakawak, Cochin China, in 1863, the intent of which perjury being to rob a poor native widow and her helpless family of a meager plantain-patch, their only stay and support in their bereavement and desolation. Mr. Twain owes it to himself, as well as to the great people whose suffrages he asks, to clear this matter up. Will he do it?

I thought I should burst with amazement! Such a cruel, heartless charge! I never had *seen* Cochin China! I never had *heard* of Wakawak! I didn't know a plantain-patch from a kangaroo! I did not know what to do. I was crazed and helpless. I let the day slip away without doing anything at all. The next morning the same paper had this—nothing more:

Satire

Significant.—Mr. Twain, it will be observed, is suggestively silent about the Cochin China perjury.

[*Mem.*—During the rest of the campaign this paper never referred to me in any other way than as "the infamous perjurer Twain."]

Next came the *Gazette,* with this:

Wanted to Know.—Will the new candidate for Governor deign to explain to certain of his fellow citizens (who are suffering to vote for him!) the little circumstance of his cabinmates in Montana losing small valuables from time to time, until at last, these things have been invariably found on Mr. Twain's person or in his "Trunk" (newspaper he rolled his traps in), they felt compelled to give him a friendly admonition for his own good, and so tarred and feathered him, and rode him on a rail, and then advised him to leave a permanent vacuum in the place he usually occupied in the camp. Will he do this?

Could anything be more deliberately malicious than that? For I never was in Montana in my life.

[After this, this journal customarily spoke of me as "Twain, the Montana Thief."]

I got to picking up papers apprehensively—much as one would lift a desired blanket which he had some idea might have a rattlesnake under it. One day this met my eye:

The Lie Nailed.—By the sworn affidavits of Michael O'Flanagan, Esq., of the Five Points, and Mr. Snub Rafferty and Mr. Catty Mulligan, of Water Street, it is established that Mr. Mark Twain's vile statement that the lamented grandfather of our noble standard bearer, Blank J. Blank, was hanged for highway robbery, is a brutal and gratuitous *lie,* without a shadow of foundation in fact. It is disheartening to virtuous men to see such shameful means resorted to to achieve political success as the attacking of the dead in their graves, and defiling their honored names with slander. When we think of the anguish this miserable falsehood must cause the innocent relatives and friends of the deceased, we are almost driven to incite an outraged and insulated public to summary and unlawful vengeance upon the traducer. But no! let us leave him to the agony of a lacerated conscience (though if passion should get the better of the public, and in its blind fury they should do the traducer bodily injury, it is but too obvious that no jury could convict and no court punish the perpetrators of the deed).

Humor as Criticism

189

The ingenious closing sentence had the effect of moving me out of bed with dispatch that night, and out at the back door also, while the "outraged and insulted public" surged in the front way, breaking furniture and windows in their righteous indignation as they came, and taking off such property as they could carry when they went. And yet I can lay my hand upon the Book and say that I never slandered Mr. Blank's grandfather. More: I had never even heard of him or mentioned him up to that day and date.

[I will state, in passing, that the journal above quoted from always referred to me afterward as "Twain, the Body-Snatcher."]

The next newspaper article that attracted my attention was the following:

A Sweet Candidate.—Mr. Mark Twain, who was to make such a blighting speech at the mass meeting of the Independents last night, didn't come to time! A telegram from his physician stated that he had been knocked down by a runaway team, and his leg broken in two places—sufferer lying in great agony, and so forth, and so forth, and a lot more bosh of the same sort. And the Independents tried hard to swallow the wretched subterfuge, and pretend that they did not know what was the *real* reason of the absence of the abandoned creature whom they denominate their standard bearer. *A certain man was seen to reel into Mr. Twain's hotel last night in a state of beastly intoxication.* It is the imperative duty of the Independents to prove that this besotted brute was not Mark Twain himself. We have them at last! This is a case that admits of no shirking. The voice of the people demands in thunder tones, *"Who was that man?"*

It was incredible, absolutely incredible, for a moment, that it was really my name that was coupled with this disgraceful suspicion. Three long years had passed over my head since I had tasted ale, beer, wine, or liquor of any kind.

[It shows what effect the times were having on me when I say that I saw myself confidently dubbed "Mr. Delirium Tremens Twain" in the next issue of that journal without a pang—notwithstanding I knew that with monotonous fidelity the paper would go on calling me so to the very end.]

By this time anonymous letters were getting to be an important part of my mail matter. This form was common:

How about that old woman you kiked of your premises which was beging.

Pol. Pry.

And this:

There is things which you have done which is unbeknow-
ens to anybody but me. You better trot out a few dols, to
yours truly, or you'll hear through the papers from
                                        Handy Andy.

This is about the idea. I could continue them till the reader
was surfeited, if desirable.

Shortly the principal Republican journal "convicted" me
of wholesale bribery, and the leading Democratic paper
"nailed" an aggravated case of blackmailing to me.

[In this way I acquired two additional names: "Twain the
Filthy Corruptionist" and "Twain the Loathsome Embracer."]

By this time there had grown to be such a clamor for an
"answer" to all the dreadful charges that were laid to me
that the editors and leaders of my party said it would be
political ruin for me to remain silent any longer. As if to
make their appeal the more imperative, the following appeared in one of the papers the very next day:

Behold the Man!—The independent candidate still main-
tains silence. Because he dare not speak. Every accusation
against him has been amply proved, and they have been
indorsed and reindorsed by his own eloquent silence, till at
this day he stands forever convicted. Look upon your candidate, Independents! Look upon the Infamous Perjurer! the
Montana Thief! the Body-Snatcher! Contemplate your incar-
nate Delirium Tremens! your Filthy Corruptionist! your
Loathsome Embracer! Gaze upon him—ponder him well—
and then say if you can give your honest votes to a creature
who has earned this dismal array of titles by his hideous
crimes, and dares not open his mouth in denial of any one
of them!

There was no possible way of getting out of it, and so, in
deep humiliation, I set about preparing to "answer" a mass
of baseless charges and mean and wicked falsehoods. But I
never finished the task, for the very next morning a paper
came out with a new horror, a fresh malignity, and seriously
charged me with burning a lunatic asylum with all its inmates, because it obstructed the view from my house. This
threw me into a sort of panic. Then came the charge of
poisoning my uncle to get his property, with an imperative
demand that the grave should be opened. This drove me to
the verge of distraction. On top of this I was accused of em-
ploying toothless and incompetent old relatives to prepare

*Humor
as Criticism*

191

the food for the foundling hospital when I was warden. I was wavering—wavering. And at last, as a due and fitting climax to the shameless persecution that party rancor had inflicted upon me, nine little toddling children, of all shades of color and degrees of raggedness, were taught to rush onto the platform at a public meeting, and clasp me around the legs and call me *Pa!*

I gave it up. I hauled down my colors and surrendered. I was not equal to the requirements of a Gubernatorial campaign in the state of New York, and so I sent in my withdrawal from the candidacy, and in bitterness of spirit signed it, "Truly yours, *once* a decent man, but now
Mark Twain, I.P., M.T., B.S., D.T., F.C., and L.E."

For Writing and Discussion

1. Mark Twain pretends to speak as himself in this selection. What kind of person does he pretend to be in the first paragraph? What does his assumption of this role foreshadow? What else is foreshadowed in the first paragraph?

2. What is Twain attacking in this monologue? Does he have a primary object of attack? What changes would he like to bring about?

3. What are the structural divisions of the story? How effective are they in keeping the reader's interest? How effective are they as satiric devices?

4. Two satiric devices, abuse and innuendo, are used against the narrator in this story. Point out examples of each. If the writer's purpose is to encourage change, are abuse and innuendo likely to be more effective when used by the narrator or when used against him? Explain.

5. To what extent is the device of exaggeration used? Think of an incident in a recent political campaign that you could turn into a satire, using the device of exaggeration.

6. Analyze the humorous devices in the following sentences. Assess the last statement in the total context of the monologue.
   a. "The ingenious closing sentence had the effect of moving me out of bed with dispatch that night, and out at the back door also, while the "outraged and insulted public" surged in the front way, breaking furniture and windows in their righteous indignation as they came, and taking off such property as they could carry when they went."
   b. "I could continue them [i.e., excerpts from malicious letters] till the reader was surfeited, if desirable."
   c. "I was not equal to the requirements of a Gubernatorial campaign in the state of New York . . ."

FROM *Tom Sawyer Abroad*

MARK TWAIN

Here, in an episode from *Tom Sawyer Abroad*, the malicious grin on the face of the author is not, as in Twain's "Running for Governor," lurking behind the figure of the narrator. In this brief excerpt from the tale of a fantastic voyage, Twain comes perhaps as close to the fable as he was temperamentally capable of doing. He uses young boys—Huck, Tom, and the untutored Jim—rather than the fable's conventional animal figures in order to mock the educational limits and the intellectual pretensions of the adult provincial of his time. The reader, along with Twain, regards the surface characters with amused affection. At worst, a reader says, "What dummies!" But that remark reveals his own limitations. The perceptive reader feels with Twain a slight degree of contempt for the pretentious figures that lurk behind the endearing trio.

Incredible as it may seem, Twain has taken three characters who are at home in the world of the Mississippi, and he has thrust them into the air to begin an improbable trip by balloon to exotic places of the world. Scarcely under way, they reveal how ill prepared they are for a flight to the next state, let alone to other continents.

**FROM
Tom Sawyer Abroad** *Not far into the journey, Huck makes a disturbing discovery.*

There was one thing that kept bothering me, and by and by I says:

"Tom, didn't we start east?"

"Yes."

"How fast have we been going?"

"Well, you heard what the professor said when he was raging round. Sometimes, he said, we was making fifty miles an hour, sometimes ninety, sometimes a hundred; said that with a gale to help he could make three hundred any time, and said if he wanted the gale, and wanted it blowing the right direction, he only had to go up higher or down lower to find it."

"Well, then, it's just as I reckoned. The professor lied."

"Why?"

Humor as Criticism

193

"Because if we was going so fast we ought to be past Illinois, oughtn't we?"

"Certainly."

"Well, we ain't."

"What's the reason we ain't?"

"I know by the color. We're right over Illinois yet. And you can see for yourself that Indiana ain't in sight."

"I wonder what's the matter with you, Huck. You know by the *color?*"

"Yes, of course I do."

"What's the color got to do with it?"

"It's got everything to do with it. Illinois is green, Indiana is pink. You show me any pink down here, if you can. No, sir; it's green."

"Indiana *pink?* Why, what a lie!"

"It ain't no lie; I've seen it on the map, and it's pink."

You never see a person so aggravated and disgusted. He says:

"Well, if I was such a numbskull as you, Huck Finn, I would jump over. Seen it on the map! Huck Finn, did you reckon the States was the same color out-of-doors as they are on the map?"

"Tom Sawyer, what's a map for? Ain't it to learn you facts?"

"Of course."

"Well, then, how's it going to do that if it tells lies? That's what I want to know."

"Shucks, you muggins! It don't tell lies."

"It don't, don't it?"

"No, it don't."

"All right, then; if it don't, there ain't no two States the same color. You git around *that,* if you can, Tom Sawyer."

He see I had him, and Jim see it too; and I tell you, I felt pretty good, for Tom Sawyer was always a hard person to git ahead of. Jim slapped his leg and says:

"I tell *you!* dat's smart, dat's right down smart. Ain't no use, Mars Tom; he got you *dis* time, sho'!" He slapped his leg again, and says, "My *lan',* but it was smart one!"

I never felt so good in my life; and yet *I* didn't know I was saying anything much till it was out. I was just mooning along, perfectly careless, and not expecting anything was going to happen, and never *thinking* of such a thing at all, when, all of a sudden, out it came. Why, it was just as much a surprise to me as it was to any of them. It was just the same way it is when a person is munching along on a hunk of cornpone, and not thinking about anything, and all of a sudden bites into a di'mond. Now all *he* knows first off is that it's some kind of gravel he's bit into; but he don't find out it's a di'mond till he gits it out and brushes off the sand and crumbs and one thing or another, and has a look at it, and then he's surprised and glad—yes, and proud too; though when you come to look the thing straight in the eye, he ain't entitled to as much credit as he would 'a' been if he'd been *hunting* di'monds. You can see the difference easy if you think it over. You see, an accident, that way, ain't fairly as big a thing as a thing that's done a-purpose. Anybody could find that di'mond in that cornpone; but mind you, it's got to be somebody that's got *that kind of a cornpone.* That's where that feller's credit comes in, you see; and that's where mine comes in. I don't claim no great things—I don't reckon I could 'a' done it again—but I done it that time; that's all I claim. And I hadn't no more idea I could do such a thing, and warn't any more thinking about it or trying to, than you be this minute. Why, I was just as ca'm, a body couldn't be any ca'mer, and yet, all of a sudden, out it come. I've often thought of that time, and I can remember just the way everything looked, same as if it was only last week. I can see it all: beautiful rolling country with woods and fields and lakes for hundreds and hundreds of miles all around, and towns and villages scattered everywheres under us, here and there and yonder; and the professor mooning over a chart on his little table, and Tom's cap flopping in the rigging where it was hung up to dry. And one thing in particular was a bird right alongside, not ten foot off, going our way and trying to keep up, but losing ground all the time; and a railroad train doing the same thing down there, sliding among the trees and farms, and pouring out a long cloud of black smoke and now and then a little puff of white; and when the white was gone so long you had almost forgot it, you would hear a little faint toot, and that was the whistle. And we left the bird and the train both behind, 'way behind, and done it easy, too.

But Tom he was huffy, and said me and Jim was a couple of ignorant blatherskites, and then he says:

"Suppose there's a brown calf and a big brown dog, and an artist is making a picture of them. What is the *main* thing that that artist has got to do? He has got to paint them so you can tell them apart the minute you look at them, hain't he? Of course. Well, then, do you want him to go and paint *both* of them brown? Certainly you don't. He paints one of them blue, and then you can't make no mistake. It's just the same with the maps. That's why they make every State a different color; it ain't to deceive you, it's to keep you from deceiving yourself."

But I couldn't see no argument about that, and neither could Jim. Jim shook his head, and says:

"Why, Mars Tom, if you knowed what chuckle-heads dem painters is, you'd wait a long time before you'd fetch one er *dem* in to back up a fac'. I's gwine to tell you, den you kin see for you'self. I see one of 'em a-paintin' away, one day, down in ole Hank Wilson's back lot, en I went down to see, en he was paintin' dat old brindle cow wid de near horn gone—you knows de one I means. En I ast him what he's paintin' her for, en he say when he git her painted, de picture's wuth a hundred dollars. Mars Tom, he could a got de cow fer fifteen, en I *tole* him so. Well, sah, if you'll b'lieve me, he jes' shuck his head, dat painter did, en went on a-dobbin'. Bless you, Mars Tom, *dey* don't know nothin'."

Tom lost his temper. I notice a person 'most always does that's got laid out in an argument. He told us to shut up, and maybe we'd feel better.

For Writing and Discussion

1. What kind of irony is revealed by Huck's statement that ". . . Tom Sawyer was always a hard person to git ahead of"?

2. What is the relationship between the diamond in the cornpone and Huck's intellectual discovery? Analyze his dissertation as to how such a great idea occurred to him. What characteristics of the provincial mind is Twain mocking here?

3. In his explanation of the map colors, Tom reveals that his sense of superiority is false. What are the flaws in his argument?

4. How would you classify Jim's contribution to logical thought?

5. What is the extent of the differences in intellectual quality and in pretensions of intellect between natural man, exemplified by Jim and Huck, and pseudolearned man, exemplified by Tom?

6. The satiric device of the fantastic or imaginary voyage reveals Twain's ironic intent. What other techniques or devices reveal the author's ironic intent?

7. Huck and Tom are trapped by the magic of print. In this episode Huck is taken in by a printed map; in other episodes they are both taken in by printed words. What evidence do you have of contemporary viewers being trapped in the province of television?

Some Fables for Our Time

JAMES THURBER

It all started with Aesop—or rather, well before Aesop appeared. And it, the fable, appealed to James Thurber, who added a few gems to the long history of fables which will most likely continue to develop as long as men write.

A fable is a brief tale which exemplifies a moral and which uses simply characterized animals as symbols for men. It seems natural that this form should have appealed to Thurber, for among its conventions are brevity and simplicity of style in both sentence structure and word choice, two characteristics of Thurber's writing in general.

Although most fables embody moral lessons, not all fables make satiric points for humans to reflect upon. By and large, however, Thurber's do just this. His fables are sharp enough to pass as satire. They focus in general on some of the meanest aspects of human behavior. The inhabitants of his fables are stupid enough, greedy enough, perverse enough to satisfy almost anyone but Jonathan Swift. True, there are contrasts, but the good inhabitants of his tales generally are exterminated. Only rarely do they prevail. Although other Thurber fables sometimes contain combinations of men and animals or even men alone, the fables which follow present only animals masquerading as men. They serve (as do all fables) to remind man not only that he is an animal but that if animals could talk, somehow they might manage individual relationships and larger social contracts better than he himself does.

The Very Proper Gander   Not so very long ago there was a very fine gander. He was strong and smooth and beautiful and he spent most of his time singing to his wife and children. One day somebody who saw him strutting up and down in his yard and singing remarked, "There is a very proper gander." An old hen overheard this and told her husband about it that night in the roost. "They said something about propaganda," she said. "I have always suspected that," said the rooster, and he went around the barnyard next day telling everybody that the very fine gander was a dangerous bird, more than likely a hawk in gander's clothing. A small brown hen remembered

Humor as Criticism

197

a time when at a great distance she had seen the gander talking with some hawks in the forest. "They were up to no good," she said. A duck remembered that the gander had once told him he did not believe in anything. "He said to hell with the flag, too," said the duck. A guinea hen recalled that she had once seen somebody who looked very much like the gander throw something that looked a great deal like a bomb. Finally everybody snatched up sticks and stones and descended on the gander's house. He was strutting in his front yard, singing to his children and his wife. "There he is!" everybody cried. "Hawk-lover! Unbeliever! Flag-hater! Bomb-thrower!" So they set upon him and drove him out of the country:

Moral: *Anybody who you or your wife thinks is going to overthrow the government by violence must be driven out of the country.*

The Rabbits
Who Caused
All the Trouble

Within the memory of the youngest child there was a family of rabbits who lived near a pack of wolves. The wolves announced that they did not like the way the rabbits were living. (The wolves were crazy about the way they themselves were living, because it was the only way to live.) One night several wolves were killed in an earthquake and this was blamed on the rabbits, for it is well known that rabbits pound on the ground with their hind legs and cause earthquakes. On another night one of the wolves was killed by a bolt of lightning and this was also blamed on the rabbits, for it is well known that lettuce-eaters cause lightning. The wolves threatened to civilize the rabbits if they didn't behave, and the rabbits decided to run away to a desert island. But the other animals, who lived at a great distance, shamed them, saying, "You must stay where you are and be brave. This is no world for escapists. If the wolves attack you, we will come to your aid, in all probability." So the rabbits continued to live near the wolves and one day there was a terrible flood which drowned a great many wolves. This was blamed on the rabbits, for it is well known that carrot-nibblers with long ears cause floods. The wolves descended on the rabbits, for their own good, and imprisoned them in a dark cave, for their own protection.

When nothing was heard about the rabbits for some weeks, the other animals demanded to know what had happened to them. The wolves replied that the rabbits had been eaten and since they had been eaten the affair was a purely internal matter. But the other animals warned that they might possibly unite against the wolves unless some reason was given for the destruction of the rabbits. So the wolves gave them one. "They were trying to escape," said the wolves, "and, as you know, this is no world for escapists."

Moral: *Run, don't walk, to the nearest desert island.*

The Birds and the Foxes

Once upon a time there was a bird sanctuary in which hundreds of Baltimore orioles lived together happily. The refuge consisted of a forest entirely surrounded by a high wire fence. When it was put up, a pack of foxes who lived nearby protested that it was an arbitrary and unnatural boundary. However, they did nothing about it at the time because they were interested in civilizing the geese and ducks on the neighboring farms. When all the geese and ducks had been civilized, and there was nothing else left to eat, the foxes once more turned their attention to the bird sanctuary. Their leader announced that there had once been foxes in the sanctuary but that they had been driven out. He proclaimed that Baltimore orioles belonged in Baltimore. He said, furthermore, that the orioles in the sanctuary were a continuous menace to the peace of the world. The other animals cautioned the foxes not to disturb the birds in their sanctuary.

So the foxes attacked the sanctuary one night and tore down the fence that surrounded it. The orioles rushed out and were instantly killed and eaten by the foxes.

The next day the leader of the foxes, a fox from whom God was receiving daily guidance, got upon the rostrum and addressed the other foxes. His message was simple and sublime. "You see before you," he said, "another Lincoln. We have liberated all those birds!"

Moral: *Government of the orioles, by the foxes, and for the foxes, must perish from the earth.*

The Tiger Who Understood People

Once upon a time there was a tiger who escaped from a zoo in the United States and made his way back to the jungle. During his captivity the tiger had learned a great deal about how men do things and he thought he would apply their methods to life in the jungle. The first day he was home he met a leopard and he said, "There's no use in you and me hunting for food; we'll make the other animals bring it to us." "How will we do that?" asked the leopard. "Easy," said the tiger, "you and I will tell everybody that we are going to put on a fight and that every animal will have to bring a freshly killed boar in order to get in and see the fight. Then we will just spar around and not hurt each other. Later you can say you broke a bone in your paw during the second round and I will say I broke a bone in my paw during the first round. Then we will announce a return engagement and they'll have to bring us more wild boars." "I don't think this will work," said the leopard. "Oh, yes it will," said the tiger. "You just go around saying that you can't help winning because I am a big palooka and I will go around saying I can't lose because you are a big palooka, and everybody will want to come and see the fight."

So the leopard went around telling everybody that he couldn't help winning because the tiger was a big palooka and the tiger went around telling everybody he couldn't lose because the leopard was a big palooka. The night of the fight came and the tiger and the leopard were very hungry because they hadn't gone out and done any hunting at all; they wanted to get the fight over as soon as possible and eat some of the freshly killed wild boars which all the animals would bring to the fight. But when the hour of the combat came none of the animals at all showed up. "The way I look at it," a fox had told them, "is this: if the leopard can't help winning and the tiger can't lose, it will be a draw and a draw is a very dull thing to watch, particularly when fought by fighters who are both big palookas." The animals all saw the logic of this and stayed away from the arena. When it got to be midnight and it was obvious that none of the animals would appear and that there wouldn't be any wild-boar meat to devour, the tiger and the leopard fell upon each other in a rage. They were both injured so badly and they were both so worn out by hunger that a couple of wild boars who came wandering along attacked them and killed them easily.

Moral: *If you live as humans do, it will be the end of you.*

The
Fairly Intelligent Fly

A large spider in an old house built a beautiful web in which to catch flies. Every time a fly landed on the web and was entangled in it the spider devoured him, so that when another fly came along he would think the web was a safe and quiet place in which to rest. One day a fairly intelligent fly buzzed around above the web so long without lighting that the spider appeared and said, "Come on down." But the fly was too clever for him and said, "I never light where I don't see other flies and I don't see any other flies in your house." So he flew away until he came to a place where there were a great many other flies. He was about to settle down among them when a bee buzzed up and said, "Hold it, stupid, that's flypaper. All those flies are trapped." "Don't be silly," said the fly, "they're dancing." So he settled down and became stuck to the flypaper with all the other flies.

Moral: *There is no safety in numbers, or in anything else.*

The Courtship
of Arthur and Al

Once upon a time there was a young beaver named Al and an older beaver named Arthur. They were both in love with a pretty little female. She looked with disfavor upon the young beaver's suit because he was a harum-scarum and a ne'er-do-well. He had never done a single gnaw of work in his life, for he preferred to eat and sleep and to swim lazily in the streams and to play Now-I'll-Chase-You with the girls. The older beaver had never done anything but work from the time he got his first teeth. He had never played anything with anybody.

When the young beaver asked the female to marry him, she said she wouldn't think of it unless he amounted to something. She reminded him that Arthur had built thirty-two dams and was working on three others, whereas he, Al, had never even made a breadboard or a pin tray in his life. Al was very sorry, but he said he would never go to work just because a woman wanted him to. Thereupon she offered to be a sister to him, but he pointed out that he already had seventeen sisters. So he went back to eating and sleeping and swimming in the streams and playing Spider-in-the-Parlor with the girls. The female married Arthur one day at the lunch hour—he could never get away from work for

Humor
as Criticism

more than one hour at a time. They had seven children and Arthur worked so hard supporting them he wore his teeth down to the gum line. His health broke in two before long and he died without ever having had a vacation in his life. The young beaver continued to eat and sleep and swim in the streams and play Unbutton-Your-Shoe with the girls. He never Got Anywhere, but he had a long life and a Wonderful Time.

Moral: *It is better to have loafed and lost than never to have loafed at all.*

The Crow and the Oriole

Once upon a time a crow fell in love with a Baltimore oriole. He had seen her flying past his nest every spring on her way North and every autumn on her way South, and he had decided that she was a tasty dish. He had observed that she came North every year with a different gentleman, but he paid no attention to the fact that all the gentlemen were Baltimore orioles. "Anybody can have that mouse," he said to himself. So he went to his wife and told her that he was in love with a Baltimore oriole who was as cute as a cuff link. He said he wanted a divorce, so his wife gave him one simply by opening the door and handing him his hat. "Don't come crying to me when she throws you down," she said. "That fly-by-season hasn't got a brain in her head. She can't cook or sew. Her upper register sounds like a streetcar taking a curve. You can find out in any dictionary that the crow is the smartest and most capable of birds—or was till you became one." "Tush!" said the male crow. "Pish! You are simply a jealous woman." He tossed her a few dollars. "Here," he said, "go buy yourself some finery. You look like the bottom of an old teakettle." And off he went to look for the oriole.

This was in the springtime and he met her coming North with an oriole he had never seen before. The crow stopped the female oriole and pleaded his cause—or should we say cawed his pleas? At any rate, he courted her in a harsh, grating voice, which made her laugh merrily. "You sound like an old window shutter," she said, and she snapped her fingers at him. "I am bigger and stronger than your gentleman friend," said the crow. "I have a vocabulary larger than his. All the orioles in the country couldn't even lift the corn I own. I am a fine sentinel and my voice can be heard for miles in case of danger." "I don't see how that could interest anybody but another crow," said the female oriole, and she laughed at him and flew on toward the North. The male oriole tossed the crow some coins. "Here," he said, "go buy yourself a blazer or something. You look like the bottom of an old coffeepot."

The crow flew back sadly to his nest, but his wife was not there. He found a note pinned to the front door. "I have gone away with Bert," it read. "You will find some arsenic in the medicine chest."

Moral: *Even the llama should stick to mamma.*

The Moth
and the Star
A young and impressionable moth once set his heart on a certain star. He told his mother about this and she counselled him to set his heart on a bridge lamp instead. "Stars aren't the thing to hang around," she said; "lamps are the thing to hang around." "You get somewhere that way," said the moth's father. "You don't get anywhere chasing stars." But the moth would not heed the words of either parent. Every evening at dusk when the star came out he would start flying toward it and every morning at dawn he would crawl back home worn out with his vain endeavor. One day his father said to him, "You haven't burned a wing in months, boy, and it looks to me as if you were never going to. All your brothers have been badly burned flying around street lamps and all your sisters have been terribly singed flying around house lamps. Come on, now, get out of here and get yourself scorched! A big strapping moth like you without a mark on him!"

The moth left his father's house, but he would not fly around street lamps and he would not fly around house lamps. He went right on trying to reach the star, which was four and one-third light years, or twenty-five trillion miles, away. The moth thought it was just caught in the top branches of an elm. He never did reach the star, but he went right on trying, night after night, and when he was a very, very old moth he began to think that he really had reached the star and he went around saying so. This gave him a deep and lasting pleasure, and he lived to a great old age. His parents and his brothers and his sisters had all been burned to death when they were quite young.

Moral: *Who flies afar from the sphere of our sorrow is here today and here tomorrow.*

Humor
as Criticism

203

For Writing and Discussion

1. Fables can satirize an individual characteristic or foible, or they can satirize society in general. What are the targets of Thurber's fables?

2. Examine the moral statements that Thurber attaches to his fables. Are they consistent in tone? explicit in message? obviously directed at humans? Which of these morals do you find most fitting for a satiric fable? Defend your choice. What happens to the fable if the moral is made explicit within the narrative rather than in a tag line at the end?

3. Animals in fables generally have only one dominant human trait. Is this true of the animals in Thurber's fables?

4. Compare the presence of the narrator in any of these fables with the presence of the narrator in "Running for Governor." Which narrator is more detached? What is the effect on the reader of a more detached narrator? Explain.

5. Generally speaking, how do the fables begin? What narrative technique does Thurber use?

6. When animals are used in satire, the device of mimicry is obviously in operation. How does the use of this device add a further dimension to satire?

7. How does the message of the fable "The Courtship of Arthur and Al" compare with the message of the short story "A Couple of Hamburgers?"

8. Compare the statements made in "The Tiger Who Understood People" and "The Moth and the Star." Which is more optimistic? by how much? How much inconsistency in outlook should one expect from a writer of satiric fables?

9. The messages of "The Very Proper Gander" and "The Rabbits Who Caused All the Trouble" are essentially the same. What is the difference?

10. About what percentage of dialogue and straight narration does Thurber use in his fables? Which of these fables seem most dramatic? Which mixture seems more effective for use in a fable: predominance of dialogue, predominance of straight narration, or an equal amount of both? Why?

11. How many of the problems touched upon in these fables might have been reversed or minimized by challenging the misuse or distortion of language? How much evidence is there that some or all of these problems go far deeper than language?

9

Aiming the Barbs

In Chapter 7 we set out to make trouble pay. Now by using satire to change someone's mind, or at least to deflate him, we are ready just to make trouble. Give your adversary a metaphorical kick first. Then, while he is still smarting, bring in the heavy artillery.

IT'S ONLY TRIVIA?—IN FABLE FORM

Purpose

Look around. What do you see that you would like to change? Don't take on the most searing problem first. Start with a situation that is aggravating but not demoralizing. Perhaps the sloppiness of people curdles your disposition. Ignoring all entreaties to "Use the litter basket" and to "Keep the country beautiful," people seem to be so benumbed by the appearance of a shopping center, say, that their only response to it is to drop flurries of paper. You would like to boot such people all the way to the litter basket—satirically.

Form

What form should the big kick take? How can you convey a message that will jolt people into a little positive action, shame them, for a few weeks at least, into attending to the appearance of their surroundings? You could write a letter to an editor and fill it with caricatures of the local offenders. Or, you could write an essay, filled with four-letter words and unpleasant comparisons, for the underground newspaper. Such masterpieces will give you a great feeling of relief, but will enough people read them? Why not, instead, put your message into fable form? The fable is short, easy to write, fun—and not overused. Present the most recent complaint in the oldest form. This will attract readers and may, without alienating them, nudge them to frenzies of cleaning up that might put a Dutch housewife to shame.

Sources of Invention

Where will you get your material? Either close your eyes and visualize, or better yet, take a first-hand look at the scene. Visit the nearest drive-in theater or shopping center—any location that people regard as a huge litter basket, a spot where they feel free to purge themselves and their cars of rubbish. Observe the husband, son, or boy friend as he patiently waits for the shopper, for example. He often makes use of the hour by undertaking a worthwhile cleanup project. He pulls the ash tray from his car and dumps the cigarette butts, dried apple cores, and gum wrappers in a neat pile beside the door. He then removes the supply of empty coffee containers, no-return bottles, and scraps of paper that have accumulated since the last trip to the litter basket. Now, turn and observe the passing parade of litterbugs. Number one offender pitches the soft-drink can into the gutter, five feet from a container. The second flips his empty cigarette pack into the bushes. Number three, her own hair littered with fat pink rollers, tosses a gum wrapper over her shoulder. Jot down these vignettes, and add any others you can remember.

So much for the scene itself. Now let's return to the fable. Its most obvious characteristic, of course, is the use of an animal to represent man. Try to think of an animal that is reputed to have the bad qualities that your litterbug people display. We generally think of rats, mice, and roaches as filthy creatures. Actually, they are probably less sloppy than most people. You might decide to choose a tidy animal, like the raccoon, and have one delinquent member of the family do all the dirty work.

Narrative Technique

Another characteristic of the fable is that it is a very short narrative. The two fables included in this chapter are each just thirteen sentences long. Not only is the fable's length a break for the writer, but the opener demands very little imagination, since, often as not, it is the familiar "Once upon a time . . ." Take another look at Thurber's fables in the previous chapter, and you will see that he made ample use of that expression. Some of his other fables begin just as simply: "Not so very long ago . . .," or, "Within the memory of man . . ." Take care, however, from this point on, for it's usually easier for beginning writers to ramble than to be concise. Notice that the fable, like the ballad, plunges right into the situation, often in the first sentence. See, for example, how Thurber does this in "The Peacelike Mongoose," another of his brief fables, which follows.

The Peacelike Mongoose In cobra country a mongoose was born one day who didn't want to fight cobras or anything else. The word spread from mongoose to mongoose that there was a mongoose who didn't want to fight cobras. If he didn't want to fight anything else, it was his own business, but it was the duty of every mongoose to kill cobras or be killed by cobras.

"Why?" asked the peacelike mongoose, and the word went around that the strange new mongoose was not only pro-cobra and antimongoose but intellectually curious and against the ideals and traditions of mongoosism.

"He is crazy," cried the young mongoose's father.

"He is sick," said his mother.

"He is a coward," shouted his brothers.

"He is a mongoosexual," whispered his sisters.

Strangers who had never laid eyes on the peacelike mongoose remembered that they had seen him crawling on his stomach, or trying on cobra hoods, or plotting the violent overthrow of Mongoosia.

"I am trying to use reason and intelligence," said the strange new mongoose.

"Reason is six-sevenths of treason," said one of his neighbors.

"Intelligence is what the enemy uses," said another.

Finally, the rumor spread that the mongoose had venom in his sting, like a cobra, and he was tried, convicted by a show of paws, and condemned to banishment.

Moral: *Ashes to ashes, and clay to clay, if the enemy doesn't get you your own folks may.*

Development

After the opening is settled upon, how is the rest of the fable developed? As you can see, Thurber generally uses a blend of straight narration and dialogue. There is very little description, not just because the fable form is short, but also because there is little need for description in synoptic forms such as myth and fable. Readers are usually familiar with a number of the elements of these forms, such as the characters and plot line of the myth and the characteristics of the animals chosen for the fable. As for concluding your tale, the fable ends with a generalization, a moral that is labeled as such and that is set down outside the framework of the story.

Devices

Before turning to specific devices, stop and check what you have already gathered together. You have a long list of litterbug incidents and details, an untidy raccoon to perpetrate the ultimate litter disaster, and "Once upon a time"—just to get your fable started. There is time enough later on to decide whether you wish to use an alternate. How shall you have your delinquent raccoon proceed to wreak havoc? Whatever he does naturally will be exaggerated. Exaggeration, one of the most frequently used devices in comic writing, often appears in the satiric fable. One of the ways Thurber achieves exaggeration is by reducing the time span and increasing the details. Notice in "The Bear Who Let It Alone," our second thirteen-sentence fable, which follows, that this particular animal could turn his home into a disaster scene every evening in only five or ten minutes.

The Bear Who Let It Alone In the woods of the Far West there once lived a brown bear who could take it or let it alone. He would go into a bar where they sold mead, a fermented drink made of honey, and he would have just two drinks. Then he would put some money on the bar and say, "See what the bears in the back room will have," and he would go home. But finally he took to drinking by himself most of the day. He would reel home at night, kick over the umbrella stand, knock down the bridge lamps, and ram his elbows through the windows. Then he would collapse on the floor and lie there until he went to sleep. His wife was greatly distressed and his children were very frightened.

At length the bear saw the error of his ways and began to reform. In the end he became a famous teetotaller and a persistent temperance lecturer. He would tell everybody that came to his house about the awful effects of drink, and he would boast about how strong and well he had become since he gave up touching the stuff. To demonstrate this, he would stand on his head and on his hands and he would turn cartwheels in the house, kicking over the umbrella stand, knocking down the bridge lamps, and ramming his elbows through the windows. Then he would lie down on the floor,

tired by his healthful exercise, and go to sleep. His wife was greatly distressed and his children were very frightened.

Moral: *You might as well fall flat on your face as lean over too far backward.*

An ordinary human drunk could scarcely duplicate this splendid effort in a month. Perhaps you can give your delinquent raccoon just five minutes to create an area of devastation. Examine your list of details, eliminating the weakest and effectively arranging those that remain.

Not only will your villain act in an exaggerated fashion, but he will give very strange excuses for his behavior. Think back to "The Birds and the Foxes" (page 199). Here is the excuse Thurber allows the foxes to give after they have killed the birds.

The next day the leader of the foxes, a fox from whom God was receiving daily guidance, got upon the rostrum and addressed the other foxes. His message was simple and sublime. "You see before you," he said, "another Lincoln. We have liberated all those birds!"

How incongruous that God should receive guidance from a fox. What are the other incongruities in the fox's statement? Although you don't have to go to the same extreme to get away with littering that you do to get away with murder, your raccoon may well make the incongruous suggestion that littering is beneficial— the latest technique, perhaps, in recycling. He may also imply, as do the neighbors of the peacelike mongoose, that those who are trying to improve their habits are politically subversive. In explaining why he did not wish to fight, the peacelike mongoose states: "I am trying to use reason and intelligence." *Reason* and *intelligence*—words with the finest connotations. But in topsy-turvy fashion, a warlike mongoose replies: "Reason is six-sevenths of treason." Another plays upon words with the suggestion that "Intelligence is what the enemy uses." Perhaps your good raccoons will say: "Please help us. Our motto is 'Keep Raccoonville Clean.'" Nasty raccoon's response will be, "Cleanliness is next to ———. What—atheism? agnosticism? godlessness? or something funny, flip, unexpected, illogical?

Give some thought also to a title and a moral for your fable. Study Thurber's titles and find a pattern that appeals to you, or put your own imagination to work. Study Thurber's moral statements: they are varied—short, long; flip, serious; prose, verse. Re-read the statements following "The Birds and the Foxes" (page 199) and "The Very Proper Gander" (page 198) for examples of positive and negative ways to write moral statements.

Before reviewing the procedures of writing a fable, let's consider other topics that you might like to pursue. For example, are you still taking a beating about your long hair? Turn yourself into an unclipped poodle and put yourself into a fable. Or slant the situation and be the only short-haired sheepdog in a kennel of conventional longhairs. Have you ever had to put up with a reformed smoker? Make him a nervous whippet instead of a bear. Have you been bored by a health-food nut? Turn him into a fussy ant and have your revenge. Are you interested in censorship? The following news story from Brazil will help you conjure up many other pictures.

Brazilian Town Has Night Clubs Shut By Police

Cabo Frio, Brazil Jan. 23 (AP)—The new police chief of Cabo Frio, one of Brazil's most fashionable resorts, dealt another blow to permissive society today, closing the town's seven night clubs.

Moacir Bellot earlier had announced a "moralization" campaign that would include killing stray dogs and shaving shaggy-haired hippies.

Chief Bellot boasted that he had killed personally more than 200 dogs "responsible for shocking scenes of immoral sex acts in front of children and young ladies."

He said he was closing the night clubs because they were operating without licenses.

The police chief toured the beaches with a squad of officers and banned more than 20 refreshment vendors.

Chief Bellot said he would continue his fight against "the excess of hippies.

"The hippies who land here will either never return or will explode," he told newsmen.

Reviewing Procedure for Writing a Fable

Different fables follow different patterns, use different techniques and devices, and thus require different procedures. The procedures that follow are those we used for the raccoon tale.

1. Gather together a series of details to illustrate your topic.
2. Choose for your villain or hero an animal known for the characteristics you will ascribe to people; or, choose an opposite, as we have done.

3. Eliminate the weakest illustrations; arrange in order those that best suit your topic and the character of the animal you have chosen.
4. State the situation in a sentence, using, at least as a start, one of the traditional opening phrases for a fairy tale or fable.
5. Molding your best illustrations into a brief plot, finish your story in about a dozen sentences.
6. Write in a blend of straight narration interspersed with dialogue; keep description to a minimum.
7. After you have written your first draft:
   a. To insure a proper degree of exaggeration, check to see that there is enough discrepancy between the period of time that passes in your story and the number of illustrations and details.
   b. Check to see that you have included some topsy-turvy or incongruous expressions.
8. Work out a moral and a title.

IT'S ONLY MONEY—A REPORT TO THE BOYS

Sources of Invention

Now that you have successfully completed a piece of satiric writing, you are ready to take on mission impossible. In an inflationary era, you have heard many complaints about the high cost of living and of getting the job done. The boss, for example, spills real tears about the expense of getting out a letter. To him each one appears to cost at least seven dollars, the stenographer's progress having been interrupted by two telephone calls from her mother, an interminable coffee break, and a conference to help plan a blind date for the new girl in the department. The stenographer, on the other hand, takes a dim view of the high cost of a box of cereal, feeling a good portion of that amount has gone to subsidize the boss's expensive sales lunches, the one-hour recovery naps, and heaven knows how many golf balls. These matters are probably just hearsay to you, but perhaps you have first-hand experience in knowing that, one way or another, there is a high cost to getting out the vote. You have worked as a volunteer: addressing envelopes, manning the telephone, standing outside the polls. And you begin to remember some of the peculiar happenings of the last election—voting machines arriving hours late in several precincts, breaking down in others. You yourself might have been challenged outside the polling place for doing what the law allowed you to do.

Purpose

Since election time will arrive soon again, you decide to try to head off repetition of such incidents. The sharpness of your satire will depend upon the kind of practices you consider dubious in your voting area.

Jot down all of the dubious practices you are aware of and search for reported incidents to add to the list. A few minutes with the *Reader's Guide* will direct you to a number of articles on poll watching and on vote fraud. If you feel that quoted details such as "unregistered voters were allowed to vote by signing an affidavit" and "rounding up nonresident derelicts at fifty cents each" reflect objectively or exaggerate somewhat the conditions in your precinct, jot them down. Take down other supporting details from newspaper and magazine articles: use of phantom names, drugging soft drinks of poll watchers, tire slashing, and registering people who have long since died. Such details will help you get ideas to include in your satire.

Form

What form will your satire take? You wish to consider writing a straight piece of exposition envisioning the peccadillos of your voting district exploding into the most corrupt practices you discovered in the articles. Perhaps you might enjoy writing a skit imitating the roasting sessions held periodically in many cities and by many associations, such as the Gridiron Club. Or you can pretend that you are the local district leader and that you are delivering your regular preelection estimate of the cost of getting out the vote, a report which will be burned or buried in the vault immediately after delivery. If you decide on the latter, the following excerpt from Chapter 28 of Mark Twain's *The Gilded Age* will give you some ideas about technique.

In this excerpt, Harry Brierly is calling on the president of the Columbus River Slack-Water Navigating Company to learn why he and Colonel Sellers haven't received their salaries and money to pay the workers. He discovers that the appropriation passed by Congress to assist in turning Goose Run into Columbus River disappeared before it reached them.

"The appropriation?—that paltry $200,000, do you mean?"

"Of course—but I didn't know that $200,000 was so very paltry. Though I grant, of course, that it is not a large sum, strictly speaking. But where is it?"

"My dear sir, you surprise me. You surely cannot have had a large acquaintance with this sort of thing. Otherwise you would not have expected much of a result from a mere *initial* appropriation like that. It was never intended for anything but a mere nest egg for the future and *real* appropriations to cluster around."

"Indeed? Well, was it a myth, or was it a reality? Whatever became of it?"

"Why the matter is simple enough. A Congressional appropriation costs money. Just reflect, for instance. A majority of the House Committee, say $10,000 apiece—$40,000; a majority of the Senate Committee, the same each—say $40,000; a little extra to one or two chairmen of one or two such committees, say $10,000 each—$20,000; and there's $100,000 of the money gone, to begin with. Then, seven male lobbyists, at $3,000 each—$21,000; one female lobbyist, $10,000; a high moral Congressman or Senator here and there—the high moral ones cost more, because they give tone to a measure—say ten of these at $3,000 each, is $30,000; then a lot of small-fry country members who won't vote for anything whatever without pay—say twenty at $500 apiece, is $10,000; a lot of dinners to members—say $10,000 altogether; lot of jimcracks for Congressmen's wives and children—those go a long way—you can't spend too much money in that line—well, those things cost in a lump, say $10,000—along there somewhere;—and then comes your printed documents—your maps, your tinted engravings, your pamphlets, your illuminated show cards, your advertisements in a hundred and fifty papers at ever so much a line—because you've *got* to keep the papers all right or you are gone up, you know. Oh, my dear sir, printing bills are destruction itself. Ours, so far amount to—let me see— 10; 52; 22; 13;—and then there's 11; 14; 33—well, never mind the details, the total in clean numbers foots up $118,- 254.42 thus far!"

"What!"

"Oh, yes indeed. Printing's no bagatelle, I can tell you. And then there's your contributions, as a company, to Chicago fires and Boston fires, and orphan asylums and all that sort of thing—head the list, you see, with the company's full name and a thousand dollars set opposite—great card, sir—one of the finest advertisements in the world—the preachers mention it in the pulpit when it's a religious charity—one of the happiest advertisements in the world is your benevolent donation. Ours have amounted to sixteen thousand dollars and some cents up to this time."

"Good heavens!"

Before the president of Columbus River Slack-Water finishes, Brierly learns that it has taken $325,000 to push through passage of an appropriation for $200,000.

Be sure to notice the matter-of-fact tone of the narrator in Twain's piece. He presents the list of expenses in so routine a manner that he might be a carpenter making out a work sheet and enumerating the cost of two-by-fours, nails, and the number of man-hours necessary to build a modest shed. This is the tone that the narrator of your satire should adopt. As district leader, he has been making this kind of report for many years. But, although the tone of the narrator is matter-of-fact, the tone of the writer is ironic, and your reader must be able to detect this irony. The clue to the reader lies in the great contrast between the narrator's tone and Twain's audacious exaggeration of facts.

Although there is no mention of the word *bribery* in this section—and neither should there be in your satire—nonetheless the simple assumption is that everything is done with money. Virtually everyone is being paid varying amounts of money in accordance with his supposed importance to the passage of the appropriations bill.

Before you start your draft, look again at the ideas you jotted down from the magazines and add some of your own if you have not already done so; then have some fun with a worksheet. On what can you spend your money?

Wheelchair rental:	to convey floaters in no condition to stand straight
Ambulance rental:	for your "corpses" who are dying to vote
Tutoring fees:	to assist in aiding nonresident illiterates
Taxi and baby-	extra fees for sitters who

sitting fees: wash dishes, dust, and
                            vacuum before the house-
                            wife returns from the
                            polls

The last item seems out of place, not that it isn't incongruous
in its own way. Perhaps you should eliminate it and include instead
a fee for the architects of construction chaos who will foil the
moving men as they attempt to deliver voting machines deep into
opposition territory. Or include the payment to the photographer
who will again come through at the last minute with a picture of
an opponent in questionable condition or company.

How should you organize these estimates? Twain organizes in
a simple way; he starts with the larger amounts of money and
works down. You may do this, or you may choose to organize by
categories.

When starting your first draft, keep your introduction as busi-
nesslike as possible. You may start with: "Is there any new
business?"

"Mr. Chairman."
"Mr. Fixer."

A bit dull? Well, no need to keep this when you revise, but
such a lead helps you, the writer, feel that this is just a routine
meeting, with, as the first order of new business, routine consideration of the estimate of funds needed for preelection activities. As
you continue your draft, be sure to keep in mind exactly what you
are doing. Basically, you are presenting a cool narrator reporting
on a hot subject. You can take care of the location in the title of
his report, and at the same time you are setting limits—one precinct, one period of time. Setting limits makes your estimates seem
even more wild. And you are already exaggerating the situation by
exaggerating the amount of money you, the writer, suspect is being
used for corrupt practices, and by exaggerating the number of par-
ticipants in the schemes and the degree of their involvement. What
else is needed?—one final smashingly incongruous idea. Use your
imagination.

IT'S ONLY LIFE—WRESTLING WITH CONSCIENCE

Since one purpose of satire is to change a condition—or if it cannot be changed, at least to expose it—let's take on something more

important and more controversial than littering, something infinitely more heartbreaking than the waste of money or even than corrupt voting practices. Let's also break away from the safety of a form as restricted as the fable or the report of a meeting.

In another century, when an individual had more reason to be aware of hunger, and in another land, one less well endowed than our own, Jonathan Swift, viewing the results of three years of crop failure and many more years of misgovernment, wrote a brilliant piece of satire. He entitled it "A Modest Proposal for Preventing the Children of Poor People in Ireland from being a Burden to their Parents or Country; and for making them beneficial to their Publick." In this essay, written in 1729, Swift suggested that the children of the poor in Ireland be raised like little pigs or chickens and that they be used as food for the population in general. A stunning suggestion, it should have put a stop to foolish suggestions for ending famine, and it should have encouraged proposals for stopping the drain out of the country of Ireland's revenue, a condition largely responsible for the famine.

A century and a half later, Mark Twain suggested an idea that was almost as preposterous as Swift's: the idea that it should take a real tussle with one's conscience to admit that one man should not be a slave to another, to admit that a man's family should not be scattered over the land in order to accommodate the economy of a ruling class of people.

Sources of Invention

Why not choose to satirize a situation that strikes you as equally preposterous? Remember, however, that no one can write effective satire, even as practice, unless he cares deeply about changing the situation he is satirizing. Contemporary examples of man's inhumanity to man abound, and your first task is simply to decide on something you consider highly objectionable. Perhaps you may want to follow up on Swift's topic and write about hunger, and perhaps you will find it possible to combine Swift's topic with Twain's method of development. If you are familiar with newspaper, magazine, or television reports on hunger in America, it may occur to you that today, centuries after Swift, you can see in your own country a sampling of what Swift saw in his. Using hunger as your topic, you are also face to face with a condition as worthy of satire as Twain's. You may be in a position to support the realities of the reports you have seen with what you see around you. Or you may simply remember being deeply moved by a documentary or by pictures and stories. At any rate, one way or another you have doubtless seen a baby as withered as an old man, or a starving mother whose child died before it was born. Hunger, then, is an effective topic for satirical writing.

Form

What form will you use to shape your contemporary modest proposal? A good choice might be to write a monologue similar to the one Mark Twain wrote for Huck Finn, one in which your speaker faces a moral dilemma as great as the one Huck faced.

Below are two excerpts from *The Adventures of Huckleberry Finn* that show something of Huck's problem. You may remember the situation. On the raft, Huck and Jim have been trying to find Cairo, a river port where the runaway Jim can escape to freedom. In the following passage Huck wrestles with his conscience. Should he help Jim, or should he turn him in to the authorities?

> Jim said it made him all over trembly and feverish to be so close to freedom. Well, I can tell you it made me all over trembly and feverish, too, to hear him, because I begun to get it through my head that he *was* most free—and who was to blame for it? Why, *me*. I couldn't get that out of my conscience, no how nor no way. It got to troubling me so I couldn't rest; I couldn't stay still in one place. It hadn't ever come home to me before, what this thing was that I was doing. But now it did; and it stayed with me, and scorched me more and more. I tried to make out to myself that *I* warn't to blame, because *I* didn't run Jim off from his rightful owner; but it warn't no use, conscience up and says, every time, "But you knowed he was running for his freedom, and you could 'a' paddled ashore and told somebody." That was so—I couldn't get around that no way. That was where it pinched. Conscience says to me, "What had poor Miss Watson done to you that you could see her nigger go off right under your eyes and never say one single word? What did that poor old woman do to you that you could treat her so mean? Why, she tried to learn you your book, she tried to learn you your manners, she tried to be good to you every way she knowed how. *That's* what she done."
> I got to feeling so mean and so miserable I most wished I was dead. I fidgeted up and down the raft, abusing my-

Aiming
the Barbs

219

self to myself, and Jim was fidgeting up and down past me. We neither of us could keep still. Every time he danced around and says, "Dah's Cairo!" it went through me like a shot, and I thought if it *was* Cairo I reckoned I would die of miserableness.

Jim talked out loud all the time while I was talking to myself. He was saying how the first thing he would do when he got to a free state he would go to saving up money and never spend a single cent, and when he got enough he would buy his wife, which was owned on a farm close to where Miss Watson lived; and then they would both work to buy the two children, and if their masters wouldn't sell them, they'd get an Ab'litionist to go and steal them.

It most froze me to hear such talk. He wouldn't ever dared to talk such talk in his life before. Just see what a difference it made in him the minute he judged he was about free. It was according to the old saying, "Give a nigger an inch and he'll take an ell." Thinks I, this is what comes of my not thinking. Here was this nigger, which I had as good as helped to run away, coming right out flat-footed and saying he would steal his children—children that belonged to a man I didn't even know; a man that hadn't ever done me no harm.

Later Huck writes a letter to Miss Watson, Jim's owner, in which he tells her exactly where Jim is hiding. After finishing his letter, Huck again finds himself wrestling with his conscience.

I felt good and all washed clean of sin for the first time I had ever felt so in my life, and I knowed I could pray now. But I didn't do it straight off, but laid the paper down and set there thinking—thinking how good it was all this happened so, and how near I come to being lost and going to hell. And went on thinking. And got to thinking over our trip down the river; and I see Jim before me all the time: in the day and in the nighttime, sometimes moonlight, sometimes storms, and we a-floating along, talking and singing and laughing. But somehow I couldn't seem to strike no places to harden me against him, but only the other kind. I'd see him standing my watch on top of his'n, 'stead of calling me, so I could go on sleeping; and see him how glad he was when I come back out of the fog; and when I come to him again in the swamp, up there where the feud was; and such-like times; and would always call me honey, and pet me, and do everything he could think of for me, and how good he always was; and at last I struck the time I saved him by telling the men we had smallpox aboard, and he was so grateful, and said I was the best friend old Jim ever had in the world, and the *only* one he's got now; and then I happened to look around and see that paper.

It was a close place. I took it up, and held it in my hand. I was a-trembling, because I'd got to decide, forever, betwixt two things, and I knowed it. I studied a minute, sort of holding my breath, and then says to myself:

"All right, then, I'll *go* to hell"—and tore it up.

Narrative and Satiric Technique

The tone of the foregoing passages is ironic, and it is this very tone that you should try to achieve in your own monologue, being sure that your reader can detect the irony. In your mock report, the idea was to have the narrator project toward his subject an attitude so matter-of-fact as to indicate a degree of cynicism that would lead the reader to question his reliability. In the kind of satire that reaches the reader indirectly through the plot, the kind you are now writing, the narrator is frequently naive, gullible, or quite stupid. Any one of these characteristics should cause the reader to question the narrator's actions and opinions and to suspect that there is a discrepancy between what he says and what the author wants the reader to believe.

Mark Twain's narrator is a very decent boy, but one we're not inclined to take seriously all the time. In planning your monologue, you too should choose a narrator as naive and conservative as Huck, yet one who, like Huck, can be moved by something intangible. We all known one or two people who fit this pattern, and can benefit from studying them. It's also important to remember that your narrator must be young enough or uneducated enough so that you the writer do not despise him for opinions that you consider benighted.

Situation

Once you have your narrator, the next step is to involve another character in an action that you the writer believe completely justified but that the narrator will find appalling. Perhaps you will decide to have a mother embarrass the government by camping out in the local courthouse with her hungry children until the authorities recognize her desperate situation. Perhaps she will bring her dead baby to town for all to see. Jot down the incident in rough form. Next, give your narrator an opportunity to tip off the local officials so they can head off the mother's plans.

Continue your jotting, this time noting the clusters of details that you will need for the different parts of your monologue. Exaggeration, a satirical device that you have used previously, can again help establish the tone of your paper. Gather together all the stereotyped responses you have heard about people who expect "too much" from the government, clichés such as:

> how much "we" have already done for "them"
> how ungrateful "that kind" always is
> that they could find work if they wanted it
> that they could manage better if they wanted to
> that people don't have any business bringing
>   children into the world if they can't
>   provide for them
> that the good life in America is available to
>   all but the lazy and shiftless
> that "those people" enjoy living "like that"

Star the responses you hear most often and consider most unfair. Exaggerate them a little beyond the present stereotype.

Next, consider whatever it is that makes your narrator hesitate to report the mother's planned sit-in, despite what he considers her unpardonable action, despite his confidence in attainability of the American Dream for all. What was it that turned Huck away from his "duty" of turning in Jim? What will it be for your narrator? List the details as you outline the incident. Add a few details about how embarrassing the planned encampment or angry visit will be to the government. The usual stereotyped remark in an instance of this sort is a variation of "what will the neighbors think?" In this case the neighbors are other counties, states, or countries. Finally, list some good physical details to describe the appearance of the mother and the children, particularly the condition of the baby. To insure the accuracy of these descriptive details, you may wish to examine relevant pictures and magazine articles.

Organization

After accumulating your clusters of details and evaluating the relative effectiveness of each, plan the organization of your satire. Consider the following: a paragraph that introduces the situation briefly, followed by a fairly lengthy paragraph that includes your narrator's opinions as to the outrageous nature of the mother's demands and the clichés about her unworthiness. Work in as contrast the details of the sad plight and the distressing appearance of the family. Be sure to include the tenderest points, for they will indicate the essential incongruity of the situation. In Twain's account, he makes clear that it is incongruous in a democracy that a man should have to think about buying his wife and children or stealing them. In your monologue, make clear the incongruity of having starving people in a country of such great wealth. To point this up, your most touching detail might be a brief description of the baby's bloated belly. The final sentence or two can allude to the embarrassing nature of such a situation for any government.

At this point, it is logical for the narrator to swing into his tentative steps to foil the plot, attempts that give rise to patriotic and righteous feelings. Here you need a psychologically sound incident or device. Observe the soundness of Twain's choice: namely, the letter he has Huck write to Miss Watson. In the end, Huck continues to help Jim because they are both decent humans who have shared good experiences. The letter to Miss Watson, however, is essential in that, whether he realizes it or not, it is a device that enables Huck to satisfy his conscience. By writing the letter, he has sublimated one part of his conscience, and thus finds it no longer necessary to follow through with the action of turning him in. In your final paragraph, include your narrator's decision to let the matter take its course without his interference, and, along with some final agonizing about his decision, give his reasons for not proceeding.

The organization proposed above is just a suggested one, of course; it follows Twain's fairly closely. Why not also consider Twain's method of developing the scene? Twain gives us Huck's memories of his thoughts and feelings. Some remembered dialogue is paraphrased; some is directly quoted. Try to offer the same variety in your own writing.

Once your plan of organization is set, examine all the details you have collected in relation to it, eliminating the weakest and arranging in logical order those that remain. Decide where some quoted dialogue should appear. Now you are ready to write your first draft. If you have planned carefully, the draft will be a good one that will need polishing rather than extensive revision, and the final monologue will be effective satire.

Hunger in America should be eliminated. Therefore, it is a worthy subject for satire. Hunger can be eliminated. Therefore, satire will suffice—no need for bitter irony. Should you prefer, however, to write a satire on another topic, there are, of course, many other topics to consider. Perhaps, you would like to present the dilemma of the narrator who wonders whether he should report the whereabouts of a friend who is avoiding the draft. Or perhaps you have strong feelings about the situation of the first black family in a neighborhood that does not want to accept them? In this situation, will your narrator put out a "For Sale" sign? Have you anything to say about the sudden collapse of bridges, walls, or wings of buildings? Is this kind of occurrence an act of God or is man responsible? Is it inevitable that every winter whole families perish in tenement fires? What to you is the most disgraceful situation in your immediate area?

Review of Procedures for Writing Satirically

1. Choose a controversial subject that requires a courageous satirical attack.
2. If you do not have first-hand evidence on your subject, be sure to seek out sources of information that will help you to verify and sharpen your details.
3. Plan to present your facts ironically and to write with a clearly ironic tone.
4. Choose as your narrator a naive individual who will strengthen your ironic tone.
5. Choose a controversial course of action for the beleaguered individual in your satire.
6. Gather together the most stereotyped and outrageous illustrations and details. Eliminate the weakest of these, and arrange the remaining ones in effective order.
7. Plan your organization. Outline the order in which you want your narrator to present his thoughts and feelings.
8. Write your draft.
9. As you revise, make sure of two things:
   a. that your choice of details indicates that the narrator has been facing a real dilemma.
   b. that your choice of details indicates the basic incongruity in the situation.

PART FIVE

"Black" Comedy:
The Scornful,
Mournful Laugh

10

Darts
from the Darkness

We said at the very beginning of this book that humor isn't always "funny," but that the stories and sketches in this collection and the suggestions for creating your own humor should help you respond to many different kinds of comedy—from the lowest and loudest belly-laugh burlesque to the "black" comedy that is closer to tragedy in many ways than it is to the spontaneous fun of jokes, jests, and tall tales or to the quiet humor of the backward glance at life's little absurdities and humiliations. The three chapters preceding this one have dealt with successively more serious kinds of humor, with progressively more subdued responses of laughter, smiles, jeers. In this chapter, you will encounter humor so serious and frequently so gloomy that it may seem closer to tragedy than to any sort of comic writing you are acquainted with. Many literary critics, in fact, consider the bitter irony and obvious pessimism of black humor to be in a different category of literature entirely from either comedy or tragedy, just as they might consider romance or tragicomedy different modes. We have agreed, however, that our object is not to classify or define comic types so much as to understand the range of the comic and the use of the humorous techniques with which to deal with subject matter of all kinds.

To indicate ways in which bitter, indignant irony is "comic" rather than "tragic," however, is not to imply that bitter comedy differs from other types of humor simply by being more serious.

Bitter humor also differs in quality and tone from the three other types of comedy. For one thing, its styles and tones are more limited in scope than those of other forms of humor. The tone of low comedy can be either boisterous, gentle, rollicking, understated, crude, subtle, earthy, or merely mundane. Retrospective, idiosyncratic humor can be amusedly tolerant or devastatingly critical, quietly funny or hilarious. Only satire comes close to black comedy.

SATIRE AND IRONY

Bitter irony uses the same devices as satire—sarcasm, invective, understatement or exaggeration, mockery, ridicule, paradox. And, like the satirist, the ironist or "black" humorist exposes human frailties and evil by methods that emphasize the reversal or topsy-turvy differences between aspiration and reality, aim and fulfillment, self-portrait and mirror image. The subject matter of black comedy, like the subject matter of satire, is human vanity and weakness. But black comedy operates in a narrower range than satire. Rarely good-natured or genial, it is most often cutting, pessimistic, insulting, and belligerent. Black comedy denies rather than affirms, rages rather than soothes, disturbs or depresses rather than relieves. Satire often concerns itself with petty as well as gross vanities; black humor deals with the seven deadly sins, with evils stripped of all disguise. Satire primarily is critical of society; irony directs its barbs at Man Universal, at "homo non-sapiens," as a species fulfilling an unconscious death wish. And irony comes close to tragedy when it deals with the contrast between man's capabilities for greatness and his suicidal perversion of perhaps his two most human and humane faculties—his reason and his language; that is, his unique way of communicating his ideas and feelings to other human beings. Black comedy comes closest to tragedy when, according to the humorist E. B. White, it "plays close to the big hot fire which is Truth, and sometimes the reader feels the heat."

As you might expect, you will observe noticeable differences in style and tone between Thurber and Twain. Twain's "heat" is more raging, inflammatory, and searing than Thurber's. But read carefully and you will feel the perhaps more tellingly persistent heat generated by Thurber's quieter fires.

To the Person Sitting in Darkness

MARK TWAIN

Mark Twain, the humorist of the American frontier—with its boisterous, optimistic, joking fun—is the Twain best known to the world. Less familiar to many readers is the moralist whose satiric darts were aimed at political corruption, social hypocrisy, financial greed, and injustices of all kinds. Least known of all is the Twain who, toward the closing years of his life, looked beyond society and politics and raised the ultimate, philosophical questions about Man. What is Man's relative place in the universe? Is it his nature to be good or evil, or both? What does man value above all other things? What is man's destiny?

Twain was a realist, a person trained in reporting and accustomed to observing the scene before drawing conclusions based on the evidence. When he looked at the state of the world at the turn of the century, he saw corruption, poverty, greed, and—most destructive of all—widespread war. The nineteenth century was the century of imperialism, when large portions of Africa and Asia came under colonial rule. The imperialistic motives for many of these invasions were often masked under the guise of taking on the "white man's burden," for the "civilized" white nations considered it their religious and moral duty to share the blessings of their culture with the so-called "primitive" races. These blessings, upon closer examination, seemed less than humane or enlightening to the benighted beneficiaries.

At the time, the British were fighting in China (the Boxer Rebellion) and the British and Dutch in Africa (the Boer War), and the Americans were soon to become engaged in the Philippines. After his trip through Africa in 1896, Twain sided with the native Africans against the Dutch Boers and the British; in the Boxer Rebellion, Twain sided with the Chinese; and in the Spanish-American War, though he had at first believed that the United States was actually trying to "free" Cuba from Spain, he finally became convinced that the fighting there and in the faraway Philippines was not undertaken to free the people. "We have gone there to conquer, not to redeem," he said. The blessings of civilization seemed to Twain to point to dire ends for men of all races; for those "sitting in darkness" could scarcely fail to resent their exploitation, fight back, and ultimately resist the "light" that brought misery and destruction. It seemed to Twain that man's destiny was to destroy himself and his kind. Man himself, not the God he professed to believe in, was to be the agent of his own damnation.

In his much-discussed commentary on the entire question of imperialism and of a Christian mission that, inadvertently perhaps, brought more hopelessness than salvation, Twain turned his ironic humor into a devastating weapon of attack on man himself. As you read the following excerpts from his famous article, "To the Person Sitting in Darkness," originally printed in the *North American Review* in 1901, keep asking yourself whether the questions Twain raises and the comments he makes are still timely. What do you think his reactions to the present-day fighting in Southeast Asia, the Middle East, and Africa would have been? Or to the concentration camps and gas chambers of the second World War? Though the term "black humor," meaning grim or bitter humor, is a comparatively recent one, one not used in Twain's time, consider whether the current connotation of the term is appropriate to the humor in this article.

FROM
To the Person
Sitting
in Darkness

Extending the Blessings of Civilization to our Brother who Sits in Darkness has been a good trade and has paid well, on the whole; and there is money in it yet, if carefully worked—but not enough, in my judgment, to make any considerable risk advisable. The People that Sit in Darkness are getting to be too scarce—too scarce and too shy. And such darkness as is now left is really of but an indifferent quality, and not dark enough for the game. The most of those People that Sit in Darkness have been furnished with more light than was good for them or profitable for us. We have been injudicious.

The Blessings-of-Civilization Trust, wisely and cautiously administered, is a Daisy. There is more money in it, more territory, more sovereignty and other kinds of emolument, than there is in any other game that is played. But Christendom has been playing it badly of late years and must certainly suffer by it, in my opinion. She has been so eager to

"Black" Comedy: The Scornful, Mournful Laugh

get every stake that appeared on the green cloth that the People who Sit in Darkness have noticed it—they have noticed it and have begun to show alarm. They have become suspicious of the Blessings of Civilization. More—they have begun to examine them. This is not well. The Blessings of Civilization are all right, and a good commercial property; there could not be a better, in a dim light. In the right kind of a light and at a proper distance, with the goods a little out of focus, they furnish this desirable exhibit to the Gentlemen who Sit in Darkness:

Love	Law and Order
Justice	Liberty
Gentleness	Equality
Christianity	Honorable Dealing
Protection to the Weak	Mercy
Temperance	Education

—and so on.

There. Is it good? Sir, it is pie. It will bring into camp any idiot that sits in darkness anywhere. But not if we adulterate it. It is proper to be emphatic upon that point. This brand is strictly for Export—apparently. *Apparently.* Privately and confidentially, it is nothing of the kind. Privately and confidentially, it is merely an outside cover, gay and pretty and attractive, displaying the special patterns of our Civilization which we reserve for Home Consumption, while *inside* the bale is the Actual Thing that the Customer Sitting in Darkness buys with his blood and tears and land and liberty. That Actual Thing is indeed Civilization, but it is only for Export. Is there a difference between the two brands? In some of the details, yes.

We all know that the Business is being ruined. The reason is not far to seek. It is because our Mr. McKinley, and Mr. Chamberlain, and the Kaiser and the Tsar[1] and the French have been exporting the Actual Thing *with the outside cover left off.* This is bad for the Game. It shows that these new players of it are not sufficiently acquainted with it.

It is a distress to look on and note the mismoves, they are so strange and so awkward. Mr. Chamberlain manufactures a war out of materials so inadequate and so fanciful that they make the boxes grieve and the gallery laugh, and he tries hard to persuade himself that it isn't purely a private raid for

[1] *Mr. McKinley . . . Tsar:* national representatives, respectively, of the United States, Great Britain, Germany, and Russia.

cash but has a sort of dim, vague respectability about it somewhere, if he could only find the spot; and that by and by he can scour the flag clean again after he has finished dragging it through the mud, and make it shine and flash in the vault of heaven once more as it had shone and flashed there a thousand years in the world's respect until he laid his unfaithful hand upon it. It is bad play—bad. For it exposes the Actual Thing to Them that Sit in Darkness, and they say: "What! Christian against Christian? And only for money? Is *this* a case of magnanimity forbearance, love, gentleness, mercy, protection of the weak—this strange and overshowy onslaught of an elephant upon a nest of field mice, on the pretext that the mice had squeaked an insolence at him— conduct which 'no self-respecting government could allow to pass unavenged'? as Mr. Chamberlain said. Was that a good pretext in a small case, when it had not been a good pretext in a large one?—for only recently Russia had affronted the elephant three times and survived alive and unsmitten. Is this Civilization and Progress? Is it something better than we already possess? These harryings and burnings and desert-makings in the Transvaal—is this an improvement on our darkness? It is, perhaps, possible that there are two kinds of Civilization—one for home consumption and one for the heathen market?"

Then They that Sit in Darkness are troubled, and shake their heads, and they read this extract from a letter of a British private, recounting his exploits in one of Methuen's victories some days before the affair of Magersfontein, and they are troubled again:

We tore up the hill and into the intrenchments, and the Boers saw we had them; so they dropped their guns and went down on their knees and put up their hands clasped, and begged for mercy. And we gave it them—*with the long spoon.*

The long spoon is the bayonet. See *Lloyd's Weekly,* London, of those days. The same number—and the same column —contained some quite unconscious satire in the form of shocked and bitter upbraidings of the Boers for their brutalities and inhumanities!

Next, to our heavy damage, the Kaiser went to playing the game without first mastering it. He lost a couple of missionaries in a riot in Shantung, and in his account he made an overcharge for them. China had to pay a hundred thousand dollars apiece for them in money; twelve miles of territory, containing several millions of inhabitants and worth twenty million dollars; and to build a monument and also a Christian church; whereas the people of China could have been depended upon to remember the missionaries without the help of these expensive memorials. This was all bad play. Bad, because it would not, and could not, and will not now or ever, deceive the Person Sitting in Darkness. He knows that it was an overcharge. He knows that a missionary is like any other man: he is worth merely what you can supply his place for and no more. He is useful, but so is a doctor, so is a sheriff, so is an editor; but a just Emperor does not charge war prices for such. A diligent, intelligent, but obscure missionary, and a diligent, intelligent country editor are worth much, and we know it; but they are not worth the earth. We esteem such an editor and we are sorry to see him go, but when he goes, we should consider twelve miles of territory and a church and a fortune overcompensation for his loss. I mean, if he was a Chinese editor and we had to settle for him. It is no proper figure for an editor or a missionary; one can get shop-worn kings for less. It was bad play on the Kaiser's part. It got this property, true; but it *produced the Chinese revolt,* the indignant uprising of China's traduced patriots, the Boxers. The results have been expensive to Germany and to the other Disseminators of Progress and the Blessings of Civilization.

The Kaiser's claim was paid, yet it was bad play, for it could not fail to have an evil effect upon Persons Sitting in Darkness in China. They would muse upon the event and be likely to say: "Civilization is gracious and beautiful, for such is its reputation, but can we afford it? There are rich Chinamen, perhaps they can afford it; but this tax is not laid upon them, it is laid upon the peasants of Shantung; it is they that must pay this mighty sum and their wages are but four cents a day. Is this a better civilization than ours, and holier and higher and nobler? Is not this rapacity? Is not this extortion? Would Germany charge America two hundred thousand dollars for two missionaries, and shake the mailed fist in her face and send warships and send soldiers, and say, "Seize twelve miles of territory, worth twenty millions of dollars, as additional pay for the missionaries, and make those peasants build a monument to the missionaries, and a costly Christian church to remember them by?' And later would Germany say to her soldiers, 'March through America and slay, *giving no quarter;* make the German face there, as has been our Hun-face here, a terror for a thousand years; march through the Great Republic and slay, slay, slay, carving a road for our offended religion through its heart and bowels?' Would Germany do like this to America, to England, to France, to Russia? Or only to China, the helpless—imitating the elephant's assault upon the field mice? Had we better invest in this Civilization—this Civilization which called Napoleon a buccaneer for carrying off Venice's bronze horses, but which steals our ancient astronomical instruments from our walls and goes looting like common bandits—that is, all the alien soldiers except America's; and (Americans again excepted) storms frightened villages and cables the result to glad journals at home every day: 'Chinese losses, 450 killed; ours, *one officer and two men wounded*. Shall proceed against neighboring village tomorrow, where a massacre is reported.' Can we afford Civilization?"

And next Russia must go and play the game injudiciously. She affronts England once or twice—with the Person Sitting in Darkness observing and noting; by moral assistance of France and Germany, she robs Japan of her hard-earned spoil, all swimming in Chinese blood—Port Arthur—with the Person again observing and noting; then she seizes Manchuria, raids its villages, and chokes its great river with the swollen corpses of countless massacred peasants—that astonished Person still observing and noting. And perhaps he is saying to himself, "It is yet *another* Civilized Power, with its banner of the Prince of Peace in one hand and its loot basket and its butcher knife in the other. Is there no salvation for us but to adopt Civilization and lift ourselves down to its level?"

And by and by comes America, and our Master of the Game plays it badly—plays it as Mr. Chamberlain was play-it in South Africa. It was a mistake to do that; also, it was one which was quite unlooked for in a Master who was playing it so well in Cuba.[1] In Cuba, he was playing the usual and regular *American* game and it was winning, for there is no way to beat it. The Master, contemplating Cuba, said, "Here is an oppressed and friendless little nation which is willing to fight to be free; we go partners, and put up the strength of seventy million sympathizers and the resources of the United States: play!" Nothing but Europe combined could call that hand, and Europe cannot combine on anything. There in Cuba he was following our great traditions in a way which made us very proud of him, and proud of the deep

[1] The Spanish-American War.

dissatisfaction which his play was provoking in continental Europe. Moved by a high inspiration, he threw out those stirring words which proclaimed that forcible annexation would be "criminal aggression," and in that utterance fired another "shot heard round the world." The memory of that fine saying will be outlived by the remembrance of no act of his but one—that he forgot it within the twelvemonth, and its honorable gospel along with it.

For presently came the Philippine temptation. It was strong, it was too strong, and he made that bad mistake: he played the European game, the Chamberlain game. It was a pity, it was a great pity, that error—that one grievous error, that irrevocable error. For it was the very place and time to play the American game again. And at no cost. Rich winnings to be gathered in, too, rich and permanent, indestructible, a fortune transmissible forever to the children of the flag. Not land, not money, not dominion—no, something worth many times more than that dross: our share, the spectacle of a nation of long harassed and persecuted slaves set free through our influence; our posterity's share, the golden memory of that fair deed. The game was in our hands. If it had been played according to the American rules, Dewey would have sailed away from Manila as soon as he had destroyed the Spanish fleet—after putting up a sign on shore guaranteeing foreign property and life against damage by the Filipinos, and warning the Powers that interference with the emancipated patriots would be regarded as an act unfriendly to the United States. The Powers cannot combine in even a bad cause, and the sign would not have been molested.

Dewey could have gone about his affairs elsewhere and left the competent Filipino army to starve out the little Spanish garrison and send it home, and the Filipino citizens to set up the form of government they might prefer and deal with the friars and their doubtful acquisitions according to Filipino ideas of fairness and justice—ideas which have since been tested and found to be of as high an order as any that prevail in Europe or America.

But we played the Chamberlain game and lost the chance to add another Cuba and another honorable deed to our good record.

The more we examine the mistake, the more clearly we perceive that it is going to be bad for the Business. The Person Sitting in Darkness is almost sure to say, "There is something curious about this—curious and unaccountable. There

Darts from the Darkness

must be two Americas, one that sets the captive free, and one that takes a once-captive's new freedom away from him, and picks a quarrel with him with nothing to found it on, then kills him to get his land."

The truth is, the Person Sitting in Darkness *is* saying things like that, and for the sake of the Business we must persuade him to look at the Philippine matter in another and healthier way. We must arrange his opinions for him. I believe it can be done, for Mr. Chamberlain has arranged England's opinion of the South African matter and done it most cleverly and successfully. He presented the facts—some of the facts—and showed those confiding people what the facts meant. He did it statistically, which is a good way. He used the formula: "Twice 2 are 14, and 2 from 9 leaves 35." Figures are effective; figures will convince the elect.

Now, my plan is a still bolder one than Mr. Chamberlain's, though apparently a copy of it. Let us be franker than Mr. Chamberlain; let us audaciously present the whole of the facts, shirking none, then explain them according to Mr. Chamberlain's formula. This daring truthfulness will astonish and dazzle the Person Sitting in Darkness, and he will take the Explanation down before his mental vision has had time to get back into focus. Let us say to him:

"Our case is simple. On the first of May, Dewey destroyed the Spanish fleet. This left the Archipelago in the hands of its proper and rightful owners, the Filipino nation. Their army numbered 30,000 men and they were competent to whip out or starve out the little Spanish garrison; then the people could set up a government of their own devising. Our traditions required that Dewey should now set up his warning sign and go away. But the Master of the Game happened to think of another plan—the European plan. He acted upon it. This was to send out an army—ostensibly to help the native patriots put the finishing touch upon their long and plucky struggle for independence, but really to take their land away from them and keep it. That is, in the interest of Progress and Civilization. The plan developed stage by stage, and quite satisfactorily. We entered into a military alliance with the trusting Filipinos and they hemmed in Manila on the land side, and by their valuable help the place, with its garrison of 8,000 or 10,000 Spaniards, was captured—a thing which we could not have accomplished unaided at that time. We got their help by—by ingenuity. We knew they were fighting for their independence and that they had been at it for two years. We knew they supposed that we also were fighting in their worthy cause—just as we had helped the Cubans fight for Cuban independence—and we allowed them to go on thinking so. *Until Manila was ours and we could get along without them.* Then we showed our hand. Of course, they were surprised—that was natural, surprised and disappointed, disappointed and grieved. To them it looked un-American, uncharacteristic, foreign to our established traditions. And this was natural, too, for we were only playing the American Game in public—in private it was the European. It was neatly done, very neatly, and it bewildered them. They could not understand it, for we had been so friendly—so affectionate, even—with those simple-minded patriots! We, our own selves, had brought back out of exile their leader, their hero, their hope, their Washington—Aguinaldo; brought him in a warship, in high honor, under the sacred shelter and hospitality of the flag; brought him back and restored him to his people and got their moving and eloquent gratitude for it. Yes, we had been so friendly to them and had heartened them up in so many ways! We had lent them guns and ammunition; advised with them; exchanged pleasant courtesies with them; placed our sick and wounded in their kindly care; intrusted our Spanish prisoners to their humane and honest hands; fought shoulder to shoulder with them against "the common enemy" (our own phrase); praised their courage, praised their gallantry, praised their mercifulness, praised their fine and honorable conduct; borrowed their trenches, borrowed strong positions which they had previously captured from the Spaniards; petted them, lied to them —officially proclaiming that our land and naval forces came to give them their freedom and displace the bad Spanish Government—fooled them, used them until we needed them no longer, then derided the sucked orange and threw it away. We kept the positions which we had beguiled them of, by and by we moved a force forward and overlapped patriot ground—a clever thought, for we needed trouble and this would produce it. A Filipino soldier, crossing the ground, where no one had a right to forbid him, was shot by our sentry. The badgered patriots resented this with arms, without waiting to know whether Aguinaldo, who was absent, would approve or not. Aguinaldo did not approve, but that availed nothing. What we wanted in the interest of Progress and Civilization was the Archipelago, unencumbered by patriots struggling for independence; and War was what we needed. We clinched our opportunity. It is Mr. Chamberlain's case over again—at least in its motive and intention;

Darts from the Darkness

and we played the game as adroitly as he played it himself."

At this point in our frank statement of fact to the Person Sitting in Darkness, we should throw in a little trade taffy about the Blessings of Civilization—for a change, and for the refreshment of his spirit—then go on with our tale:

"We and the patriots having captured Manila, Spain's ownership of the Archipelago and her sovereignty over it were at an end—obliterated—annihilated—not a rag or shred of either remaining behind. It was then that we conceived the divinely humorous idea of *buying* both of these specters from Spain! [It is quite safe to confess this to the Person Sitting in Darkness, since neither he nor any other sane person will believe it.] In buying those ghosts for twenty millions, we also contracted to take care of the friars and their accumulations. I think we also agreed to propagate leprosy and smallpox, but as to this there is doubt. But it is not important, persons afflicted with the friars do not mind other diseases.

"With our Treaty ratified, Manila subdued, and our Ghosts secured, we had no further use for Aguinaldo and the owners of the Archipelago. We forced a war and we have been hunting America's guest and ally through the woods and swamps ever since."

At this point in the tale, it will be well to boast a little of our war work and our heroisms in the field, so as to make our performance look as fine as England's in South Africa, but I believe it will not be best to emphasize this too much. We must be cautious. Of course, we must read the war telegrams to the Person, in order to keep up our frankness, but we can throw an air of humorousness over them and that will modify their grim eloquence a little, and their rather indiscreet exhibitions of gory exultation. Before reading to him the following display heads of the dispatches of November 18, 1900, it will be well to practice on them in private first, so as to get the right tang of lightness and gayety into them:

"*Administration Weary of
Protracted Hostilities!*"

"*Real War Ahead for Filipino
Rebels!*"[1]

"*Will Show No Mercy!*"

"*Kitchener's Plan Adopted!*"

"Black" Comedy:
The Scornful,
Mournful Laugh

[1] "Rebels!" Mumble that funny word—don't let the Person catch it distinctly. [Twain's note.]

238

Kitchener[1] knows how to handle disagreeable people who are fighting for their homes and their liberties, and we must let on that we are merely imitating Kitchener and have no national interest in the matter, further than to get ourselves admired by the Great Family of Nations, in which august company our Master of the Game has bought a place for us in the back row.

Of course, we must not venture to ignore our General MacArthur's reports—oh, why do they keep on printing those embarrassing things?—we must drop them trippingly from the tongue and take the chances:

During the last ten months our losses have been 268 killed and 750 wounded; Filipino loss, *three thousand two hundred and twenty-seven killed,* and 694 wounded.

We must stand ready to grab the Person Sitting in Darkness, for he will swoon away at this confession, saying, "Good God! those 'niggers' spare their wounded, and the Americans massacre theirs!"

We must bring him to and coax him and coddle him, and assure him that the ways of Providence are best and that it would not become us to find fault with them; and then, to show him that we are only imitators, not originators, we must read the following passage from the letter of an American soldier lad in the Philippines to his mother, published in *Public Opinion,* of Decorah, Iowa, describing the finish of a victorious battle:

"We never left one alive. If one was wounded, we would run our bayonets through him."

Having now laid all the historical facts before the Person Sitting in Darkness, we should bring him to again and explain them to him. We should say to him:

"They look doubtful but in reality they are not. There have been lies, yes, but they were told in a good cause. We have been treacherous, but that was only in order that real good might come out of apparent evil. True, we have crushed a deceived and confiding people; we have turned against the weak and the friendless who trusted us; we have stamped out a just and intelligent and well-ordered republic; we have stabbed an ally in the back and slapped the face of a guest; we have bought a Shadow from an enemy that hadn't it to sell; we have robbed a trusting friend of his land and his

[1] *Kitchener:* Horatio Herbert Kitchener (1850–1916) served as the British Army's Chief of Staff in South Africa.

Darts
from the
Darkness

239

liberty; we have invited our clean young men to shoulder a discredited musket and do bandits' work under a flag which bandits have been accustomed to fear, not to follow; we have debauched America's honor and blackened her face before the world; but each detail was for the best. We know this. The Head of every State and Sovereignty in Christendom and 90 per cent of every legislative body in Christendom, including our Congress and our fifty state legislatures, are members not only of the church but also of the Blessings-of-Civilization Trust. This world-girdling accumulation of trained morals, high principles, and justice cannot do an unright thing, an unfair thing, an ungenerous thing, an unclean thing. It knows what it is about. Give yourself no uneasiness; it is all right."

Now then, that will convince the Person. You will see. It will restore the Business. Also, it will elect the Master of the Game to the vacant place in the Trinity of our national gods, and there on their hign thrones the Three will sit, age after age, in the people's sight, each bearing the Emblem of his service: Washington, the Sword of the Liberator; Lincoln, the Slave's Broken Chains; the Master, the Chains Repaired.

It will give the Business a splendid new start. You will see.

Everything is prosperous now; everything is just as we should wish it. We have got the Archipelago, and we shall never give it up. Also, we have every reason to hope that we shall have an opportunity before very long to slip out of our congressional contract with Cuba and give her something better in the place of it. It is a rich country and many of us are already beginning to see that the contract was a sentimental mistake. But now—right now—is the best time to do some profitable rehabilitating work—work that will set us up and make us comfortable, and discourage gossip. We cannot conceal from ourselves that, privately, we are a little troubled about our uniform. It is one of our prides, it is acquainted with honor, it is familiar with great deeds and noble, we love it, we revere it, and so this errand it is on makes us uneasy. And our flag—another pride of ours, our chiefest! We have worshiped it so, and when we have seen it in far lands—glimpsing it unexpectedly in that strange sky, waving its welcome and benediction to us—we have caught our breaths and uncovered our heads and couldn't speak for a moment, for the thought of what it was to us and the great ideals it stood for. Indeed, we *must* do something about these things; it is easily managed. . . .

And we do not need that Civil Commission out there.

Having no powers, it has to invent them, and that kind of work cannot be effectively done by just anybody; an expert is required. Mr. Croker[1] can be spared. We do not want the United States replaced there, but only the Game.

By help of these suggested amendments, Progress and Civilization in that country can have a boom, and it will take in the Persons who are Sitting in Darkness, and we can resume Business at the old stand.

[1] *Mr. Croker:* Richard Croker (1843?–1922), New York City politician, and Tammany Hall leader (1886–1902).

For Writing and Discussion

1. What is Twain's purpose in writing this article for a well-known journal of his day? Do you think he was hopeful about man's ability to change? What evidence in the article do you find to support your opinion?

2. Andrew Carnegie, a millionaire industrialist and philanthropist, put up one-thousand dollars (a considerable sum in those days) to reprint this story for circulation by the Anti-Imperialist League. He said it was the "only missionary work" he had ever been responsible for. What is ironic about these remarks, considering the fact that Carnegie considered himself a religious man? Do you think he had more hope for the "damned human race" than Twain? To what use is much of Carnegie's wealth put now?

3. "To the Person Sitting in Darkness" is commentary based on factual data, which is used to support a strong position. It is "argumentative" in nature. What facts are presented? What is the author's opinion as to the actions of the nations which ostensibly are assuming the "white man's burden?"

4. Not all satire is ironic; but all irony is satiric. Which of the techniques of satire does Twain use in this article? What are the purposes of the article? How is the tone different from that of the satiric pieces you read in the preceding chapter?

5. Twain does not always directly and explicitly state his opinion, yet only a completely unsophisticated reader would not be aware of his viewpoint. He presents it indirectly, using most of the devices of black humor. Point out examples of each of these devices in the article: (1) sarcasm, or verbal irony—that is, saying the opposite of what is meant; (2) irony of situation—that is, the reversal of events from what is expected, so that the outcome is opposite from what is predicted; (3) paradox, a seeming contradiction in meaning, or the combining of opposites that results in an unmasking of the truth.

6. Considerable use of understatement is made in this essay. It is

Darts from the Darkness

used as a linguistic contrast to the overstated, outrageous, dark and evil acts. Point out at least three instances where the most inoffensive language is used to comment on the most offensive realities.

7. The basic device illustrated in the essay is that of the "mock encomium." An encomium is a "song of praise," usually delivered on some occasion of public rejoicing in honor of a national victory or hero. The "mock" encomium uses the same techniques, but it uses them in mockery rather than in praise. Using this article as a model of the form, list some of the characteristics of the mock encomium. When you have completed your list, compare it with that of other readers. Later on, you can refer to it for aid in writing a mock encomium of your own. How is the form basically a satiric, ironic literary form?

8. The mocking tone of seeming praise is occasionally interrupted by a more obviously bitter, denunciatory comment. Locate places where this change of tone and method occurs. Trace the increasingly insulting attitude from the beginning to the end of the essay.

9. Assuming that tragedy presupposes man's ability, through his greatness and nobility, to rise above his fate, and that comedy, acting as a caustic reminder of man's frailties, deals more realistically with human weaknesses, justify the inclusion of an article like "To the Person Sitting in Darkness" as humor rather than tragedy, bitter humor though it may be.

A Box to Hide In

JAMES THURBER

Mark Twain died before the first World War and therefore did not have the opportunity to comment on that conflict, nor on the extended period of modern wars that it ushered in. No doubt he would have considered them, in the ironic manner of his mock encomium "To the Person Sitting in Darkness," the "crowning achievement" of the "damned" human race. One wonders what resources of language that he had not already tapped would be available to him today. Perhaps he would have turned again to fiction to express even more indirectly than does the ironic mock encomium his bitterness and dismay at the spectacle of man's cruelty to man.

For Thurber, short fiction and fiction-enriched essays were the genres most congenial to his talent. We would not expect Thurber to go to the extremes of boisterousness in low comedy nor to the extremes of "bitter" mockery and insult that were reflections of Twain's more flamboyant, intense personality. But that is not to say that Thurber did not react with as much pessimism, if not with as much vituperation, about the human race as did Twain. As we recognize when reading satire, Thurber was one of the most devastating unmaskers of vanity and hypocrisy in our time.

In the very brief story that follows, Thurber uses the elements of fiction—character, situation, setting, and theme—to comment on the "darkness" at the heart of modern life. In the story, he deals, as was his custom, not with Man as a species, but with Man's plight from the point of view of each unique individual who reacts *as* an individual to the world scene. Evidently, he too is aware of the darkness in the world, but he suggests that darkness may be preferable to the light that forces man to see himself and others, not as he once aspired to be, but as he has become.

A Box
to Hide In

I waited till the large woman with the awful hat took up her sack of groceries and went out, peering at the tomatoes and lettuce on her way. The clerk asked me what mine was.

"Have you got a box," I asked, "a large box? I want a box to hide in."

"You want a box?" he asked.

"I want a box to hide in," I said.

"Whatta you mean?" he said. "You mean a big box?"

I said I meant a big box, big enough to hold me.

"I haven't got any boxes," he said. "Only cartons that cans come in."

I tried several other groceries and none of them had a box big enough for me to hide in. There was nothing for it but to face life out. I didn't feel strong, and I'd had this overpowering desire to hide in a box for a long time.

"Whatta you mean you want to hide in this box?" one grocer asked me.

"It's a form of escape," I told him, "hiding in a box. It circumscribes your worries and the range of your anguish. You don't see people, either."

"How in the hell do you eat when you're in this box?" asked the grocer. "How in the hell do you get anything to eat?" I said I had never been in a box and didn't know, but that that would take care of itself.

"Well," he said, finally, "I haven't got any boxes, only some pasteboard cartons that cans come in."

It was the same every place. I gave up when it got dark and the groceries closed, and hid in my room again. I turned out the light and lay on the bed. You feel better when it gets dark. I could have hid in a closet, I suppose, but people are always opening doors. Somebody would find you in a closet. They would be startled and you'd have to tell them why you were in the closet. Nobody pays any attention to a big box lying on the floor. You could stay in it for days and nobody'd think to look in it, not even the cleaning-woman.

My cleaning-woman came the next morning and woke me up. I was still feeling bad. I asked her if she knew where I could get a large box.

"How big a box you want?" she asked.

"I want a box big enough for me to get inside of," I said. She looked at me with big, dim eyes. There's something wrong with her glands. She's awful but she has a big heart, which makes it worse. She's unbearable, her husband is sick and her children are sick and she is sick too. I got to thinking how pleasant it would be if I were in a box now, and didn't have to see her. I would be in a box right there in the room and she wouldn't know. I wondered if you have a desire to bark or laugh when someone who doesn't know walks by the box you are in. Maybe she would have a spell with her heart, if I did that, and would die right there. The officers and the elevatorman and Mr. Gramadge would find us. "Funny doggone thing happened at the building last night," the doorman would say to his wife. "I let in this woman to clean up 10-F and she never come out, see? She's never there more'n an hour, but she never come out, see? So when it got to be time for me to go off duty, why I says to Crennick, who was on the elevator, I says what the hell you suppose has happened to that woman cleans 10-F? He says he didn't know; he says he never seen her after he took her up. So I spoke to Mr. Gramadge about it. 'I'm sorry to bother you, Mr. Gramadge,' I says, 'but there's something funny about that woman cleans 10-F.' So I told him. So he said we better have a look and we all three goes up and knocks on the door and rings the bell, see, and no-body answers so he said we'd have to walk in so Crennick

opened the door and we walked in and here was this woman cleans the apartment dead as a herring on the floor and the gentleman that lives there was in a box." . . .

The cleaning-woman kept looking at me. It was hard to realize she wasn't dead. "It's a form of escape," I murmured. "What say?" she asked, dully.

"You don't know of any large packing boxes, do you?" I asked.

"No, I don't," she said.

I haven't found one yet, but I still have this overpowering urge to hide in a box. Maybe it will go away, maybe I'll be all right. Maybe it will get worse. It's hard to say.

For Writing and Discussion

1. What keeps this story from being tragic, or even pathetic?

2. What view of man underlies the story? How is man reduced in stature, as he is in all comedy except, perhaps, in the childlike exaggerations of the tall tale?

3. Why do you think Thurber chose to tell this story in the first person? Is he narrating a personal experience, or is he implying a certain kind of identity with other people? If so, what feeling or emotion common to us all is highlighted?

4. The gentleman in this story is a compulsive type similar to many Thurber chose for characters. His compulsion is not "funny," however. Why not?

5. Does the reader feel involved with the protagonist? What does this say about the maintenance of a tone and point of view typical of all humor?

6. Understatement to describe the unusual or exaggerated situation or

*Darts
from the
Darkness*

245

motive is the key device that Thurber uses in a humorous way. Locate several examples of understatement in the story. How does it "reduce" the "I" of the story as well as the people he deals with casually?

7. What picture of human relationships do you get from this story?

8. How do remarks about the "awful" cleaning-woman represent a reversal of the mock encomium technique?

9. Compare the use of the words "dark" or "darkness" and "light" with their use in Twain's article. How do you account for the fact that using these same words in a different context helps considerably to alter the tone of Thurber's story?

FROM *The Lowest Animal*

MARK TWAIN

One of the nineteenth-century scientific theories that shook the complacent Western colonial powers was the theory of evolution advanced by Charles Darwin, a British naturalist. The Darwinian hypothesis, as it is more properly called, attempted to relate man as an animal species to the entire living world, to show how man is integrated into this world, and how his origins arise from it. Although Darwin realized and pointed out the similarities of man's physical structure to that of the higher primates, he never implied that man "ascended" or "descended" from the lower animals. He did remark on the complexity of man's emotional and mental apparatus, but he made no value judgments as to man's "superiority" over animals. Darwin's theory had a disastrous effect on man's ego, since it stressed his animal relationships rather than his godlike origins and aspirations. Not since the Copernican theory did man feel so small both in the universe and on his own planet.

Evidently Mark Twain either shared in the popular misconception of man as the "highest" animal in the evolutionary scale, or else he took advantage of the general reader's erroneous conception for purely literary purposes. Obviously the assumption that man is superior to all other forms of life is capable of inversion, the use of that "upside-down" technique so often used by humorists to make apparent the contrast between what *is* and what is *professed* or *hoped*. And the ultimate irony for man is, of course, that far from being a god, he is in fact "worse"—in an ethical or humane sense—than the lower forms of animal life, for, whether or not he acts upon it, at least he is capable of recognizing his own limitations through that very intelligence that sets him apart from other animals.

The form Twain chose to use for his comments on man as an animal is the letter, a form well suited to making ironic observations. But instead of writing an open letter to the editor of a current publication, Twain chose to develop a series of fictional letters purported to have been written to the inhabitants of heaven by Satan, an emissary to earth who was reporting his observations about men. The fact that the angel who soon thereafter became the symbol of evil, the devil, was so condemnatory of man compounds the bitterness of the irony; for if the worst example of evil is horrified at the spectacle of man's degradation, how "damned" the human race must be!

The excerpt that follows is from the fifth of Satan's *Letters from the Earth*. The specific events that gave rise to these reactions on Twain's part were the religious persecutions in Crete that were taking place at the time. But the massacres in the name of religion were only a sample of an interminable list of man's depravities—acts which placed man, in Twain's judgment, at the bottom rather than at the top of the animal kingdom.

FROM
The Lowest Animal   I have been studying the traits and dispositions of the "lower animals" (so-called), and contrasting them with the traits and dispositions of man. I find the result humiliating to me. For it obliges me to renounce my allegiance to the Darwinian theory of the Ascent of Man from the Lower Animals; since it now seems plain to me that that theory ought to be vacated in favor of a new and truer one, this new and truer one to be named the *Descent* of Man from the Higher Animals.

In proceeding toward this unpleasant conclusion I have not guessed or speculated or conjectured, but have used what is commonly called the scientific method. That is to say, I have subjected every postulate that presented itself to the crucial test of actual experiment, and have adopted it or rejected it according to the result. Thus I verified and established each step of my course in its turn before advancing to the next. These experiments were made in the London

Darts from the Darkness

Zoological Gardens, and covered many months of painstaking and fatiguing work.

Before particularizing any of the experiments, I wish to state one or two things which seem to more properly belong in this place than further along. This in the interest of clearness. The massed experiments established to my satisfaction certain generalizations, to wit:

1. That the human race is of one distinct species. It exhibits slight variations—in color, stature, mental caliber, and so on—due to climate, environment, and so forth; but it is a species by itself, and not to be confounded with any other.

2. That the quadrupeds are a distinct family, also. This family exhibits variations—in color, size, food preferences and so on; but it is a family by itself.

3. That the other families—the birds, the fishes, the insects, the reptiles, etc.—are more or less distinct, also. They are in the procession. They are links in the chain which stretches down from the higher animals to man at the bottom.

Some of my experiments were quite curious. In the course of my reading I had come across a case where, many years ago, some hunters on our Great Plains organized a buffalo hunt for the entertainment of an English earl—that, and to provide some fresh meat for his larder. They had charming sport. They killed seventy-two of those great animals; and ate part of one of them and left the seventy-one to rot. In order to determine the difference between an anaconda and an earl—if any—I caused seven young calves to be turned into the anaconda's cage. The grateful reptile immediately crushed one of them and swallowed it, then lay back satisfied. It showed no further interest in the calves, and no disposition to harm them. I tried this experiment with other anacondas; always with the same result. The fact stood proven that the difference between an earl and an anaconda is that the earl is cruel and the anaconda isn't; and that the earl wantonly destroys what he has no use for, but the anaconda doesn't. This seemed to suggest that the anaconda was not descended from the earl. It also seemed to suggest that the earl was descended from the anaconda, and had lost a good deal in the transition.

I was aware that many men who have accumulated more millions of money than they can ever use have shown a rabid hunger for more, and have not scrupled to cheat the ignorant and the helpless out of their poor servings in order to partially appease that appetite. I furnished a hundred different kinds of wild and tame animals the opportunity to accumulate vast stores of food, but none of them would do it. The squirrels and bees and certain birds made accumulations, but stopped when they had gathered a winter's supply, and could not be persuaded to add to it either honestly or by chicane. In order to bolster up a tottering reputation the ant pretended to store up supplies, but I was not deceived. I know the ant. These experiments convinced me that there is this difference between man and the higher animals: he is avaricious and miserly, they are not.

In the course of my experiments I convinced myself that among the animals man is the only one that harbors insults and injuries, broods over them, waits till a chance offers, then takes revenge. The passion of revenge is unknown to the higher animals.

Roosters keep harems, but it is by consent of their concubines; therefore no wrong is done. Men keep harems, but it is by brute force, privileged by atrocious laws which the other sex were allowed no hand in making. In this matter man occupies a far lower place than the rooster.

Cats are loose in their morals, but not consciously so. Man, in his descent from the cat, has brought the cat's looseness with him but has left the unconsciousness behind—the saving grace which excuses the cat. The cat is innocent, man is not.

Indecency, vulgarity, obscenity—these are strictly confined to man; he invented them. Among the higher animals there is no trace of them. They hide nothing; they are not ashamed. Man, with his soiled mind, covers himself. He will not even enter a drawing room with his breast and back naked, so alive are he and his mates to indecent suggestion. Man is "The Animal that Laughs." But so does the monkey, as Mr. Darwin pointed out; and so does the Australian bird that is called the laughing jackass. No—Man is the Animal that Blushes. He is the only one that does it—or has occasion to.

Man—when he is a North American Indian—gouges out his prisoner's eyes; when he is King John, with a nephew to render untroublesome, he uses a red-hot iron; when he is a religious zealot dealing with heretics in the Middle Ages, he skins his captive alive and scatters salt on his back; in the first Richard's time he shuts up a multitude of Jew families in a tower and sets fire to it; in Columbus's time he captures a family of Spanish Jews and—but *that* is not printable; in our day in England a man is fined ten shillings for beating his mother nearly to death with a chair, and another man is fined forty shillings for having four pheasant eggs in his possession without being able to satisfactorily explain how he got them. Of all the animals, man is the only one that is cruel. He is the only one that inflicts pain for the pleasure of doing it. It is a trait that is not known to the higher animals. The cat plays with the frightened mouse; but she has this excuse, that she does not know that the mouse is suffering. The cat is moderate—unhumanly moderate: she only scares the mouse, she does not hurt it; she doesn't dig out its eyes, or tear off its skin, or drive splinters under its nails—man-fashion; when she is done playing with it she makes a sudden meal of it and puts it out of its trouble. Man is the Cruel Animal. He is alone in that distinction.

The higher animals engage in individual fights, but never in organized masses. Man is the only animal that deals in that atrocity of atrocities, War. He is the only one that gathers his brethren about him and goes forth in cold blood and with calm pulse to exterminate his kind. He is the only animal that for sordid wages will march out, as the Hessians did in our Revolution, and as the boyish Prince Napoleon did in the Zulu war, and help to slaughter strangers of his own species who have done him no harm and with whom he has no quarrel.

Man is the only animal that robs his helpless fellow of his country—takes possession of it and drives him out of it or destroys him. Man has done this in all the ages. There is not an acre of ground on the globe that is in possession of its rightful owner, or that has not been taken away from owner after owner, cycle after cycle, by force and bloodshed.

Man is the only Slave. And he is the only animal who enslaves. He has always been a slave in one form or another, and has always held other slaves in bondage under him in one way or another. In our day he is always some man's slave for wages, and does that man's work; and this slave has other slaves under him for minor wages, and they do *his* work. The higher animals are the only ones who exclusively do their own work and provide their own living.

Man is the only Patriot. He sets himself apart in his own country, under his own flag, and sneers at the other nations, and keeps multitudinous uniformed assassins on hand at heavy expense to grab slices of other people's countries, and keep *them* from grabbing slices of *his*. And in the intervals between campaigns he washes the blood off his hands and works for "the universal brotherhood of man"—with his mouth.

Man is the Reasoning Animal. Such is the claim. I think it is open to dispute. Indeed, my experiments have proven to me that he is the Unreasoning Animal. Note his history, as sketched above. It seems plain to me that whatever he is he is *not* a reasoning animal. His record is the fantastic record of a maniac. I consider that the strongest count against his intelligence is the fact that with that record back of him he blandly sets himself up as the head animal of the lot: whereas by his own standards he is the bottom one.

In truth, man is incurably foolish. Simple things which the other animals easily learn, he is incapable of learning. Among my experiments was this. In an hour I taught a cat and a dog to be friends. I put them in a cage. In another hour I taught them to be friends with a rabbit. In the course of two days I was able to add a fox, a goose, a squirrel and some doves. Finally a monkey. They lived together in peace; even affectionately.

Next, in another cage I confined an Irish Catholic from Tipperary, and as soon as he seemed tame I added a Scotch Presbyterian from Aberdeen. Next a Turk from Constantinople, a Greek Christian from Crete; an Armenian; a Methodist from the wilds of Arkansas; a Buddhist from China; a Brahman from Benares. Finally, a Salvation Army Colonel from Wapping. Then I stayed away two whole days. When I came back to note results, the cage of Higher Animals was all right, but in the other there was but a chaos of gory odds and ends of turbans and fezzes and plaids and bones and flesh—not a specimen left alive. These Reasoning Animals had disagreed on a theological detail and carried the matter to a Higher Court.

One is obliged to concede that in true loftiness of character, Man cannot claim to approach even the meanest of the Higher Animals.

And so I find that we have descended and degenerated, from some far ancestor—some microscopic atom wandering at its pleasure between the mighty horizons of a drop of water perchance—insect by insect, animal by animal, reptile by reptile, down the long highway of smirchless innocence, till we have reached the bottom stage of development—namable as the Human Being. Below us—nothing.

Man seems to be a rickety poor sort of a thing, any way you take him; a kind of British Museum of infirmities and inferiorities. He is always undergoing repairs. A machine that

*Darts
from the
Darkness*

251

was as unreliable as he is would have no market. On top of his specialty—the Moral Sense—are piled a multitude of minor infirmities; such a multitude, indeed, that one may broadly call them countless. The higher animals get their teeth without pain or inconvenience. Man gets his through months and months of cruel torture; and at a time of life when he is but ill able to bear it. As soon as he has got them they must all be pulled out again, for they were of no value in the first place, not worth the loss of a night's rest. The second set will answer for a while, by being reinforced occasionally with rubber or plugged up with gold; but he will never get a set which can really be depended on till a dentist makes him one. This set will be called "false" teeth—as if he had ever worn any other kind.

In a wild state—a natural state—the Higher Animals have a few diseases; diseases of little consequence; the main one is old age. But man starts in as a child and lives on diseases till the end, as a regular diet. He has mumps, measles, whooping cough, croup, tonsilitis, diphtheria, scarlet fever, almost as a matter of course. Afterward, as he goes along, his life continues to be threatened at every turn: by colds, coughs, asthma, bronchitis, itch, cholera, cancer, consumption, yellow fever, bilious fever, typhus fevers, hay fever, ague, chilblains, piles, inflammation of the entrails, indigestion, toothache, earache, deafness, dumbness, blindness, influenza, chicken pox, cowpox, smallpox, liver complaint, constipation, bloody flux, warts, pimples, boils, carbuncles, abscesses, bunions, corns, tumors, fistulas, pneumonia, softening of the brain, melancholia and fifteen other kinds of insanity; dysentery, jaundice, diseases of the heart, the bones, the skin, the scalp, the spleen, the kidneys, the nerves, the brain, the blood; scrofula, paralysis, leprosy, neuralgia, palsy, fits, headache, thirteen kinds of rheumatism, forty-six of gout, and a formidable supply of gross and unprintable disorders of one sort and another. Also—but why continue the list? The mere names of the agents appointed to keep this shackly machine out of repair would hide him from sight if printed on his body in the smallest type known to the founder's art. He is but a basket of pestilent corruption provided for the support and entertainment of swarming armies of bacilli—armies commissioned to rot him and destroy him, and each army equipped with a special detail of the work. The process of waylaying him, persecuting him, rotting him, killing him, begins with his first breath, and there is no mercy, no pity, no truce till he draws his last one.

Look at the workmanship of him, in certain of its particulars. What are his tonsils for? They perform no useful function; they have no value. They have no business there. They are but a trap. They have but the one office, the one industry: to provide tonsilitis and quinsy and such things for the possessor of them. And what is the vermiform appendix for? It has no value; it cannot perform any useful service. It is but an ambuscaded enemy whose sole interest in life is to lie in wait for stray grapeseeds and employ them to breed strangulated hernia. And what are the male's mammals for? For business, they are out of the question; as an ornament, they are a mistake. What is his beard for? It performs no useful function; it is a nuisance and a discomfort; all nations hate it; all nations persecute it with the razor. And because it is a nuisance and a discomfort, Nature never allows the supply of it to fall short, in any man's case, between puberty and the grave. You never see a man bald-headed on his chin. But his hair! It is a graceful ornament, it is a comfort, it is the best of all protections against certain perilous ailments, man prizes it above emeralds and rubies. And because of these things Nature puts it on, half the time, so that it won't stay. Man's sight, smell, hearing, sense of locality—how inferior they are. The condor sees a corpse at five miles; man has no telescope that can do it. The bloodhound follows a scent that is two days old. The robin hears the earthworm burrowing his course under the ground. The cat, deported in a closed basket, finds its way home again through twenty miles of country which it has never seen.

For style, look at the Bengal tiger—that ideal of grace, beauty, physical perfection, majesty. And then look at Man —that poor thing. He is the Animal of the Wig, the Trepanned Skull, the Ear Trumpet, the Glass Eye, the Pasteboard Nose, the Porcelain Teeth, the Silver Windpipe, the Wooden Leg—a creature that is mended and patched all over, from top to bottom. If he can't get renewals of his bric-a-brac in the next world, what will he look like?

He has just one stupendous superiority. In his intellect he is supreme. The Higher Animals cannot touch him there. It is curious, it is noteworthy, that no heaven has ever been offered him wherein his one sole superiority was provided with a chance to enjoy itself. Even when he himself has imagined a heaven, he has never made provision in it for intellectual joys. It is a striking omission. It seems a tacit confession that heavens are provided for the Higher Animals alone. This is a matter for thought; and for serious thought.

And it is full of grim suggestion: that we are not as important, perhaps, as we had all along supposed we were.

For Writing and Discussion

1. What evidence can you find in this bitter letter to support the following statement by Bernard De Voto, the editor of Twain's *Letters from the Earth*?

    The humor that was the essential Mark Twain remains; it is interstitial; it is the breathing of his mind. Whether it be exuberance, an individual way of letting light in, the passion of a man hardly able to contain his wrath, or the deadlier laughter in suspension that means a tortured mind's adaptation to reality, it is the fundamental attribute of Mark Twain. The critic who for a moment forgets that Mark was a humorist is betrayed.

2. Point out examples of the following types of humorous devices in the letter: understatement, exaggeration, sarcasm, invective, paradox, ridicule, verbal irony.

3. How does Twain ape the scientific method, turning it "topsy-turvy" for ironic purposes? How does his imitation of scientific procedures and terms add a mock-serious tone of objectivity that is essential to humor? Where does he abandon this tone? Why?

4. What are some of the contrasts Twain establishes between man's stated values and goals in life and his actions? between what man calls "civilized" and what Satan calls "civilized"? Which of the humor techniques mentioned in question 2 above seem to you most effective in dramatizing these contrasts?

5. In what way is the entire letter an exercise in reversals?

6. One of the dangers of writing bitter irony is that the writer, as critic, places himself above the subjects of his anger, and sets himself apart from his own kind. Do you feel that Twain does this in this letter? Or do you believe that he is actually trying to present, in Satan's narration, an objective picture of what man's earthly existence had become? What evidence can you find in the letter to support your opinion?

7. Repetition is used as a rhetorical device throughout the letter—in repeated ideas, repeated devices, repeated words. What examples can you think of? List all the adjectives Twain uses to vary the repeated sentence: "Man is the_____animal." How does this sentence function as a unifying element in the letter?

8. Do you find any redeeming optimistic notes in the letter? If so, where?

9. Do you agree or disagree with Twain's estimate of man? Explain.

The Trouble With Man Is Man

In case you are feeling morbidly pessimistic about the "lowest animal," you may find a breezier comparison of man and other animals in Thurber's short piece, "The Trouble With Man Is Man." As you would anticipate, Thurber manages to convey a dim view of man's possibilities and accomplishments with a much lighter touch than does Twain. Note the interesting comparisons and contrasts between Twain's and Thurber's use of repetition, reversal, and paradox. The greatest difference, however, is in tone.

The Trouble With Man Is Man

Man has gone long enough, or even too long, without being man enough to face the simple truth that the trouble with Man is Man. For nearly three thousand years, or since the time of Aesop, he has blamed his frailties and defects on the birds, the beasts, and the insects. It is an immemorial convention of the writer of fables to invest the lower animals with the darker traits of human beings, so that by age-old habit, Man has come to blame his faults and flaws on the other creatures in this least possible of all worlds.

The human being says that the beast in him has been aroused, when what he actually means is that the human being in him has been aroused. A person is not pigeon-toed, either, but person-toed, and what the lady has are not crow's-feet but woman-wrinkles. It is our species, and not any other, that goes out on wildcat strikes, plays the badger game, weeps crocodile tears, sets up kangaroo courts. It is the man, and not the shark that becomes the loan shark; the cat burglar, when caught, turns out not to be a cat but a man; the cock-and-bull story was not invented by the cock and the bull; and the male of our species, at the height of his arrogant certainties, is mansure and not cocksure, just as, at his most put-upon, he is woman-nagged and not hen-pecked.

It is interesting to find in one dictionary that "cowed" does not come from "cow" but means, literally, "with the tail between the legs." I had naturally assumed, too, that Man blamed his quailing, or shrinking with fear, on the quail, but the dictionary claims that the origin of the verb "to quail" is uncertain. It is nice to know that "duck," meaning to avoid an unpleasant task, does not derive from our web-

Darts from the Darkness

255

"There go the most intelligent of all animals"

footed friend but from the German verb "*tauchen*," meaning "to dive." We blame our cowardice, though, on poultry, when we say of a cringing man that he "chickened out."

Lest I be suspected by friends and colleagues, as well as by the F.B.I. and the American Legion, of wearing fur or feathers under my clothing, and acting as a spy in the midst of a species that is as nervous as a man and not as a cat, I shall set down here some of the comparatively few laudatory phrases about the other animals that have passed into general usage. We say, then, that a man has dogged determination, bulldog tenacity, and is the watchdog of this or that public office, usually the Treasury. We call him lionhearted or as brave as a lion, as proud as a peacock, as lively as a cricket, as graceful as a swan, as busy as a bee, as gentle as a lamb, and we sometimes observe that he has the memory of an elephant and works like a beaver. (Why this should make him dog-tired instead of beaver-tired I don't know.)

As I sit here, I suddenly, in my fevered fancy, get a man's-eye view, not a bird's-eye view, of a police detective snooping about a brownstone house, back in the prohibition days. He has been tipped off that the place is a blind tiger that sells white mule, or tiger sweat, and he will not believe the denials of the proprietor, one Joe, whose story sounds fishy.

The detective smells a rat and begins pussy-footing around. He is sure that this is a joint in which a man can drink like a fish and get as drunk as a monkey. The proprietor may be as wise as an owl and as slippery as an eel, but the detective is confident that he can outfox him.

"Don't hound me. You're on a wild-goose chase," insists Joe, who has butterflies in his stomach, and gooseflesh. (The goose has been terribly maligned by the human being, who has even gone so far as to pretend that the German jack-boot strut is the goose step. Surely only the dog, cat, and the bug are more derogated than the goose.) "You're as crazy as a loon," Joe quavers.

"Don't bug me," says the cop, and the bloodhound continues his search. Suddenly he flings open a door, and there stands the proprietor's current mouse, a soiled dove, as naked as a jay bird. But the detective has now ferreted out a secret panel and a cache of currency. "There must be ten thousand clams here," he says. "If you made all this fish legitimately, why do you hide it? And don't try to weasel out."

"In this rat race it's dog eat dog," the proprietor says, as he either is led off to jail or pays off the cop.

The English and American vocabularies have been vastly enlarged and, I suppose, enriched by the multitudinous figures of speech that slander and libel the lower animals, but the result has been the further inflation of the already inflated human ego by easy denigration of the other species. We have a thousand disparaging nouns applicable only to human beings, such as scoundrel, rascal, villain, scalawag, varlet, curmudgeon, and the like, but an angry person is much more apt to use, instead of one of these, such words as jackal, jackass, ape, baboon, gorilla, skunk, black sheep, louse, worm, lobster, crab, or shrimp. Incidentally, the word "curmudgeon" seems to derive from the French "coeur méchant," so that an old curmudgeon is nothing worse than an old naughty heart.

The female of our species comes out of slight, slur, insult, and contumely wearing more unfavorable tags and labels than the male. The fishwife, for example, has no fishhusband. The "shrew" derives from the name of a small furred mammal with a malignant reputation, based on an old, mistaken notion that it is venomous. Shrews are, to be sure, made up of both males and females, but the word is applied only to the female human being. Similarly, "vixen," meaning an ill-tempered person, was originally applied to both sexes (of

human beings, not foxes), but it is now aimed only at the woman. When a man, especially a general or other leader, is called a fox, the word is usually employed in a favorable sense.

Both "shrew" and "vixen" are rarely used any more in domestic altercations. For one thing, neither implies mental imbalance, and our species is fond of epithets and invective implying insanity. The list of such slings and arrows in Roget's Thesaurus contains, of course, such expressions as "off one's rocker" and "off one's trolley," but once again the lower forms of life are accused of being "disturbed," as in "mad as a March hare," "bats," "batty," "bats in the belfry," "crazier than a bedbug," and so on. (My favorite phrase in this Roget category gets away from bugs and bats, and rockers and trolleys; it is "balmy in the crumpet.")

Every younger generation, in its time and turn, adds to our animalistic vocabulary of disparagement. A lone male at a dance is no longer a stag turned wolf when he dogs the steps of a girl; he's a bird dog. And if the young lady turns on him, she no longer snaps, "Get lost!" or "Drop dead!" but, I am told, "Clean out your cage!" Since I heard about this two years ago, however, it may well be old hat by now, having given way to something like "Put your foot back in the trap!" or "Go hide under your rock!" or "Crawl back into the woodwork!"

I am afraid that nothing I can say will prevent mankind from being unkind to catkind, dogkind, and bugkind. I find no record of any cat that was killed by care. There are no dogs where a man goes when he goes to the dogs. The bugs that a man gets out of his mechanisms, if he does get them out, are not bugs but defects caused by the ineptitude, haste, or oversight of men.

Let us all go back to counting sheep. I think that the reason for the prevalent sleeplessness of Americans must be that we are no longer counting sheep but men.

For Writing and Discussion

1. If wit, as differentiated from humor, is essentially a playing on and with words, then this essay is beautifully "witty." Point out at least ten examples where Thurber's playing with words for the purpose of coining new expressions from trite idioms provides the main element of "surprise" that points up the contrast between what *is* and what is *professed*.

2. Which of the expressions that Thurber coins to describe man's behavior as a reversal of animal behavior do you find "funny?" Is the subject of the essay "funny?" How does the use of broad humor contrast with the content that Thurber is dealing with?

3. Compare the subject matter and tone of the essay with that of Twain's "The Lowest Animal." Which treatment of man's inadequacies do you find more accurate? Which caused you to think seriously about man's values and opinions of himself?

4. One of the attributes of "black comedy" is its tendency to reduce man's self-image to the lowest possible degree. How does Thurber achieve his reduction of man? How does he avoid the "blackness" of bitter irony that is perhaps more characteristic of this kind of humor than his own more tolerant way of putting things?

5. Do you feel that Thurber "includes himself in" when he discusses the vanities and evil of all men? Explain.

Here Come the Dolphins

JAMES THURBER

Thurber, unlike Twain, lived through the atrocities of both world wars. Since those two major wars, the evidence against man has continued to pile up. The darkness that eliminated six million Jews in the gas chambers and concentration camps of Hitler's Third Reich, and that burst in mushroom disguise on Hiroshima and Nagasaki, spread into a series of limited wars, killing hundreds of thousands. Man is still pitted against man throughout the world, and still with the approval, aid, and even active participation, of the civilized nations. And if man is lucky or intelligent and well meaning enough to prevent his own nuclear self-destruction, he has still to risk the polluted atmosphere and the threats of hunger and overpopulation.

Like Twain, Thurber looked with jaundiced eye on man's

Darts from the Darkness

"progress," and was aware of his increasingly slim margin of opportunity to make a better world. But in his quieter way, Thurber paints a devastatingly and deceptively "funny" possibility for optimism in the takeover from man by an animal like him in at least one respect—the ability to communicate in a language distinctively his own.

Here Come the
Dolphins

How sharper than a sermon's truth it must have been for many human beings when they learned that bottle-nosed Dolphin may, in time, succeed battle-poised Man as the master species on earth. This prophecy is implicit in the findings of those scientists who have been studying, and interviewing, dolphins in laboratories. It neither alarms nor surprises me that Nature, whose patience with our self-destructive species is giving out, may have decided to make us, if not extinct, at least a secondary power among the mammals of this planet.

Clarence Day, in his *This Simian World,* prefigured, in turn, the tiger and the dog as the master species, if their evolution, instead of ours, had turned them into People. He did not think of the dolphin, that member of the whale family sometimes called, inaccurately, the porpoise or the grampus. As far back as 1933 I observed a school of dolphins (their schools increase as ours decline) romping, as we carelessly call it, alongside a cruise ship in the South Atlantic, and something told me that here was a creature, all gaiety, charm, and intelligence, that might one day come out of the boundless deep and show us how a world can be run by creatures dedicated not to the destruction of their species but to its preservation.

We shall, alas, not be on earth to hear the lectures, and to read the reports, on Man by a disinterested intelligence equal, and perhaps superior, to our own. I should like to hear a thoughtful and brilliant dolphin cutting us down to our true size, in that far day when the much-vaunted Dignity of Man becomes a footnote to history, a phrase lifted from the dusty books of human sociologists and the crumbling speeches of obliterated politicians.

Anyone, even a human being, capable of contemplation and the exercise of logic, must realize that what has been called the neurotic personality of our time is rapidly becoming psychopathic. One has but to look at and listen to those

"Black" Comedy:
The Scornful,
Mournful Laugh

anti-Personality Cultists, Khrushchev and Castro, to identify them as the most notorious personality cultists of our era. I mourn the swift mortality of Man that will prevent him from reading *The Decline and Fall of Man* by Professor B.N. Dolphin. What I am saying will, of course, be called satire or nonsense. Professor Dolphin can deal with that when the time comes.

Almost all of Man's self-praise is exaggerated and magnified by the muddled and conflicting concepts of religion, sociology, and philosophy. We are not, for instance, the most adjustable of creatures, but the most helpless and desperate, so that we have had to develop ingenuity of a high and flexible kind in order to survive. All the other creatures of earth, with the exception of those we have made dependent by domestication, are more adjusted than we are, and can, and must, get along without us. But we depend upon many of them for our existence as we depend upon vegetables. It is impossible to imagine a female seal saying to another female seal "What a charming ladyskin! Where did you get it?" And I have just learned from a doctor friend of mine who spent six months in the Antarctic that the human being down there invariably suffers from Big Eye—that is, the inability to sleep well, or at all. And everybody knows that the penguins adjusted to their climate and that they never develop stomach ulcers since they long ago discovered a wholesome and nurturing diet, which we couldn't do even if we had another million years to live.

The penguin eats plankton, a nourishing if somewhat despondent food, charmingly described by the dictionary as "the passively floating and weakly swimming animal and plant life of a body of water." Man, being Man, doesn't care much for submissive victuals, but loves to beat the hell out of some of his main dishes, and has devised a dozen weapons with which to kill them, on sea or land or in the air, from the fish hook and the harpoon to the rifle and the shotgun. The penguin and dolphin, beholding the dismaying spectacle of human beings at table, will surely exclaim when they learn English, "What foods these mortals eat!"

I cannot be there to see, but I can clearly visualize what will happen when dolphinity has replaced humanity as the primary power. I can picture the dolphins' first ambassador to Washington or to the Court of St. James's coming into the presence of the President or the Prime Minister and saying with a wink and a whistle, "Ours is a porpoiseful society.

Good-by, and sorry, and may there be a proper moaning of the bar when you, who came from out the boundless deep, return again home."

Oh, but there is still time, gentlemen! Let's uncork the bottles, call up the ladies, exchange with our enemies the well-worn accusations of imperialistic ambitions, and lean back. Let us have fun before we are officially advised that, as Henley put it, our little job is done. And make mine a double Scotch and soda while you're at it. I have become a touch jittery myself, meditating that human marriage, whose success and failure both have helped to put us where we are, will seem, one fine century in the future, as quaint and incredible to the dolphins as the hipbone of a dinosaur.

For Writing and Discussion

1. An ironic sequel to Thurber's little tale appeared in the September 1970 issue of *Travel* magazine, in a column by Bob Gordon called "Travel Oddities": "Porpoises are believed to be closer to man's level of intelligence than almost any other animal. Pity the poor porpoise, though, for along with this distinction, he suffers from ulcers, stomach aches, and nervous breakdowns." If Thurber were alive today to read this same bit of information, how do you think he might have ended his essay? When thinking about Thurber's possible new ending, take into consideration the possibility that because, through the dolphin's intelligence, he can acquire illnesses similar to man's, he might ultimately fail to make the world safe for porpoises.

2. In this essay, Thurber goes further than you have seen him go thus far in making explicit, direct criticisms of man. Point out some examples of these direct statements. Then look at the sentences immediately preceding and following these direct statements. What techniques does Thurber use to provide contrast, both in tone and in method, to these explicit denunciations?

3. One of Thurber's favorite humorous devices is the misquoted allusion. Give at least two examples of these. What are the originals on which Thurber's deliberate bloopers are based? How do these misquotes contribute to the humor of the essay and, at the same time, make telling points?

4. Puns, often coupled with misquoted allusions, are another favorite Thurber device. Point out some puns and explain the double meanings.

5. Examples of antithesis abound in this little essay, and many of them appear in grammatically balanced, or parallel, constructions. The

"Black" Comedy: The Scornful, Mournful Laugh

contrast of "bottle-nosed Dolphin" with "battle-poised Man" is one example of this device. Point out others. How do they contribute to humor and, at the same time, convey the contrast between what man professes to be or believe and what he actually does?

6. In what sense is Thurber's hope for the universe, if not for man as a species, more optimistic than Twain's?

7. Comment on the following statement in relation to Thurber's essay: "Language can be as much of a barrier to understanding and survival as it can be a contributor to world peace and unity."

8. What evidence is there that Thurber again "includes himself in" with all other men rather than sets himself apart as their critic?

11

Masking the Tears

Both exaggerated jokes and quietly retrospective stories of former discomforts are often told in intimate, or at least fairly small, social groups. They are "personal" humor in this sense, and also in the sense that they depend so much upon the individuality of the teller or performer. Satire is a more "public" form of comedy because it frequently makes fun of man's political or social hypocrisies and is often presented in a more formal literary way than either low comedy or quiet humor, which lend themselves to informal, talky situations. "Black comedy" is often private in origin, resulting from the interaction of one's personal philosophy with one's perceptions of the state of the world. The forms of this kind of humor, however, are most often public and literary, and include the drama, the essay, letters, and public commentaries of various kinds.

On the other hand, the devices and techniques of black humor —invective, sarcasm, ironic understatement, mockery, and ridicule —are frequently interjected verbally into small social gatherings. Unfortunately, bitter comments tend to make one's listeners uncomfortable, either because of the topic or because of the implications that the speaker who is delivering himself of his rage or pessimistic prognoses is placing himself above his listeners, and is asserting his superior intellectual grasp of the hopelessness, ignorance, or malice in the world around him. But because the ironist's purpose is precisely to voice his own discomfort and to create discomfort or at least recognition in his audience, he can accomplish his aims better in writing or in a public form of oral literature—drama.

The Purpose

"Black comedy" is essentially a way of masking the jeers of impotent rage or hopelessness in the disguises of humor. It is a hostile kind of humor that recognizes man's impotence while at the same time providing him with a weapon against utter defeat. It shakes a fist at life or men, but in so doing, it shakes up the reader or listener by communicating the writer's discomfort without offering the consolations of tragic transcendence. The ultimate response to black humor is to ignore it as too depressing, or to react to it by thinking through in terms of one's own experience and observations the problems the writer has presented. If the condition being deplored is not irremediable, then some hope for improvement in positive action may result.

The Situation

Bitter humor is a response to a situation or person so inhuman or wrong-headed as to be beyond belief in demonstrating the bottomless depths of human depravity and selfishness. Facts that recount such acts and describe these people appear in the newspapers and on television each day. When enough evidence that is incontrovertible piles up, we are forced into shocked belief. We read of the deliberate starvation of whole groups of people in war, of the torture of prisoners and the injuring of children and old people, of the neglect of the aged, of the mistreatment of racial and religious minorities—and we resist, at first, the knowledge of our own vulnerability, of the possibilities in each of us for cruelty, ignorance, and cowardice. For the belief that all men are brothers implies the capacity of all men for evil as well as for good. Perhaps this is why we find the atrocities of our "enemies," the cruel acts of strangers or alien nations, easier to believe in and scorn. These are terrible, yes; but the atrocities that we ourselves perpetrate make us recoil in horror. During all wars, for instance, the enemy is usually painted as quite different from ourselves, more like cruel and cunning animals than like men. But after the wars are over, and the "facts" gradually come out, we often find that our own allies and our own defenders perpetrated acts as grim as those of the other side. To the sins of our enemies we react emotionally; to those of strangers we react with rage. To our own evil, we react with bitterness and hopeless dismay. And the path to recognition of evil is often through the most commonly used device of black humor—irony.

Sources of Invention

We have all felt gloomy on a number of occasions, and perhaps we have all had times when we wondered whether we would have done better to stay in bed rather than get up to face life's responsibilities. But this sort of casual, frequent, and easily dispelled "blueness" isn't the same sort of gloom that overpowers us when we become aware of evil in all its myriad forms. The recognition that this is not, indeed, the best of all possible worlds and that we perhaps are far from being the best of animal species is an insight not easily ignored or forgotten. Bitter irony and hostile rage accompany our persistent questions about man's ultimate values and abilities, questions that often evoke negative answers or, at the very least, skeptical doubts. Some of us have had, at an early age, a shattering experience of a personal nature that, when related to similar experiences we read or hear about, has undermined our optimistic faith that man will indeed survive. Others of us who are more fortunate arrive at the same questions and experience the same doubts by viewing atrocities in paintings, on television, or in films. We empathize with the protagonist of a play, or story, or the latest news reports.

Indeed, the newspaper report, told in the classic objectivity of journalistic style, presents the best source for materials on which to base black humor. Its very distance and matter-of-fact narration lend themselves to the ironist's purpose of pointing out the awful contrast between the facts and the aspirations, between the emotional commitments to certain principles and beliefs and the cold display of acts devoid of feeling. One of our current social concerns is the conditions in our prisons, where men are brutalized beyond redemption before being released, after which some former prisoners find themselves committing even greater crimes against society and themselves than those for which they were originally convicted. The following article could very well be found in a newspaper today. Originally published in January 1917, it was written by Harold A. Littledale, an enterprising reporter for the New York *Evening Post*, who made a thorough investigation of the New Jersey State Prison at Trenton.

Masking the Tears

Prisoners with midnight in their hearts

New York *Evening Post,* January 12, 1917. Copyright, 1917, New York Evening Post Co.

Bad prisons breed crime, and the New Jersey State Prison at Trenton is among the worst in the country. It is bad in its structure, bad in its influence, and bad in its management. By comparison Sing Sing is a cozy corner, for Trenton is monstrous, medieval, unhealthy and overcrowded.

It is hard to believe that in the twentieth century, one hundred years after Elizabeth Fry visited Newgate[1] and the English convict ships, man's inhumanity to man should express itself as it does express itself at Trenton. It is hard to believe that for infractions of the rules men are placed face to the wall for punishment and deprived of their meals. It is hard to believe that their labor is farmed out to private contractors for a pittance while their families are in want. It is hard to believe that the state's wards are cast into dungeons. It is hard to believe that women are placed with men. It is hard to believe that the insane mingle with the sane, the consumptive with the healthy, the pervert with the pure. But this, and much more, obtains at Trenton; this and much more exists and is sanctioned and permitted to be.

Here is the indictment:

It is a fact that two, three, and even four men are confined together in the same cell in violation of the law.

It is a fact that dungeons exist and that men are incarcerated therein and given only bread and water twice a day.

It is a fact that men have been chained to the walls of underground dungeons.

It is a fact that every day a man serves in a dungeon is added to his minimum sentence.

It is a fact that women convicts are confined with men, and that cell 55, wing 4, is kept for that purpose.

It is a fact that women prisoners eat, sleep, and live in their cells and work on sewing machines in the corridor outside their cells.

It is a fact that there is no dining hall and that men are fed in their cells or in the corridor.

It is a fact that cries of convicts protesting against their food have been heard by those who passed through the streets outside.

It is a fact that these wards of the state save the scraps of one meal to eat at the next.

It is a fact that the men have only half an hour's

[1] In the early nineteenth century the chief prison of London, Newgate, was in a disgraceful state of privation, filthiness, and neglect. Appalled by the horrible conditions, Elizabeth Fry (1780–1845), a courageous philanthropist, demanded and obtained a measure of reform.

*"Black" Comedy:
The Scornful,
Mournful Laugh*

recreation a week and that the recreation yard for fourteen women convicts is larger than the recreation yard for 1200 men.

It is a fact that many cells are dark and ill-ventilated.

It is a fact that in the newest wing seventy cells are so damp that they cannot be used, and that on occasions the corridor is so wet that the keepers have to wear rubbers.

It is a fact that a cell building erected in 1835 is in use today.

It is a fact that the state's wards were confined up to last Monday in an old wing that the State Board of Health had condemned as unfit for human habitation.

It is a fact that consumptives circulate with the well, exposing them to contagion.

It is a fact that the degenerate, the pervert, and the homosexual are placed with other convicts, with what result can well be imagined.

It is a fact that the first offender is thrown with the habitual criminal.

It is a fact that a youth was released in December who came to the prison a boy of thirteen years, wearing short trousers.

It is a fact that men are punished by being put face to the wall and that sometimes they are kept there all day without food.

It is a fact that convicts may not receive fruit.

It is a fact that a commodious bathhouse, with hot- and cold-water supply, is used only two months in the year.

It is a fact that for ten months in the year the convicts are given only a bucket of water once a week in which to bathe, that after bathing they must wash their clothes in this water and then wash out their cells.

It is a fact that the lights in the cells are extinguished at 8:30 P.M., and that on Sunday evenings there is no light at all.

It is a fact that the hospital is too small and its equipment inadequate.

It is a fact that the management of the prison is vested in a Board of Inspectors who meet only once a month, and whose members are from scattered parts of the state.

It is a fact that the Board of Inspectors of six members appointed six committees, a chairmanship for each member, creating so much more interference.

It is a fact that paroles can be granted by two independent bodies—the Board of Inspectors and the Court of Pardons.

It is a fact that a salaried school teacher is employed, but that there is no schoolroom or furniture, in violation of the law.

It is a fact that three chaplains are employed, but that the chapel seats only 350 persons, while the prison population is usually in excess of 1300.

It is a fact that the salaried moral instructor is the Reverend Thomas R. Taylor, father of Leon R. Taylor, ex-Speaker of the Assembly, and that he was appointed by his son while

Acting Governor of the state.

It is a fact that contract labor exists, if not in violation of the law, certainly against the spirit of it.

It is a fact that some of the shops where convicts are employed by private contractors are ill-ventilated and dark.

It is a fact that one contract shop is in the cellar.

It is a fact that more than one hundred men are employed on a contract in violation of the law.

It is a fact that much space is given over to these private contractors for use as storerooms.

It is a fact that the Board of Inspectors turns the convicts over for work on the public roads at the rate of $1.25 a day, which is paid by the taxpayers, but that the board turns the convicts over to private contractors at thirty-five cents a day.

It is a fact that free light, heat, and power are furnished to the contractors.

It is a fact that goods made in the prison for private contractors are not marked "Manufactured in New Jersey State Prison," and that this is a violation of the law.

It is a fact that while the contract shops are put in operation daily, the shop, equipped at a cost of more than $12,000 to make socks and underwear for inmates of state institutions, is idle and has been idle for some months, and that the salaried instructor has nothing to do.

It is a fact that the graded and meriting system was recommended in 1911 and that nothing was done.

It is a fact that the employment of a dietarian was recommended in 1911 by the State Commissioner of Charities and Corrections and that nothing was done.

It is a fact that the keepers are underpaid and overworked.

It is a fact that the powers of the Principal Keeper (Warden) are little more than those of janitor.

It is a fact that convicts are supposed to be paid $2\frac{1}{2}$ cents a day for their work in prison and that they do not get it.

That, then, is the New Jersey State Prison at Trenton, where 1300 men are confined at a net cost in 1915 (the last available report) of more than $253,-000. That is how the state's wards are kept. That is how they are punished. That is how they are "reformed." That is how society is "protected." That is the state of affairs in this year of grace, 1917. Is it really one hundred years since Elizabeth Fry found men and women shut together, found them in rags, found them dirty, and inveighed so against the malice and all uncharitableness that the English conscience was stirred and the era of reform begun? In the state of New Jersey today is there no Elizabeth Fry who will come forward and fight this thing? Or is it "molly-coddling" convicts to permit them to see the sun in the day, to give them better food, to give them light in their cells at night that they may read or study as they would, to provide them with dining halls where they might eat like human beings instead of having their food thrust into their cages as if they were wild and dangerous beasts, to end forever the vicious system of contract labor as Chapter 372 of the Laws of 1911 intended it should be ended, to permit them to receive fruit from their friends who wish to bring them fruit, to try to bring out the good that is in each and every one of them, for good there is in all of them, and it is like pure gold. If this is "mollycoddling" convicts it is best to leave them as they are with midnight in their hearts.

Littledale's dramatic report, attributing the evils to a muddled system of management, stirred up a hornets' nest in the state of New Jersey. The new governor immediately appointed a commission to investigate the charges, and within three weeks he found a report on his desk listing a series of eleven basic reforms, such as bricking up the dungeons, separate confinement of prisoners, establishment of a psychiatric clinic, and introduction of a grades and merit system.

Like John Howard of England, who in 1769 began his ceaseless labors in behalf of prison reform, Littledale achieved results by awakening the public conscience to a sense of guilt for its inhumanity. For his exposé he was awarded the 1918 Pulitzer Prize in reporting.

INDIGNANT MOCKERY

Expressing Your True Feelings

As a first step toward writing a mock encomium similar in tone, though not in length, to Twain's "To the Person Sitting in Darkness," write a statement in the form of an explicit opinion, something like an editorial, in which you express directly your own reactions to the facts Littledale presented in his article.

When you have completed this preliminary draft, you might want to compare your reactions to those of Littledale, as expressed in the first two and in the concluding paragraphs of his article.

For Writing and Discussion

1. As you compare your own statements about the facts Littledale presented, do you find that any of the adjectives you used are identical to or synonymous with words like *monstrous, medieval, bad*?

Masking the Tears

2. How is repetition of word, sentence, and phrase used effectively throughout the article? Is it used for emphasis or for humorous effect? How do you know?

3. In the concluding paragraph of the article, the reporter begins to use sarcasm, one of the main devices of bitter humor and of satire. Point out examples of this device.

Writing a Mock Encomium

Suppose you were to turn your direct statement of your reactions, or to use Littledale's statement of his reactions, into an example of black humor in the form of a mock encomium. If you recall Twain's comments on the "person sitting in darkness," you know that the mock encomium praises what it is actually criticizing. The form itself is therefore a "topsy-turvy" form, using most of the devices that reverse and reduce. You might begin by using the reporter's key words of sarcasm—*reformed, protected,* and *molly-coddling*—and listing four or five facts that might be used to dramatize the irony of the methods used to achieve the results of reforming the criminal and protecting society. For example, one would suppose that chaining men to walls of underground dungeons was intended to make them reconsider the evil of their ways and resolve never to sin again. If you are writing a mock encomium, then, you might single out this most inhuman punishment and present it as the best form of improving the prisoner's character. And compared to this punishment, the society of four of five men together in a cell would indeed be a kind of "mollycoddling," as would the placement of men and women in the same cell.

Try your hand now at some statements that could be included where the fact you choose to present is used as an example of a praiseworthy practice. You might choose sarcasm, such as: "Providing bread twice a day instead of once, or even every other day, and in the company of one's own fellows, seems charitable, unnecessarily generous." Or you might choose understatement: "Perhaps a few of the prisoners' families, less well off than the average family, would not object to receiving the thirty-five cents a day paid to the contractors for their husbands' labor." Or you can capitalize on the many paradoxical situations the reporter supplies—the three chaplains and the chapel with seats for fewer than a fourth of the inmates, the teacher with no classroom, the "commodious" baths used only two months of the year. The irony of the prison board's own violations of legal provisions for prisoners is only one of the many ironic circumstances presented, surpassed, of course, by the supreme irony of the results of such treatment.

After you have considered the possibilities for using devices such as sarcasm, paradox, invective, ridicule, and ironic under-statement or exaggeration, write an open letter to the newspaper editor in which you state your reactions in the form of mock praise. Share your letter with others who are doing the same assignment in order to be sure your "praise" is transparent enough to be taken finally for anger and criticism.

If you wish, locate some current news articles dealing with abhorrent social conditions that are still unalleviated—such as the welfare system, slum housing, care of the aged, current prison conditions, conditions in mental hospitals run by the state and local authorities—and prepare a letter to an editor of a local paper using the devices and form of a mock encomium.

ROLE-PLAYING THE DEVIL'S ADVOCATE

Mock encomiums incline to heavy-handedness, for subtlety in truly black comedy easily misses its mark and is frequently mistaken for praise instead of mockery, especially by readers unskilled in detecting the signals of irony and sarcasm. James Thurber shows us another way, however, of expressing a serious and threatening viewpoint; namely, by assuming a role in a situation that is a seemingly minor manifestation of a major theme or philosophical problem. In "A Box to Hide In," for example, the "I" narrating the story is featured in a slim plot involving his attempts to find a box big enough to hide in, dark enough to shut out the light that represents the character's recognition that men have made a de-humanized and frightening world for themselves. In this case, we can identify with the man and assume his role; for most of us, at some time in our lives, have been loath to face the unpleasant truths and have tried to escape knowledge.

The Key Techniques

Thurber's technique of creating a fictional situation and a charac-ter who epitomizes some quality we either share with regret or re-coil from in horror, can be useful in creating a story of black humor. In this case, the writer assumes the role of the "villain" in the plot and narrates the story from the point of view of the people he is actually criticizing. This technique is based on two major devices of humor—the topsy-turvy or "reversal" syndrome, and the imposition of an individual or dreamlike wishful thinking on the cold facts and logic of the world.

Pitfalls

If, for instance, Twain had assumed the role of a person on Earth, being interviewed by Satan perhaps, and giving his view of man's values, he could have made the same points that he makes by using Satan as narrator, except that he would have sacrificed the obvious irony of using the devil as a critic of men. The difficulty in role-playing the part of your adversary is somewhat similar to the difficulty in mock encomiums; that is, if you really play the role "straight," the reader may mistake your purpose and may instead try to understand and tolerate what you are trying to make him abhor. You can avoid this pitfall in two ways—first, by creating a character that is a prototype of a group rather than a highly individualized character such as those that appear in Thurber's and Twain's humorous sketches. The man who wanted to hide in a box, for example, is not developed as an individual we empathize with except insofar as his particular fear may also be ours. The people Satan describes are groups rather than individuals. Second, you must insert into your narrator's monologue the most telling humorous devices you can command—but *in reverse* of the way you would use these same devices if you were the reporter or critic. Where you would use ironic understatement, try exaggeration; where you would use sarcasm, tell it "straight."

An illustration may be helpful here. Mr. Littledale, in his report on prisons, uses the word *mollycoddling* sarcastically. Although he makes clear the way he is using the word by placing it in quotation marks, any reader who responds to the examples of mollycoddling he gives in his article understands that he is using the word ironically. If the prison board representative had been describing the same prison conditions, however, he might have used the same word and intended it to be taken literally. Instead of saying that the prisoners had *only* one bucket of water in which to bathe, wash their clothes, and clean their cells, he might have said that each prisoner was given a *full* bucket of water, with soap. The facts might be the same, but the interpretation of the facts is different—in this case, nonobjective. The narrator's prejudgments and his own peculiar brand of logic must show through your story so that in the end the reader condemns him for exactly the reasons and the data he presents for your commendation. If you have read Browning's "My Last Duchess," an often-cited example of the dramatic monologue, you know something of this technique. To begin with, it might be easier for you, however, to prepare a story in dialogue, in the form of an interview, in which an objective observer, such as a reporter, is interviewing a participant in a destructive action and listening to his slanted report.

Sources of Invention

A good source of raw data for such an interview is a well-written, completely objective description of an incident, one that is as nearly objective as any eyewitness account can be. Such a report was written on September 23, 1957, outside the high school at Little Rock, Arkansas, where eight black students were attempting to enter what had formerly been an all-white school. The Governor of Arkansas had sent the National Guard to the school, but had withdrawn it after a federal injunction that forbade his use of the guard under these conditions. When the black students entered the school under escort, an Associated Press reporter, Relman Morin, was stationed in a phone booth opposite the school. His report, dictated into the phone as the events unfolded, won for him a Pulitzer Prize in 1958 for national reporting.

Morin's report follows. Read it carefully and then make a list of the objective "facts" Morin presents. You might, for example, begin by writing: "It is a fact that . . ."

"Oh, God, the niggers are in the school!"— Relman Morin

The Associated Press, September 23, 1957

LITTLE ROCK, ARKANSAS, SEPTEMBER 23 (AP) — A howling, shrieking crowd of men and women outside Central High School, and disorderly students inside, forced authorities to withdraw eight Negro students from the school Monday, three and one-half hours after they entered it.

At noon, Mayor Woodrow Wilson Mann radioed police officers on the scene, telling them to tell the crowd: "The Negro students have been withdrawn."

Almost immediately, the three Negro boys and five girls left the school under heavy police escort. The officers took them away in police cars.

Crowds clustered at both ends of the school set up a storm of fierce howling and surged toward the lines of police and state troopers. They were beaten back.

The explosive climax came, after the school had been under siege since 8:45 A.M., when the Negroes walked quietly through the doors. Police armed with riot guns and tear gas, had kept the crowd under control.

Inside, meanwhile, students reported seeing Negroes with blood on their clothes. And some whites who came out—in protest against integration — pictured wild disorder, with policemen chasing white students through the halls, and attacks on Negroes in the building.

The break came shortly before noon.

Virgil Blossom, school superintendent, said he asked Gene Smith, assistant chief of police at the scene, if he thought it would be best to pull out the Negroes. Smith said he did.

Mann's announcement, ordering the police to notify the crowd, came minutes afterward.

Three newspapermen were beaten by the crowd before the sudden turn in the situation. They were Paul Welch, a reporter, and Gray Villette and Francis Miller, photographers. All three are employed by *Life* Magazine. A man smashed Miller in the face while he was carrying an armful of camera equipment. Miller fell, bleeding profusely.

Even after the Negroes left the school, the crowds remained. Teenagers in two automobiles cruised on the outskirts yelling, "Which way did the niggers go?"

During the hours while the Negroes were in the school an estimated thirty to fifty white students left. The crowd yelled, cheered, and clapped each time a white student left the school. "Don't stay in there with the niggers," people yelled.

Four Negroes were beaten and some arrests were made before the eight students went into the school.

The initial violence outside the school was a frightening sight. Women burst into tears and a man, hoisted up on a wooden barricade, roared, "Who's going through?"

"We all are," the crowd shouted. But they didn't

The drama-packed climax of three weeks of integration struggle in Little Rock came just after the buzzer sounded inside the 2,000-pupil high school at 8:45, signaling the start of classes.

Suddenly, on a street leading toward the school the crowd spotted four Negro adults, marching in twos, down the center of the street. A man yelled, "Look, here come the niggers!"

They were not the students. One appeared to be a newspaperman. He had a card in his hat and was bearing a camera.

I jumped into a glass-windowed telephone booth on the corner to dictate the story. As the crowd surged toward the four Negroes they broke and ran.

They were caught on the lawn of a home nearby. Whites jumped the man with the camera from behind and rode him to the ground, kicking and beating him. They smashed the camera.

This, obviously, was a planned diversionary movement to draw the crowd's attention away from the school. While I was dictating, someone yelled, "Look! They're going into the school!"

At that instant, the eight Negroes — the three boys and five girls—were crossing the schoolyard toward a side door at the south end of the school. The girls were in bobby sox and the boys were dressed in shirts open at the neck. All were carrying books.

They were not running, not even walking fast. They simply strolled toward the steps, went up and were inside before all but a few of the two hundred people at that end of the street knew it.

"They're gone in," a man roared. "Oh, God, the niggers are in the school."

A woman screamed, "Did they get in? Did you see them go in?"

"They're in now," some other men yelled.

"Oh, my God," the woman screamed. She burst into tears and tore at her hair. Hysteria swept the crowd. Other women began weeping and screaming.

At the moment a tall, gray-haired man in a brown hunting shirt jumped on the barricade. He yelled, waving his arms: "Who's going through?"

"We all are," the people shouted.

They broke over and around the wooden barricades, rushing the policemen. Almost a dozen police were at that corner of the street. They raised their billy clubs.

Some grabbed men and women and hurled them back. Two chased a dark-haired man who slipped through their line, like a football player. They caught him in the schoolyard, whipped his coat down his arms, pinning them, and hustled him out of the yard.

Another man, wearing a construction worker's hard hat, suddenly raised his hands high in front of a policeman. It was only a dozen yards or so in front of the phone booth.

I couldn't see whether the officer had a gun in the man's stomach, but he stopped running abruptly and went back. Two men were arrested.

Meanwhile, a cavalcade of cars carrying state troopers in their broad-brimmed campaign hats and Sam Browne belts, wheeled into the street from both ends. They came inside the barricades, and order was restored for a moment.

The weeping and screaming went on among the women. A man said, "I'm going in there and get my kid out."

An officer said, "You're not going anywhere."

Suddenly another roar—and cheering and clapping—came from the crowd. A white student, carrying his books, came down the front steps. He was followed by two girls wearing bobby sox. In the next few minutes, other students came out. Between fifteen and twenty left the school within the next half hour.

Each time they appeared, the people clapped and cheered. "Come on out," they yelled. "Don't stay in there with the niggers. Go back and tell all of them to come out."

Inside, it was reported, the eight Negro students were in the office of the principal. A moment later, two policemen suddenly raced into the building through the north door. When they came out, they were holding a girl by both arms, rushing her forcibly toward a police prisoners' wagon.

For an instant it looked as though the crowd would try to break the police lines again to rescue her. But the police put her in the car and drove swiftly down the street. Screams, catcalls, and more yelling broke out as the car raced down the street.

A man, distraught, came sprinting after it. "That's my kid in there," he yelled. "Help me get my kid out."

But the car was gone. Soon afterward four white students ran down the steps of the school and across the street. Policemen were chasing them.

One of the boys said they had caught a Negro boy outside the principal's office in the school. "We walked him half the length of the building and we were going to get him out of there," they said. They refused to give their names.

Meanwhile, on the streets, at both ends of the school, clusters of troopers took up their stations, reinforcing the police. The crowd heckled them, hurling insults and some obscenity.

"How you going to feel tonight when you face your neighbors?" a man shouted.

The people called the police "nigger lovers" and insulted them. The officers stood, poker-faced, making no response.

Then the crowd, lacking any other object, turned on the newspapermen and photographers. A boy jumped up, caught the telephone wire leading from one of the three booths to the main wire and swung on it, trying to break it. The booth swayed and nearly toppled to the street.

Someone said, "We ought to wipe up the street with these Yankee reporters."

"Let's do it right now," another replied.

But it was only words. Nothing happened. The same woman who had first burst into tears buttonholed a reporter and said, "Why don't you tell the truth about us? Why don't you tell them we are peaceful people who won't stand to have our kids sitting next to niggers?"

People in the crowd reported gleefully — and shouted it at the other officers—that one policeman had torn off his badge and thrown it on the ground.

"There's one white man on the police force," a burly slick-haired youth in a T shirt yelled at the policeman in front of him.

Sporadic tussles broke out, from time to time, when men tried to pass the police and trooper lines. The police wrestled one man to the street and then, taking him by the hands and arms, hauled him into the squad car and drove off.

A number of plainclothesmen—some reported to be FBI agents—kept circulating up and down in front of the school.

Inside there was no sign that this was different from any other school day. Students who came out at the 10:30 recess said that, in one class of thirty students, only one stayed in the classroom when a Negro entered.

For Writing and Discussion

1. Select the facts that you feel are most important in order to convey to the reader your own reaction to the incident. Select facts that can be used in "straight" invective or editorializing to point up the behavior of the crowd.

2. Prepare a list of questions that a reporter interviewing one of the most active demonstrators in the crowd might ask.

3. Assume the role of one of the most vehement demonstrators in the crowd and answer the questions you listed above, being sure to use the devices of overstatement, understatement, and the giveaway insult of others that is actually a condemnation of the interviewee's own behavior. Remember that the basic device will be to illustrate the participant's personal "logic."

4. If you wish, select any news article that reflects the major problem of man's values in conflict with man's actions. Select *major* problems of national or international import that have an underlying universality because they raise the ultimate questions about man's ability to survive with his fellows. Prepare a dramatic monologue or a dialogue-interview in which you use the devices and techniques of bitter humor to express your own attitudes.

PART SIX

*The
Parroting
Humorist*

12

Parodies
on
Parade

Now that you have sampled the main kinds of comic writing and have tried your hand at doing your own thing with humor, here are a group of parodies that use all the devices you have been observing and trying out. The selections that follow provide a review and also a "happy ending"—which is certainly more appropriate to a book about humor than the bitter irony that precedes this final chapter. In its general sense, a *parody* is a caricature, a travesty of an action, style, or person originally meant to be taken seriously. If an actor is deliberately "hamming" Hamlet with the intention of being funny, he is parodying the role. In this general sense, much of the humor in this book parodies certain stereotypes such as politicians, pompous senators, or unhappily married couples. But in its stricter sense, the sense in which we are using the word in this chapter, a parody is a deliberate imitation of a particular literary work or of a general class of writing. It is written for pure entertainment or for the satiric purpose of ridiculing the original. It must imitate slavishly in detail and form the particular piece of literature or literary genre it mocks.

Each of the following examples of parody is accompanied by a suggestion for a composing assignment. After reading through the entire chapter, choose one or two of the parodies you like best as models for your own parodies.

POETIC PARODIES

The simplest kind of poetic parody duplicates the exact verse form and rhyme scheme of a particular poem with enough similarity to the original diction and organization to make the identity of the poem being parodied easily recognizable. If you don't know the original, you might think the imitation funny, but you wouldn't recognize it as a parody. The parodist, therefore, has a problem in selection; he must accompany his parody with the original poem, or choose a poem so well known that its ghostly presence in his mock version is apparent to his reading audience. If the poem is famous and often quoted, there is no problem. Any poem, for example, that began with this line: "T'was the night before Easter, and all through the hutch . . ." would immediately announce its debt to the original. But if the verse form is one quite commonly used (like the ballad quatrain, for instance), and the poem being parodied is not likely to be familiar to everyone, then the original may be provided along with the accompanying parody. Mark Twain evidently wanted to be on the safe side when he parodied a poem called "Those Evening Bells."

A COUPLE OF POEMS BY TWAIN AND MOORE

Those Evening Bells

by Thomas Moore

Those evening bells! those evening bells!
How many a tale their music tells
Of youth, and home, and that sweet time
When last I heard their soothing chime.

Those joyous hours are passed away;
And many a heart that then was gay,
Within the tomb now darkly dwells,
And hears no more those evening bells.

And so 'twill be when I am gone—
That tuneful peal will still ring on;
While other bards shall walk these dells,
And sing your praise, sweet evening bells.

Those Annual Bills

by Mark Twain

These annual bills! these annual bills!
How many a song their discord trills

Of "truck" consumed, enjoyed, forgot,
Since I was skinned by last year's lot!

Those joyous beans are passed away;
Those onions blithe, O where are they?
Once loved, lost, mourned—*now* vexing ILLS
Your shades troop back in annual bills!

And so 'twill be when I'm aground—
These yearly duns will still go round,
While other bards, with frantic quills.
Shall damn and *damn* these annual bills!

Suggested Assignment: Select any short poem you like, regardless of its familiarity to most readers. Write a parody similar to Twain's, using a topic that rhymes, or nearly rhymes, with the topic of the original. (Twain might have written about "pills," for example, instead of "bills.")

James Thurber was no more a poet than Twain, though he was an excellent parodist. He takes a novel approach to parody in his "illustrations" for one of A. E. Housman's poems, one of a group from his *Famous Poems Illustrated.* Not all the illustrations in this particular collection are parodies; some are merely humorous illustrations of the poems. But his illustrations for "Oh When I Was . . ." seem to be visual caricatures of the verbal content. Read the printed version first; then reread it while looking at the accompanying drawings. What is parodied? How does Thurber accomplish his burlesque?

*Parodies
on
Parade*

"Oh When I Was . . ."

A. E. Housman

Oh when I was in love with you,
Then I was clean and brave,
And miles around the wonder grew
How well did I behave.

And now the fancy passes by,
And nothing will remain,
And miles around they'll say that I
Am quite myself again.

Suggested Assignment: If you can draw, use Thurber's parody-in-pictures as a model for your own parody of a short, serious poem. Or, look for a magazine illustration that suggests a humorous version of a well-known poem.

A more usual kind of poetic parody is the caricaturing of a particular type of verse rather than the mocking duplication of an individual poem. Mark Twain includes such a parody in one of the most amusing chapters of *The Adventures of Huckleberry Finn:* Chapter 17, "The Grangerfords Take Me In." The Grangerfords are the family who sheltered Huck after his raft sank in the Mississippi, and the entire chapter is a kind of burlesque of a particular life-style of the middleclass but well-to-do Southern gentry. The poet in the family had been a young woman, who died at the age of fifteen. Judging from the poem Twain attributes to her, she was already on her way to becoming one of the "mob of scribbling women" that Nathaniel Hawthorne had bemoaned as early as 1855.

If you like "sick" humor and "sick" jokes, you will feel right at home with Emmeline Grangerford. She undoubtedly took herself quite seriously, as many of the writers of "sick" literature do today. Because Twain's poetess is a parody of the same women scribblers who poured their sentimental floods of tears into the popular magazines of the time, Twain's description of her, viewed through Huck's eyes, follows along with her poem.

FROM *The Adventures of Huckleberry Finn*

MARK TWAIN

They [the Grangerfords] had pictures hung on the walls—mainly Washingtons and Lafayettes, and battles, and Highland Marys, and one called "Signing the Declaration." There was some that they called crayons, which one of the daughters which was dead made her own self when she was only fifteen years old. They was different from any pictures I ever see before—blacker, mostly, than is common. One was a woman in a slim black dress, belted small under the armpits, with bulges like a cabbage in the middle of the sleeves, and a large black scoop-shovel bonnet with a black veil, and white slim ankles crossed about with black tape and very wee black slippers, like a chisel, and she was leaning pensive on a tombstone on her right elbow under a weeping willow, and her other hand hanging down her side holding a white handkerchief and a reticule, and underneath the picture it said "Shall I Never See Thee More Alas." Another one was a young lady with her hair all combed up straight to the top of her head and knotted there in front of a comb like a chair-back, and she was crying into a handkerchief and had a dead bird laying on its back in her other hand with its heels up, and underneath the picture it said "I Shall Never Hear Thy Sweet Chirrup More Alas." There was one where a young lady was at a window looking up at the moon, and tears running down her cheeks; and she had an open letter in one hand with black sealing wax showing on one edge of it, and she was mashing a locket with a chain to it against her mouth and underneath the picture it said "And Art Thou

*Parodies
on
Parade*

287

Gone Yes Thou Art Gone Alas." These was all nice pictures, I reckon, but I didn't somehow seem to take to them, because if ever I was down a little they always give me the fantods. Everybody was sorry she died, because she had laid out a lot more of these pictures to do and a body could see by what she had done what they had lost. But I reckoned that with her disposition she was having a better time in the graveyard. She was at work on what they said was her greatest picture when she took sick, and every day and every night it was her prayer to be allowed to live till she got it done, but she never got the chance. It was a picture of a young woman in a long white gown, standing on the rail of a bridge all ready to jump off, with her hair all down her back, and looking up to the moon with tears running down her face, and she had two arms folded across her breast and two arms stretched out in front and two more reaching up towards the moon—and the idea was to see which pair would look best and then scratch out all the other arms; but, as I was saying, she died before she got her mind made up and now they kept this picture over the head of the bed in her room, and every time her birthday come they hung flowers on it. Other times it was hid with a little curtain. The young woman in the picture had a kind of a nice sweet face but there was so many arms it made her look too spidery, seemed to me.

This young girl kept a scrapbook when she was alive, and used to paste obituaries and accidents and cases of patient suffering in it out of the *Presbyterian Observer*, and write poetry after them out of her own head. It was very good poetry. This is what she wrote about a boy by the name of Stephen Dowling Bots that fell down a well and was drowned:

Ode to Stephen Dowling Bots, Dec'd

And did young Stephen sicken,
  And did young Stephen die?
And did the sad hearts thicken,
  And did the mourners cry?

No; such was not the fate of
  Young Stephen Dowling Bots;
Though sad hearts round him thickened,
  'Twas not from sickness' shots.

No whooping-cough did rack his frame,
  Nor measles drear with spots;

Not these impaired the sacred name
   Of Stephen Dowling Bots.

Despised love struck not with woe
   That head of curly knots,
Nor stomach troubles laid him low,
   Young Stephen Dowling Bots.

O no. Then list with tearful eye,
   Whilst I his fate do tell.
His soul did from this cold world fly
   By falling down a well.

They got him out and emptied him;
   Alas it was too late;
His spirit was gone for to sport aloft
   In the realms of the good and great.

If Emmeline Grangerford could make poetry like that before she was fourteen, there ain't no telling what she could 'a' done by and by. Buck said she could rattle off poetry like nothing. She didn't ever have to stop to think. He said she would slap down a line, and if she couldn't find anything to rhyme with it she would just scratch it out and slap down another one and go ahead. She warn't particular; she could write about anything you choose to give her to write about just so it was sadful. Every time a man died or a woman died or a child died, she would be on hand with her "tribute" before he was cold. She called them tributes. The neighbors said it was the doctor first, then Emmeline, then the undertaker—the undertaker never got in ahead of Emmeline but once, and then she hung fire on a rhyme for the dead person's name, which was Whistlor. She warn't ever the same after that; she never complained but she kind of pined away and did not live long. Poor thing, many's the time I made myself go up to the little room that used to be hers and get out her poor old scrapbook and read in it when her pictures had been aggravating me and I had soured on her a little. I liked all that family, dead ones and all, and warn't going to let anything come between us. Poor Emmeline made poetry about all the dead people when she was alive, and it didn't seem right that there warn't nobody to make some about her now she was gone; so I tried to sweat out a verse or two myself but I couldn't seem to make it go somehow.

Suggested Assignment: Write a poem about Emmeline, using as the basis for your parody the poem that Emmeline wrote about Stephen

Dowling Bots. Or, select an exceptionally morbid or romantically optimistic and trite poem from a local newspaper or magazine, and use it as the basis for a parody. If you prefer, build up the setting in which the poet (as you imagine him to be) is working, and then insert the poem.

One of the most frequently parodied poems is the soliloquy "To be or not to be . . ." from Shakespeare's *Hamlet*. The speech makes a good target for humorists because the subject matter—whether or not to take one's own life—is deadly serious, and the tone of Shakespeare's verse is consistently elevated. This soliloquy, along with certain parts of the King James version of the Bible, is one of the best known passages in English. In *Huckleberry Finn* Twain uses this passage for humorous purpose, but he uses it only loosely as "parody." In his version, Twain uses both the verse structure and enough similarity (or exact duplication) of phrasing throughout to maintain the familiar pattern of the original soliloquy. But instead of substituting his own words or his own topic, he has mixed up the order of the original and inserted here and there some lines from other sources—from *Macbeth*, in particular. The result is called "patch poetry," a term accurately descriptive of this kind of parody. The resulting mixture makes a kind of sensible non-sense which could easily fool the reader who has only limited knowledge of Shakespeare's great tragedies. We suggest, therefore, that you refresh your own background by reading the "To be or not to be . . ." speech from *Hamlet* (Act III, Scene 1). Although familiarity with the complete texts of *Hamlet* and *Macbeth* would be helpful as background, even if you haven't read these plays you will enjoy the lapses into absurdity that occur throughout the following selection from *Huckleberry Finn*.

The scene takes place on the raft. The "duke" and the "king" are about to put on a show in a riverside village, and the duke is brushing up on his Shakespeare.

FROM *The Adventures of Huckleberry Finn*

MARK TWAIN

After dinner the duke says:
"Well, Capet, we'll want to make this a first-class show,

you know, so I guess we'll add a little more to it. We want a little something to answer encores with, anyway."

"What's onkores, Bilgewater?"

The duke told him, and then says:

"I'll answer by doing the Highland fling or the sailor's hornpipe, and you—well, let me see—oh, I've got it—you can do Hamlet's soliloquy."

"Hamlet's which?"

"Hamlet's soliloquy, you know; the most celebrated thing in Shakespeare. Ah, it's sublime, sublime! Always fetches the house. I haven't got it in the book—I've only got one volume—but I reckon I can piece it out from memory. I'll just walk up and down a minute and see if I can call it back from recollection's vaults."

So he went to marching up and down, thinking, and frowning horrible every now and then; then he would hoist up his eyebrows; next he would squeeze his hand on his forehead and stagger back and kind of moan; next he would sigh and next he'd let on to drop a tear. It was beautiful to see him. By and by he got it. He told us to give attention. Then he strikes a most noble attitude, with one leg shoved forwards and his arms stretched away up and his head tilted back, looking up at the sky, and then he begins to rip and rave and grit his teeth, and after that, all through his speech, he howled and spread around and swelled up his chest and just knocked the spots out of any acting ever *I* see before. This is the speech—I learned it easy enough while he was learning it to the king:

To be, or not to be; that is the bare bodkin
That makes calamity of so long life;
For who would fardels bear, till Birnam Wood do come to
    Dunsinane,
But that the fear of something after death
Murders the innocent sleep,
Great nature's second course,
And makes us rather sing the arrows of outrageous fortune
Than fly to others that we know not of.
There's the respect must give us pause:
Wake Duncan with thy knocking! I would thou couldst;
For who would bear the whips and scorns of time,
The oppressor's wrong, the proud man's contumely.
The law's delay, and the quietus which his pang's might take,
In the dead waste and middle of the night, when church-
    yards yawn

In customary suits of solemn black,
But that the undiscovered country from whose bourne no
    traveler returns,
Breathes forth contagion on the world,
And thus the native hue of resolution, like the poor cat i' the
    adage,
Is sicklied o'er with care,
And all the clouds that lowered o'er our housetops,
With this regard their currents turn away,
And lose the name of action.
'Tis a consummation devoutly to be wished. But soft you, the
    fair Ophelia:
Ope not thy ponderous and marble jaws,
But get thee to a nunnery—go!

    Well, the old man he liked that speech and he mighty soon got it so he could do it first-rate.

Suggested Assignment: Using as your framework two or three very familiar ballads, or several verses from a longer poem like "The Rime of the Ancient Mariner," try your hand at patch poetry.

CORRESPONDENCE

Another of the general types of writing that is frequently parodied is the advice column, the kind that consists of questions directed to an editor who is an "expert" in medicine, child care, teenage problems, etiquette, or general counseling. This kind of correspondence is a "natural" for parodists because the subject matter is often serious (at least in the eyes of the person sending in the queries), and because there is a rather set pattern of question and response that is easy to imitate. In addition, the parodist can readily capture a tone of interest in a particular problem, no matter how outlandish or mundane, and he can also attempt to offer practical solutions even when they are impossible or inappropriate to the problem.

    We offer two groups of correspondence of this type. In the first group Twain is evidently assuming the role of a general adviser to those in all sorts of difficulties.

FROM *Answers to Correspondents*

MARK TWAIN

"YOUNG AUTHOR." Yes, Agassiz *does* recommend authors to eat fish, because the phosphorus in it makes brain. So far you are correct. But I cannot help you to a decision about the amount you need to eat—at least, not with certainty. If the specimen composition you send is about your fair usual average, I should judge that perhaps a couple of whales would be all you would want for the present. Not the largest kind, but simply good middling-sized whales.

"MELTON MOWBRAY."[1] Dutch Flat.—This correspondent sends a lot of doggerel, and says it has been regarded as very good in Dutch Flat. I give a specimen verse:

"The Assyrian came down like a wolf on the fold,
And his cohorts were gleaming with purple and gold;
And the sheen of his spears was like stars on the sea,
When the blue wave rolls nightly on deep Galilee."[2]

There, that will do. That may be very good Dutch Flat poetry, but it won't do in the metropolis. It is too smooth and blubbery; it reads like buttermilk gurgling from a jug. What the people ought to have is something spirited—something like "Johnny Comes Marching Home." However, keep on practicing, and you may succeed yet. There is genius in you, but too much blubber.

"ST. CLAIR HIGGINS." Los Angeles.—"My life is a failure; I have adored, wildly, madly, and she whom I love has turned coldly from me and shed her affections upon another. What would you advise me to do?

You should set your affections on another also—or on sev-

[1] Author's Note: This piece of pleasantry, published in a San Francisco paper, was mistaken by the country journals for seriousness, and many and loud were the denunciations of the ignorance of author and editor, in not knowing that the lines in question were "written by Byron."

[2] Editor's Note: This famous passage is from Byron's poem "The Destruction of Sennacherib."

Parodies on Parade

293

eral, if there are enough to go round. Also, do everything you can to make your former dame unhappy. There is an absurd idea disseminated in novels, that the happier a girl is with another man, the happier it makes the old lover she has blighted. Don't allow yourself to believe any such nonsense as that. The more cause that girl finds to regret that she did not marry you, the more comfortable you will feel over it. It isn't poetical, but it is mighty sound doctrine.

"ARITHMETICUS." Virginia, Nevada.—"If it would take a cannon ball $3\frac{1}{3}$ seconds to travel four miles, and $3\frac{3}{8}$ seconds to travel the next four, and $3\frac{5}{8}$ to travel the next four, and if its rate of progress continued to diminish in the same ratio, how long would it take it to go fifteen hundred million miles?

I don't know.

"AMBITIOUS LEARNER." Oakland.—Yes; you are right—America was not discovered by Alexander Selkirk.

"DISCARDED LOVER." I loved, and still love, the beautiful Edwitha Howard, and intended to marry her. Yet, during my temporary absence at Benicia, last week, alas! she married Jones. Is my happiness to be thus blasted for life? Have I no redress?"

Of course you have. All the law, written and unwritten, is on your side. The *intention* and not the *act* constitutes crime—in other words, constitutes the *deed*. If you call your bosom friend a fool, and *intend* it for an insult, it *is* an insult; but if you do it playfully, and meaning no insult, it is *not* an insult. If you discharge a pistol *accidentally,* and kill a man, you can go free, for you have done no murder; but if you try to kill a man, and manifestly *intend* to kill him, but fail utterly to do it, the law still holds that the *intention* constituted the crime, and you are guilty of murder. Ergo, if you had married Edwitha *accidently,* and without really *intending* to do it, you would not actually be married to her at all, because the *act* of marriage could not be complete without the *intention*. And ergo, in the strict spirit of the law, since you deliberately *intended* to marry Edwitha, and didn't do it, you are married to her all the same—because, as I said before, the *intention* constitutes the crime. It is as clear as day that Edwitha is your wife, and your redress lies in taking a club and mutilating Jones with it as much as you can. Any man has a right to protect his own wife from the advances of other men. But you have another alternative—you were married to Edwitha *first*, because of your deliberate intention, and now you can prosecute her for bigamy, in subsequently marrying Jones. But there is another phase in this complicated case: You *intended* to marry Edwitha, and consequently, according to law, she is your wife—there is no getting around that; but she didn't marry you, and if she *never intended* to marry you, *you are not her husband,* of course. Ergo, in marrying Jones, she was guilty of bigamy, because she was the wife of another man at the time; which is all very well as far as it goes—but then, don't you see, she had no other *husband* when she married Jones, and consequently she was *not guilty* of bigamy. Now, according to this view of the case, Jones married a *spinster,* who was a *widow* at the same time and another man's *wife* at the same time, and yet who had no *husband* and *never had one,* and never had any *intention* of getting married, and therefore, of course, *never had* been married; and by the same reasoning you are a *bachelor,* because you have never been any one's *husband;* and a *married man,* because you have a wife living; and to all intents and purposes a *widower,* because you have been deprived of that wife; and a consummate *ass* for going off to Benicia in the first place, while things were so mixed. And by this time I have got myself so tangled up in the intricacies of this extraordinary case that I shall have to give up further attempt to advise you—I might get confused and fail to make myself understood. I think I could take up the argument where I left off, and by following it closely a while, perhaps I could prove to your satisfaction, either that you never existed at all, or that you are dead now, and consequently don't need the faithless Edwitha—I think I could do that, if it would afford you any comfort.

Suggested Assignment: Select any question and answer from an advice column in your local newspaper, and write a parody of the original.

As you might expect, Thurber's correspondence includes his inimitable drawings. The parodies that follow appeared originally in a collection entitled *The Owl in the Attic.* Here Thurber's "persona" assumes the role of an adviser to owners of pets. Notice that the drawings are indispensable adjuncts to the questions posed.

The Pet Department

JAMES THURBER

Q. I enclose a sketch of the way my dog William has been lying for two days now. I think there must be something wrong with him. Can you tell me how to get him out of this?

Mrs. L. L. G.

A. I should judge from the drawing that William is in a trance. Trance states, however, are rare with dogs. It may just be ecstasy. If at the end of another twenty-four hours he doesn't seem to be getting anywhere, I should give him up. The position of the ears leads me to believe that he may be enjoying himself in a quiet way, but the tail is somewhat alarming.

Q. Our gull cannot get his head down any farther than this, and bumps into things.

H. L. F.

A. You have no ordinary gull to begin with. He looks to me a great deal like a rabbit backing up. If he *is* a gull, it is impossible to keep him in the house. Naturally he will bump into things. Give him his freedom.

Q. No one has been able to tell what kind of dog we have. I am enclosing a sketch of one of his two postures. He only has two. The other one is the same except he faces in the opposite direction.

Mrs. Eugenia Black

A. I think that what you have is a cast-iron lawn dog. The expressionless eye and the rigid pose are char-

Parodies on Parade

acteristic of metal lawn animals. And that certainly is a cast-iron ear. You could, however, remove all doubt by means of a simple test with a hammer and a cold chisel, or an acetylene torch. If the animal chips, or melts, my diagnosis is correct.

Q. Mr. Jennings bought this beast when it was a pup in Montreal for a St. Bernard, but I don't think it is. It's grown enormously and is stubborn about letting you have anything, like the bath towel it has its paws on, and the hat, both of which belong to Mr. Jennings. He got it that bowling ball to play with but it doesn't seem to like it. Mr. Jennings is greatly attached to the creature.

Mrs. Fanny Edwards Jennings

A. What you have is a bear. While it isn't my bear, I should recommend that you dispose of it. As these animals grow older they get more and more adamant about letting you have anything, until finally there might not be anything in the house you could call your own—except possibly the bowling ball. Zoos use bears. Mr. Jennings could visit it.

The Parroting Humorist

Q. Sometimes my dog does not seem to know me. I think
he must be crazy. He will draw away, or show his fangs,
when I approach him.

H. M. Morgan, Jr.

A. So would I, and I'm not crazy. If you creep up on
your dog the way you indicate in the drawing, I can
understand his viewpoint. Put your shirt in and
straighten up; you look as if you had never seen a dog
before, and that is undoubtedly what bothers the animal. These maladjustments can often be worked out
by the use of a little common sense.

Q. My husband paid a hundred and seventy-five dollars for this moose to a man in Dorset, Ontario, who said he had trapped it in the woods. Something is wrong with his antlers, for we have to keep twisting them back into place all the time. They're loose.

Mrs. Oliphant Beatty

A. You people are living in a fool's paradise. The animal is obviously a horse with a span of antlers strapped onto his head. If you really want a moose, dispose of the horse; if you want to keep the horse, take the antlers off. Their constant pressure on his ears isn't a good idea.

Suggested Assignment: Make a drawing to illustrate a problem of some sort—a gardening mishap, a battered musical instrument, a piece of equipment gone wrong. Don't worry about your drawing ability. Just do the best you can. Then write a question about your drawing. Exchange your question with someone and, with your partner, prepare answers to share with other sets of partners engaged in the same task.

The
Parroting
Humorist

SCHOLARLY MISTREATMENTS

In doing research for reports or library papers, you have probably come across chapters in textbooks, articles in reference works, and learned articles or critical essays in periodicals that you found difficult to understand. Perhaps your own background in the subject matter was limited. Or, more probably, the writer's style was filled with technical jargon, allusions to unfamiliar or esoteric scholarship in the field, detailed footnotes or insertions into the text of complicated examples—all of which may have done more to impress you with the writer's knowledge than remedy your own lack of it.

Such scholarly writing is a favorite butt of parodists' jokes. It is fairly easy to imitate. Notice how Thurber, in the selection that follows, parodies the technical terms, the allusions to presumably pioneering scholars, and the drawings that frequently accompany "scientific" material. Observe, too, how often he achieves humorous "surprise" by his very informal asides inserted directly into the ostensibly serious discussion.

Prehistoric Animals of the Middle West

JAMES THURBER

Many residents of that broad, proud region of the United States known as the Middle West are, I regret to say, woefully ignorant of, not to say profoundly incurious about, the nature and variety of the wild life which existed, however precariously in some instances, in that part of North America before the coming of the Red Man (*Homo Rufus*), or of anybody else.

The only important research which has been done in this fascinating field was carried on for the better part of thirty-two years by the late Dr. Wesley L. Millmoss.[1] For the last twenty years of the great man's life, I served as his artist, companion, counsellor and assistant. In this last capacity, I did a great deal of heavy lifting, no doubt more than was good for me. During the years I spent with Dr. Millmoss, he

[1] Author's Note: While on a field trip in Africa in 1931, Dr. Millmoss was eaten by a large piano-shaped animal, to the distress of his many friends and colleagues.

devoted most of his time to digging in all parts of the Middle West for the fossilized remains of extinct animals. From bits of a thigh bone, or one vertebra, he would reconstruct the whole animal. My drawings of his most famous reconstructions accompany this treatise.

For the past twelve years I have striven without success to have his findings, together with their accompanying illustrative plates, published in one or another of the leading scientific journals of this and other countries. I lay my failure directly at the door of Dr. Wilfred Ponsonby who, at the meeting of the American Scientific Society in Baltimore in 1929, made the remark, "The old boy (Dr. Millmoss) has never dug up half as many specimens as he has dreamed up."

Although Dr. Millmoss, quite naturally, was unable to perceive the wit in this damaging observation, which hung like a cloud over his last days, he was not without a sense of humor, and I believe, if he were alive today, he would take no little satisfaction in the fact that for the last five years Dr. Ponsonby has labored under the delusion that he is married to a large South African butterfly.

However, this is scarcely the place for an exploration of the little feuds and fantasies of the scientific world. Let us proceed to an examination of the remarkable fauna of the prehistoric Middle West. If in doing so, I present no formal defense of the Millmoss discoveries, put it down to a profound reverence for the memory of Wesley Millmoss, who used so often to say, "A Millmoss assumption is more important than a Ponsonby proof."

All the plates reproduced here were drawn by me from photographs of original life-size models constructed by Dr. Millmoss out of wire, *papier mâché* and other materials. These models were all destroyed by fire in 1930. "All that I have to show for them," the good doctor once told a friend, "is two divorces."

According to all scientists except Dr. Millmoss, the famous mounds of Ohio were built by an early race of men known as Mound Builders. The doctor, on the other hand, contended that the mounds were built by the Mound Dweller (Plate I). This primitive creature was about the size of the modern living room. The Mound Dweller's body occupied only one third of the space inside his shell, the rest of which was used to carry the earth as he dug it up. The creature's eye was an integral part of its shell, a mistake made by Mother Nature and not, as has been claimed,[1] "a bit of

[1] Author's Note: Dr. W. Ponsonby, in the *Yale Review*, 1933.

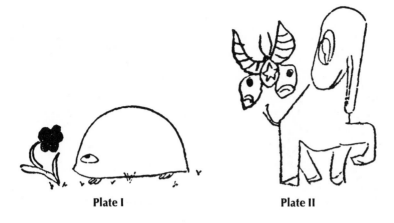

Plate I   **Plate II**

Millmoss butchery-botchery." The Mound Dweller is of interest today, even to me, principally because it was my friend's first reconstruction, and led to his divorce from Alma Albrecht Millmoss.

In Plate II, I have drawn the Thake, a beast which Dr. Millmoss was wont to refer to lovingly as "Old Laughing Ears." It represents perhaps the most controversial of all the ancient creatures reconstructed by the distinguished scientist. Dr. Millmoss estimated that the Thake had inhabited the prairies of Illinois approximately three million years before the advent of the Christian era. Shortly after Dr. Millmoss gave his model of the Thake to the world, Dr. Ponsonby, in a lecture at Williams College that was notable for its lack of ethical courtesy, asserted that the Thake bones which Dr. Millmoss had found were in reality those of a pet airedale and a pet pony buried together in one grave by their owner *circa* 1907. My own confidence in the authenticity of the Thake has never been shaken, although occasionally it becomes a figure in my nightmares, barking and neighing.

In Plate III, we have the Queech, also known as the Spotted, or Ringed, Queech—the only prehistoric feline ever discovered by Dr. Millmoss in his midwestern researches. I find no record in the doctor's notes as to the probable epoch in which it flourished. Like so many of Dr. Millmoss' restorations, the Queech was made the object of a particularly unfriendly and uncalled-for remark by Dr. Ponsonby. At a dinner of the New York Society of Zoologists, held at the old Waldorf-Astoria some fifteen years ago,

Parodies on Parade

303

Plate III

Plate IV

Ponsonby observed, "There is no doubt in my mind but that this pussy cat belongs to the Great Plasticine Age."

As to the authenticity of the Cobble-tufted Wahwah (Plate IV), even the sardonic Dr. Ponsonby could offer no slighting insinuations.[1] Like all other scientists, he was forced tacitly to admit the brilliant precision with which the old master had restored this antediluvian fowl. The Wahwah bird, in spite of its mammoth size, measured nothing at all from wing tip to wing tip, since it had only one wing. Because of its single wing, its obviously impractical feet and its tendency to walk over high rocks and fall, it is probable, Dr. Millmoss believed, that the species did not exist for more than a hundred and seventy-five years. Dr. Millmoss once told me that, if the bird made any sound at all, it probably "went 'wahwah.'" Since this embarrassed me for some reason, the celebrated scientist did not press the point.

In Plate V, we come upon my favorite of all the Millmoss discoveries, the Hippoterranovamus. One of Nature's most colossal errors, the Hippoterranovamus ate only stork meat and lived in a land devoid of storks. Too large to become jumpy because of its predicament, the 'novamus took out its frustration in timidity. It almost never came out completely from behind anything. When I asked Dr. Millmoss how long he figured the 'novamus had existed as a species, he gave me his infrequent but charming smile and said in his slow drawl, "Well, it never lived to vote for William Jennings

[1] Author's Note: My research staff has since established that Dr. Ponsonby was enjoying a two-year sabbatical in Europe at the time the Wahwah model was completed.

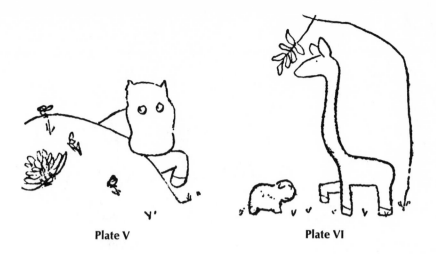

Plate V   **Plate VI**

Bryan." This was the only occasion on which I heard the great man mention politics.

Plates VI and VII represent, respectively, the Ernest Vose, or Long-necked Leafeater, and the Spode, or Wood-wedger. Neither of these animals has ever interested me intensely, and it is only fair to say that I am a bit dubious as to the utter reality of their provenance. At the time he constructed these models, Dr. Millmoss was being divorced by his second wife, Annette Beggs Millmoss, and he spent a great deal of his time reading children's books and natural histories. The tree at the back of the Spode is my own conception of a 3,000,-000-year-old tree. The small animal at the feet of the Ernest Vose is a Grod. Dr. Millmoss' notes are almost entirely illegible, and I am not even sure that Ernest Vose is right. It looks more like Ernest Vose than anything else, however.

The final plate (Plate VIII) was one of the last things Wesley Millmoss ever did, more for relaxation, I think, than in the interests of science. It shows his idea, admittedly a trifle fanciful, of the Middle-Western Man and Woman, three and a half million years before the dawn of history. When I asked him if it was his conviction that Man had got up off all fours before Woman did, he gave me a pale, grave look and said simply, "He had to. He needed the head start."

Even in death, Dr. Wesley Millmoss did not escape the sharp and envious tongue of Dr. Wilfred Ponsonby. In commenting upon the untimely passing of my great employer and friend, the *New York Times* observed that explorers in

Parodies on Parade

Plate VII   Plate VIII

Africa might one day come upon the remains of the large, piano-shaped animal that ate Dr. Millmoss, together with the bones of its distinguished and unfortunate prey. Upon reading this, Ponsonby turned to a group of his friends at the Explorers' Club and said, "Too bad the old boy didn't live to reconstruct *that*."

Suggested Assignment: Select any chapter from a school text, and parody a small section of it. Be sure to choose a topic closely related to the subject of the original, so that your parody is more one of technique than of content.

And now, to close this book on a note of humorous surprise, we offer you Mark Twain in a most novel role—the role of the artist explaining and exemplifying his artistry.

Instructions in Art WITH ILLUSTRATIONS BY THE AUTHOR

MARK TWAIN

The Parroting Humorist

The great trouble about painting a whole gallery of portraits at the same time is, that the housemaid comes and dusts, and does not put them back the way they were before, and so when the public flock to the studio and wish to know which is Howells and which is Depew and so on, you have to dissemble, and it is very embarrassing at first. Still, you know they are there, and this knowledge presently gives you more or less confidence, and you say sternly, "*This* is Howells," and watch the visitor's eye. If you see doubt there, you correct yourself and try another. In time you find one that will satisfy, and then you feel relief and joy, but you have suffered much in the meantime; and you know that this joy is only temporary, for the next inquirer will settle on another Howells of a quite different aspect, and one which you suspect is Edward VII or Cromwell, though you keep that to yourself, of course. It is much better to label a portrait when you first paint it, then there is no uncertainty in your mind and you can get bets out of the visitor and win them.

I believe I have had the most trouble with a portrait which I painted in installments—the head on one canvas and the bust on another.

The housemaid stood the bust up sideways, and now I don't know which way it goes. Some authorities think it belongs with the breastpin at the top, under the man's chin; others think it belongs the reverse way on account of the collar, one of these saying, "A person can wear a breastpin on his stomach if he wants to, but he can't wear his collar anywhere he dern pleases." There is a certain amount of sense in that view of it. Still, there is no way to determine the matter for certain; when you join the installments, with the pin under the chin, that seems to be right; then when you reverse it and bring the collar under the chin it seems as right as ever; whichever way you fix it the lines come together snug and convincing, and either way you do it the portrait's face looks equally surprised and rejoiced, and as if it wouldn't be satisfied to have it any way but just that one; in fact, even if you take the bust away altogether the face seems surprised and happy just the same—I have never seen an expression before, which no vicissitudes could alter. I wish I could remember who it is. It looks a little like Washington, but I do not think it can be Washington, because he had as many ears on one side as the other. You can always tell Washington by that; he was very particular about his ears, and about having them arranged the same old way all the time.

By and by I shall get out of these confusions, and then it will be plain sailing; but first-off the confusions were natural and not to be avoided. My reputation came very suddenly and tumultuously when I published my own portrait, and it turned my head a little, for indeed there was never anything

The head on one canvas

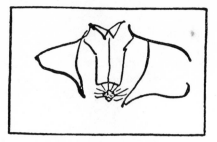

And the bust on another

like it. In a single day I got orders from sixty-two people not to paint their portraits, some of them the most distinguished persons in the country—the President, the Cabinet, authors, governors, admirals, candidates for office on the weak side— almost everybody that was anybody, and it would really have turned the head of nearly any beginner to get so much notice and have it come with such a frenzy of cordiality. But I am growing calm and settling down to business, now; and pretty soon I shall cease to be flurried, and then when I do a portrait I shall be quite at myself and able on the instant to tell it from the others and pick it out when wanted.

I am living a new and exalted life of late. It steeps me in a sacred rapture to see a portrait develop and take soul under my hand. First, I throw off a study—just a mere study, a few apparently random lines—and to look at it you would hardly ever suspect who it was going to be; even I cannot tell, myself. Take this picture, for instance:

First you think it's Dante; next you think it's Emerson; then you think it's Wayne Mac Veagh. Yet it isn't any of them; it's the beginnings of Depew. Now you wouldn't believe Depew could be devolved out of that; yet the minute it is finished here you have him to the life, and you say, yourself, "If that isn't Depew it isn't anybody."

Some would have painted him speaking, but he isn't always speaking, he has to stop and think sometimes.

That is a *genre* picture, as we say in the trade, and differs from the encaustic and other schools in various ways, mainly technical, which you wouldn't understand if I should explain them to you. But you will get the idea as I go along, and little by little you will learn all that is valuable about Art without knowing how it happened, and without any sense of strain or effort, and then you will know what school a picture belongs to, just at a glance, and whether it is an

First you think it's Dante; next you think it's Emerson; then you think it's Wayne Mac Veagh. Yet it isn't any of them; it's the beginnings of Depew.

---

animal picture or a landscape. It is then that the joy of life will begin for you.

When you come to examine my portraits of Mr. Joe Jefferson and the rest, your eye will have become measurably educated by that time, and you will recognize at once that no two of them are alike. I will close the present chapter with an example of the nude, for your instruction.

This creation is different from any of the other works. The others are from real life, but this is an example of still-life; so called because it is a portrayal of a fancy only, a thing which has no actual and active existence. The purpose of a still-life picture is to concrete to the eye the spiritual, the intangible, a something which we feel, but cannot see with the fleshy vision—such as joy, sorrow, resentment, and so on. This is best achieved by the employment of that treatment which we call the impressionist, in the trade. The present example is an impressionist picture, done in distemper, with a chiaroscuro motif modified by monochromatic technique, so as to secure tenderness of feeling and

Parodies on Parade

309

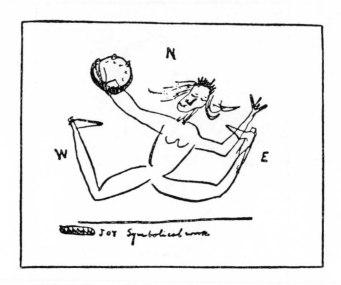

That thing in the right hand is not a skillet; it is a tambourine.

spirituality of expression. At a first glance it would seem to be a Botticelli, but it is not that; it is only a humble imitation of that great master of longness and slimness and limb-fulness.

The work is imagined from Greek story, and represents Proserpine or Persepolis, or one of those other Bacchantes doing the solemnities of welcome before the altar of Isis upon the arrival of the annual shipload of Athenian youths in the island of Minos to be sacrificed in appeasement of the Dordonian Cyclops.

The figure symbolizes solemn joy. It is severely Greek, therefore does not call details of drapery or other factitious helps to its aid, but depends wholly upon grace of action and symmetry of contour for its effects. It is intended to be viewed from the south or southeast, and I think that that is best; for while it expresses more and larger joy when viewed from the east or the north, the features of the face are too much foreshortened and wormy when viewed from that point. That thing in the right hand is not a skillet; it is a tambourine.

This creation will be exhibited at the Paris Salon in June, and will compete for the *Prix de Rome*.

The portrait reproduces
Mr. Joseph Jefferson,
the common friend of
the human race.

The above is a marine picture, and is intended to educate the eye in the important matters of perspective and foreshortening. The mountainous and bounding waves in the foreground, contrasted with the tranquil ship fading away as in a dream the other side of the fishing-pole, convey to us the idea of space and distance as no words could do. Such is the miracle wrought by that wondrous device, perspective.

The portrait reproduces Mr. Joseph Jefferson, the common friend of the human race. He is fishing, and is not catching anything. This is finely expressed by the moisture in the eye and the anguish of the mouth. The mouth is holding back words. The pole is bamboo, the line is foreshortened. This foreshortening, together with the smoothness of the water away out there where the cork is, gives a powerful impression of distance, and is another way of achieving a perspective effect.

We now come to the next portrait, which is either Mr. Howells or Mr. Laffan. I cannot tell which, because the label is lost. But it will do for both, because the features are Mr. Howells's, while the expression is Mr. Laffan's. This work will bear critical examination.

The next picture is part of an animal, but I do not know the name of it. It is not finished. The front end of it went around a corner before I could get to it.

Parodies on Parade

Either Mr. Howells or Mr. Laffan. I cannot tell which because the label is lost.

We will conclude with the portrait of a lady in the style of Raphael. Originally I started it out for Queen Elizabeth, but was not able to do the lace hopper her head projects out of, therefore I tried to turn it into Pocahontas, but was again baffled, and was compelled to make further modifications, this time achieving success. By spiritualizing it and turning it into the noble mother of our race and throwing into the countenance the sacred joy which her first tailor-made out-fit infuses into her spirit, I was enabled to add to my gallery the best and most winning and eloquent portrait my brush has ever produced.

The most effective encouragement a beginner can have is the encouragement which he gets from noting his own progress with an alert and persistent eye. Save up your works and date them; as the years go by, run your eye over them from time to time, and measure your advancing stride. This will thrill you, this will nerve you, this will inspire you as nothing else can.

It has been my own course, and to it I owe the most that I am today in Art. When I look back and examine my first

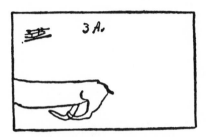

The front end of it went around
a corner before I could get to it.

The best and most winning and eloquent portrait
my brush has ever produced.

---

effort and then compare it with my latest, it seems unbelievable that I have climbed so high in thirty-one years. Yet
so it is. Practice—that is the secret. From three to seven
hours a day. It is all that is required. The results are sure;
whereas indolence achieves nothing great.

It seems unbelievable that I have climbed
so high in thirty-one years.

Suggested Assignment: Find in your local newspaper or in a monthly
or weekly periodical a criticism of a recent film, theatrical production,

concert, or ballet. Parody this review, using as your subject another performance of a similar type that you have recently attended and that you disliked or considered poorly done. If you have as much confidence in your drawing as Twain had in his, add explanatory illustrations.

B 2
C 3
D 4
E 5
F 6
G 7
H 8
I 9
J 0